LORD,
TEACH US
TO PRAY

A PRAYER CLASSIC
MORRIS CERULLO

Prayer Classic

All Scripture references are from the KJV of the Bible unless otherwise noted.

Published by:

MORRIS CERULLO WORLD EVANGELISM

P.O. Box 85277 • San Diego, California 92186-5277
(858) 277-2200

E-mail: morriscerullo@mcwe.com
Website: www.mcwe.com

MORRIS CERULLO WORLD EVANGELISM OF CANADA
P.O. Box 3600 • Concord, Ontario L4K-1B6
(905) 669-1788

MORRIS CERULLO WORLD EVANGELISM OF GREAT BRITAIN
P.O. Box 277 Hemel Hempstead, HERTS HP2-7DH
(0) 1 442 232432

INTRODUCTION

There has never been a greater time in history; from the time when God said, "Let there be light" until now for the necessity of the people of God to learn how to pray, and to pray.

The cry of the Spirit coming from the Throne room of God is a divine, universal call to prayer.

Although we are witnessing the greatest prayer movement in Church history, with millions of Christians being mobilized to pray, never before has there been a greater need for Christians to know how to pray with power, to pray prayers that are beyond ordinary prayer and that are divinely energized and charged by the Holy Spirit.

I am convinced that the normal prayers of Christians are insufficient to provide this world with the spiritual breakthroughs that we must have now.

Something supernatural must occur and begin to take place in our praying that will literally demolish Satan's strongholds over the nations.

Ordinary prayer will not do it!

Before the last remaining strongholds of Satan are torn down there must be a supernatural manifestation of God's Spirit within the Body of Christ moving us to a higher dimension of prayer.

God has given me a mandate – a powerful end-time strategy for reaching the world and fulfilling His will in the nations before Christ returns.

God said, "Raise up a prayer covering over the world."

God is going to raise up a prayer army of invincible spiritual warriors who will pray on a new level as if the salvation of the world depended on them. These spiritual warriors will get under a prayer burden for this world. They will pray until this world shakes with the power of God.

Today there are terrorists in the natural world. After 9/11 God spoke to me and said that He is raising up "Spiritual Terrorists."

God is raising up men and women who will move up to a new level of strategic spiritual warfare prayer!

This dimension of prayer is beyond the normal, traditional type of prayer. It is prayer that supercedes our natural minds and moves into the supernatural to take hold of the impossible!

Introduction

There are multiplied thousands of good books that have been written on prayer. My desire is not to just produce another book on prayer that will be read and placed on a shelf somewhere to gather dust.

It is my prayer that as you read the pages of this book, regardless of your current level of experience in prayer, you will receive a new all-consuming passion for prayer and the cry of your heart will be, "Lord, teach me to pray!"

The Holy Spirit, Who is a Spirit of intercession, is our teacher.

As you read, ask the Holy Spirit to take you beyond the limitations of your natural mind.

Ask Him to open your spiritual understanding and teach you how to pray prayers that touch the heart of God and result in His will being accomplished in your life, family, ministry and the nations of the world.

Ask Him to anoint your mouth with the fire of His Spirit, release a new prayer anointing upon you and bring you into this new level of strategic warfare prayer.

Draw near to Him with your whole heart and begin a spiritual journey into the Holy of Holies where He is waiting for you.

Get ready to receive more answers to prayer than you have ever experienced in your life!

TABLE OF CONTENTS

8

CHAPTER ONE

BEYOND ORDINARY PRAYER

We are on a spiritual journey in the passionate pursuit of Christ, to learn how to pray in the same powerful, unlimited dimension He taught and demonstrated.

We know it is possible!

We know Christ desires for us to live in a powerful, supernatural dimension of prayer where nothing is impossible to us!

We are not satisfied with the status quo or living below the full potential of the true power of prayer Christ intended for His Church to possess!

The cry welling up from deep inside our innermost being is: "Lord, teach us to pray!"

Regardless of your current level of experience in prayer, Christ is calling you to rise up and join Him, at His side, in strategic prayer and intercession that will result in entire cities, nations and people groups being transformed by His power!

Are you ready and willing to move beyond ordinary prayer into this new strategic level of prayer?

How hungry are you for a fresh manifestation of His Presence?

How hungry are you to receive a fresh anointing and impartation of His Spirit?

Are you hungry enough to die to yourself and your dependence upon your natural mind and abilities?

The first thing you must be willing to do is lay aside all pre-conceived ideas, man-made traditions and religious ideologies concerning prayer. These things will only weigh you down and prevent you from advancing in the Spirit to a new revelation and experience in prayer.

"Prevailing prayer is God's ordained means for extending His kingdom, for defeating Satan and his empire of darkness and evil, and for fulfilling God's eternal plan and bringing into effect His good will on earth."
Wesley L. Duewel

True prayer is much more than a formal repetition of eloquent words strung together to impress the hearers. It is more than just repeating or quoting prayers from a prayer book.

Prayer that moves the hand of God to produce His will upon earth is not based upon the well-planned strategies developed by our natural minds.

In fact, true prayer transcends the limitations of our natural minds because it is born of the Spirit.

"Prayer itself, is an art that only the Holy Spirit can teach us. He is the giver of all prayer."
Charles Spurgeon

There are many great books and sermons on prayer. However, the best way to learn how to pray is to come alongside the Great Intercessor, Who ever lives to make intercession for us! We must look to the Holy Spirit as not only our Teacher, but also our Divine Enabler,

Who makes it possible to pray prayers that are motivated, directed and divinely energized by Him.

Just as the disciples cried out to Jesus, "Lord, teach us to pray!" we must look carefully at what Jesus taught and demonstrated concerning prayer.

"And it came to pass, that, as he was praying in a certain place, when he ceased, one of his disciples said unto him, Lord, teach us to pray, as John also taught his disciples" (Luke 11:1).

More than likely, the only kind of prayer the disciples knew was the traditional prayers they learned from their worship in the synagogues under the priests.

Imagine for a moment being in the Presence of the Son of God and hearing Him pray. The atmosphere is electrified as the windows of Heaven open and He begins to commune with His Father.

There is something different about His prayer. Unlike the priests standing in the Synagogue reciting words, the words He speaks are alive and pulsate with life. The tone in which He speaks resonates with power.

One of the most outstanding things in Christ's life that the Disciples closest to Him had observed was His life of prayer. Jesus lived in unbroken communion and fellowship with the Father. He would often rise while everyone was sleeping and slip away before daybreak to pray. One of His favorite places of prayer was the Mount of Olives. I can almost see Him there, kneeling under one of the olive trees with His eyes lifted toward Heaven talking with the Father, listening to hear the Father's heart and receiving His instruction.

Before every major event in His life, Christ spent time alone with the Father. He said, *"...The Son can do nothing of himself, but what he seeth the Father do: for what things soever he doeth, these also doeth the Son likewise"* (John 5:19).

The great victories Jesus experienced out on the "frontlines" as He ministered to the needs of the people...teaching, opening blind eyes, unstopping deaf ears, healing all manner of diseases, raising the dead…were not automatic. They were won **before** He went out on the "frontlines"…**in prayer!**

"Prayer is the key that unlocks all the storehouses of God's infinite grace and power." **R.A. Torrey**

Although He was the Son of God, Jesus did not win these victories in His own strength. He had stripped Himself of His divine abilities and was subject to the same human limitations as you and me. He did absolutely nothing independent of the Father. None of the tremendous miracles and healings He did was automatic.

Everything Jesus did was a result of what the Father revealed to Him while He was in His Presence…while He was in **prayer!**

Before He went out onto the "frontlines," Jesus spent time in His Father's Presence where the Father revealed His will to Him. **Through prayer He penetrated** the "enemy lines," fought the battle and won it!

- BEFORE Jesus began His ministry, He spent 40 days in **fasting** and **prayer** and returned in the "…power of the Spirit into Galilee" (Luke 4:14).

- BEFORE feeding the five thousand by multiplying five loaves of bread and two fish, He went by boat out into a solitary place where He **prayed** (See Matthew 14:13).

- BEFORE a great healing campaign in Gennesaret where the people brought the sick to Him, Jesus went up on a mountainside by himself where He prayed (See Matthew 14:22-23).

- BEFORE choosing the 12 apostles, Jesus *"Went off to the mountain to pray, and He spent the whole night in prayer to God"* (Luke 6:12 NAS).

12

- BEFORE He began His ministry throughout Galilee where He preached and cast out demons, Jesus **prayed.** *"Very early in the morning, while it was still dark, Jesus got up, left the house and went off to a solitary place, where He prayed"* (See Mark 1:35 NIV).

- BEFORE going to the cross...on the road to Jerusalem...Jesus, knowing that He was going to be taken and crucified went up onto a mountain where He prayed (See Luke 9:28).

- BEFORE He was arrested, beaten, mocked and crucified, Jesus went into the garden of Gethsemane where He **prayed**...where He wrestled and agonized in prayer (See Matthew 26:36-46).

Before you take any steps that will affect your life or family, shouldn't you enter into spiritual warfare through prayer, penetrate the "enemy lines" and win the battle?

"Would you pray with mighty results? Seek the mighty workings of the Holy Spirit in your own spirit."
E. M Bounds

Now let us go back to Luke 11:1, where Jesus was praying and His disciples had come to Him asking that He teach them how to pray.

As they listened to Jesus praying, it was so awesome they could not stand by any longer and be content to just listen. I imagine hearing them cry out, "We want what you have! Lord Jesus, teach us how to pray. You are doing something we have never experienced before. We are hearing you touch heaven. We are hearing you in relationship with the God of Abraham, Isaac and Jacob. It's not just tradition, but what we are hearing is reality, and we want to know how to pray as you pray!"

PRAY "OUR FATHER..."

In answer to their heart's cry, Jesus began to teach them how to pray with what we refer to as The Lord's Prayer. This beautiful prayer is probably the most widely known and loved prayer ever prayed. Untold millions throughout the ages have repeated it. Books have been written about it. It has been sung in stately stained glass cathedrals and houses of worship of all denominations.

Jesus never intended for His prayer to become another traditional prayer to simply be repeated as part of a liturgy.

In this prayer He set forth a heavenly pattern upon which to base our prayers. One of the great truths from Jesus' prayer that I want us to focus our attention on is that He broke through the traditional barriers and for the first time taught them to acknowledge and pray to God as their Father.

Jesus said, *"When ye pray say, Our Father which art in heaven..."* (Luke 11:2).

No longer was prayer to be just a form or ritual!

No longer was it to be relegated to vain repetitions as it was with the heathen nations.

No longer was it to be a religious exercise to impress others.

Prayer was to be based upon a new revelation of recognizing and coming to the God of Israel as their Father!

A RADICAL NEW CONCEPT OF PRAYER

Jesus broke through the tradition and formalism of the religious leaders and Pharisees by teaching a radical new concept of prayer. In one of His first references to prayer, during His Sermon on the Mount, Christ taught the people to love their enemies and to pray for them. In fact, He taught praying for one's enemies as a natural response of those who are truly one of God's children.

Jesus said, *"You have heard it was said, 'Love your neighbor and hate your enemy. But I tell you: Love your enemies, and pray for those who persecute you that you may be sons of your Father in heaven"* (Matthew 5:43-45 NIV).

It is interesting to note that in His first references to prayer He emphasized prayer that goes beyond the ordinary.

How often have you spent time in prayer for your enemies, those who stab you in the back, betray your confidence, lie about you and have hurt you deeply? In the average Christian's prayer experience, very little time, if any, is spent in prayer for his enemies. Yet, Jesus emphasized the importance of this type of prayer.

"It is only as we give ourselves to the Spirit living and praying in us, that the glory of the prayer-hearing and most effective mediation of the Son can be made known by us in their power." Andrew Murray

Notice that Jesus said, *"...pray for those who persecute you THAT you may be sons of your Father in heaven"* (Matthew 5:44-45). In the natural, it is not difficult to pray for friends, family and other Christians in need. But prayer for our enemies is not easy and cannot be done in the natural because it originates in the Father's heart. It involves His love and forgiveness and those who are truly His sons and daughters, born of His Spirit, will follow His example.

LORD, TEACH US TO PRAY!

Not only through His Words but also through His example, Jesus taught that we must be willing to forgive and to pray for our enemies.

Jesus, the holy, pure, Son of God, was despised, rejected and betrayed even by those closest to Him. He was falsely accused, spit upon, made

15

a public spectacle of shame and disgrace, and nailed to a cross. Hanging there in pain and agony, He prayed the greatest prayer ever prayed: "*...Father, forgive them; for they know not what they do...*" (Luke 23:34).

This prayer falling from the lips of the Son of God, ascended unto the Father Who heard His cry, received the sacrifice of His life's blood and responded by extending to man the priceless gift of salvation.

His prayer transcended every natural limitation. It was not ordinary prayer.

It has transcended time.

As a result of that one prayer, countless multitudes throughout the ages stand acquitted, forgiven, restored into fellowship with God as their Father.

Lord, teach us to pray! Teach us to go beyond ordinary prayer, to love our enemies, to forgive and to pray for them as you have taught us through your Word and through your example as our Great Intercessor.

BEYOND HEAD KNOWLEDGE AND TRADITION

"Prayer is 'the breathing of a soul inflamed for God, and inflamed for humanity.' " E. M. Bounds

True prayer must be from the heart. It is not just the words or phrases a person repeats as a mere routine or formality. It involves coming before God, as our Father, with our hearts—our entire beings, in an attitude of humble submission. God requires our whole heart! In His dealings with the children of Israel, He spoke through the Prophet Jeremiah, "*And ye shall seek me, and find me, when ye shall search for me with all your heart*" (Jeremiah 29:13).

Jesus exposed the hypocrisy and religious tradition of those who prayed in the synagogues and street corners to be seen of men. He called the Pharisees hypocrites. He said, "*...rightly did Isaiah prophesy of you, saying 'This people honors Me with their lips, but their heart is far away from Me. But in vain do they worship Me, Teaching as doctrines the precepts of men'*" (Matthew 15:7-9 NAS).

We must be careful not to become bound by religion or the traditions taught by men. There are many Christians sitting in our churches who pray on a regular basis. The words coming out of their mouths are what they have learned, but the words are empty and hollow because they are coming from their heads and not from their hearts.

To go beyond ordinary prayer, we cannot be content with head knowledge or religious tradition. The cry of our hearts must be, "Lord, break through the dead, dry tradition and formalism and teach us how to pray as you prayed!"

The Pharisees were committed to and preoccupied with strict adherence to the Law and the oral tradition, with its rules for interpreting the Law, purification rites and man-made laws handed down by their fathers. With minute attention to detail they observed all the sacred times laid down by God. They gave tithes of all they possessed and fasted twice a week on Mondays and Thursdays. They were doing all the right things but they were so bound by tradition they did not really know God and could not receive the truths Christ spoke to them.

Their understanding of God was primarily as the Law-giver and their pre-occupation with fulfilling His commands exactly became an end in itself. When they went to the Temple to pray, their prayers were formal and legalistic. And, they went there to be seen and heard of men, not to meet with God.

Public prayers were offered daily in the synagogue which included the Shema, consisting of three passages from the Old Testament: Deuteronomy 6:4-9; Deuteronomy 11:13-21; and Numbers 15:37-41.

The Shema was repeated both morning and evening with benedictions.

In addition, the Tephillah, or Eighteen Benedictions, was repeated three times a day. Much of this was incorporated into the Hebrew Prayer Book that is still used in Jewish Synagogues today.

In sharp contrast to the hypocrisy of the Pharisees, Jesus broke through the rigid, formal tradition of man's religious forms, rituals and concepts of prayer and established it upon **a relationship with the Father!**

He taught the people the importance of shutting themselves away in a secret place to pray. Jesus said:

> *And when you pray, do not be like the hypocrites, for they love to pray standing in the synagogues and on the street corners to be seen by men. I tell you the truth, they have received their reward in full. But when you pray, go into your room, close the door and pray to your Father, who is unseen. Then your Father, who sees what is done in secret, will reward you.*
>
> Matthew 6:5-6 NIV

PRAYER – A LIVING RELATIONSHIP WITH THE FATHER

No longer was God to be known as a Supreme Being far removed in the heavens somewhere: inaccessible and unapproachable, but as a loving, Heavenly Father Who desires to live in intimate fellowship and communion with His children.

Throughout the ages, Abraham, Moses, Joshua, Elijah, David and the other Old Testament prophets and saints directed their prayers to the One true and living God, the all powerful Jehovah, the Holy One of Israel. They knew Him as the Almighty God Who revealed Himself with signs and wonders, rolled back the Red Sea, led them through the wilderness, rained down manna from heaven, caused the water to gush forth from the rock, rained down fire from Heaven, delivered them in the fiery furnace, shut the mouths of lions and fought for and delivered them out of the hands of their enemies.

But, they did not have an intimate relationship with Him as their Heavenly Father. None of the Old Testament saints ever prayed to Him as their Father.

Listen to their prayers:

Solomon prayed: *"O Lord, the God of Israel, there is no God like You in Heaven above or on earth beneath, keeping covenant and showing mercy and loving-kindness to Your servants who walk before You with all their heart;"* (1 Kings 8:23 AMP).

Hezekiah cried unto the God of Israel: *"O Lord, God of Israel, enthroned between the cherubim, you alone are God over all the kingdoms of the earth. You have made heaven and earth"* (2 Kings 19:15 NIV).

Elijah called upon the God of Abraham, Isaac and Israel. He prayed: *"O Lord, God of Abraham, Isaac and Israel, let it be known today that you are God in Israel and that I am your servant and have done all these things at your command"* (1 Kings 18:36 NIV).

The Old Testament prophets and saints were unable to know God intimately in a relationship as a Father because the Holy Spirit had not yet been given. God promised that He would make a new covenant with Israel and that He would place His Spirit within them. He said, *"A new heart will I give you, and a new spirit will I put within you"* (Ezekiel 36:26 AMP).

Under the New Covenant Jesus came not only to redeem man from His sins, but to bring man into a new, intimate relationship with God. Six different times in His Sermon on the Mount, Christ emphasized prayer based upon a living relationship with the Almighty God of Israel, Creator of the heavens and earth, **as a Father.**

Jesus said, *"...pray to your Father"* (Matthew 6:6 AMP); *"...your Father who sees what is done in secret will reward you"* (Matthew 6:6 NIV); *"...your Father knows what you need, before you ask Him"* (Matthew 6:8 NAS); *"This, then, is how you should pray: 'Our Father in heaven...'"* (Matthew 6:9 NIV).

BEYOND SELFISH PRAYERS

In Matthew, 6:31-33 Jesus teaches us not to be concerned about the basic necessities of life: what to eat, drink or how we will be clothed. He said, *"...for your heavenly Father knoweth that ye have need of all these things:"*

In these verses Jesus reveals our priority in prayer. Our major concern when we come before the Father is not to bombard Him with our needs.

Yet, in the life of the average Christian, the majority of his prayer time is spent focusing on his immediate needs and the needs of his family. We often become so occupied with our urgent petitions that we forget that our Father sees and knows.

Jesus didn't say these things aren't important to the Father or that we should not ask Him to meet our needs. He said that our Father already knows what we need before we even ask Him.

We must not allow our minds to become preoccupied or to worry about the basic necessities of life. Worry is sin because at the root of it is really a lack of faith in the Father's love and concern for us, or the fear that He will fail to meet our needs. When we pray we do not need to try to compel an unwilling God to listen to us with the urgency of our words. As a loving Heavenly Father, He not only hears our prayers but is just waiting for us to ask!

"All that God is, and all that God has, is at the disposal of prayer." R. A. Torrey

The key to having our needs met is found in verse Matthew 6:33.

Jesus said, *"But seek ye first the kingdom of God, and his righteousness; and all these things shall be added unto you."* When we know and are confident in the Father's love for us, and know that He already is aware of our needs, we will set our focus upon seeking Him...seeking to know Him, seeking to be filled with His Presence and His righteousness.

Our priority in prayer will be focused upon the Father and seeing that His will and plan is fulfilled in our lives and upon this earth.

In Matthew, 7:7-11, Jesus again stresses the fact that when we come to God in prayer, we are to come as a loving, trusting child asking in confidence knowing that our father will give us whatever we ask. Jesus said, *"If ye then, being evil, know how to give good gifts unto your children, how much more shall your Father which is in heaven give good things to them that ask him?"* (Matthew 7:11).

GOD'S UNIVERSAL LAW CONCERNING PRAYER

"God does nothing, but in answer to prayer."
John Wesley

In His teaching on prayer, Jesus taught God's Universal Law concerning prayer. He said. *"Ask, and it shall be given you; seek, and ye shall find; knock, and it shall be opened unto you: For every one that asketh receiveth; and he that seeketh findeth; and to him that knocketh it shall be opened"* (Matthew 7:7-9).

Just as God has a Universal Law concerning giving in Luke 6:38, His Universal Law concerning prayer is found here in these verses: everyone who asks in faith receives!

This law God has established is irrevocable! Knowing that God has bound Himself to His Word to answer prayer is the very basis and foundation for our prayers.

When we come to the Father we must believe that we are going to receive or we might as well not even ask! *"But without faith it is impossible to please him: for he that cometh to God must believe that he is, and that he is a rewarder of them that diligently seek him"* (Hebrews 11:6).

Too many times when the answer does not come immediately, Christians are willing to resign themselves to the fact that their prayer was unanswered supposing it was not God's will. God's law is that everyone who asks in faith receives! We must continue to persevere in faith, accept and believe His promise until we receive what we have asked.

Jesus said, *"How much more will your Father give good gifts to those who ask him?"* Our Father is a REWARDER of those who come to Him in faith. He will do all that He has promised and far beyond anything we can ever imagine or ask. He will do *"exceeding abundantly above all that we ask or think, according to the power that worketh in us"* (Ephesians 3:20).

THE TRUE FOUNDATION AND BASIS OF PRAYER

To go beyond ordinary prayer we must have a fresh revelation of God, as our Heavenly Father Who desires to pour good things into our lives. He has provided everything we need and is just waiting for us to ask. He is just looking for opportunities to manifest His power on behalf of His children. *"For the eyes of the Lord run to and fro throughout the whole earth, to shew himself strong in the behalf of them whose heart is perfect toward him"* (2 Chronicles 16:9). When we live in this intimate relationship with the Father, the prayer of faith and its answer will be the natural result!

Moses, who talked with God face to face and was known as a friend of God, did not have the privilege we have today of calling upon God as our Father! Elijah who prayed and shut the heavens so that it did not rain for 3-1/2 years, who prayed and opened the heavens, who prayed and God responded by sending fire from heaven, did not have the awesome relationship we have with God as our Father. David, who had an intimate relationship with God, and was known as a man after God's own heart, did not know Him as Father!

Today, through Christ, we have been restored into fellowship with Almighty God and enjoy the awesome privilege and blessing our spiritual forefathers did not have. Through prayer we have intimacy with Him and call Him our Father!

To go beyond ordinary prayer and live in the powerful dimension of prayer that Jesus taught, you must come before the Father with your whole heart and know Him intimately as **your Father.** This is the foundation and basis of all true prayer. Jesus said, *"After this manner therefore pray ye: Our Father which art in heaven, Hallowed be thy name"* (Matthew 6:9).

True prayer—beyond ordinary prayer—is much more than asking God for things. It is a living, vital relationship with our Heavenly Father. We must learn to come before Him with a childlike simplicity, in faith, trusting and knowing He desires to pour into our lives all that we need.

> *Father, how we praise you for this glorious privilege of coming into Your Presence and knowing You intimately as our Father! As Your children, we want to pour out our love upon You, and to know You in the fullness of Your glory. We want to know Your Father's heart, to hear Your voice and to walk in obedience and intimate fellowship with You. Draw us near to Your heart so that we can learn how to live in unbroken communion and fellowship with You.*

PRAYER THAT REACHES THE FATHER MUST BE IN THE SPIRIT!

It is through Christ that we have divine access to the Father by the Spirit. *"For through him we both have access by one Spirit unto the Father"* (Ephesians 2:18).

Paul, the great Apostle of prayer, stressed that true prayer must originate in the Spirit. He said, *"Pray at all times (on every occasion, in every season) in the Spirit, with all [manner of] prayer and entreaty. To that end keep alert and watch with strong purpose and perseverance, interceding in behalf of all the saints (God's consecrated people)"* (Ephesians 6:18 AMP).

R. A. Torrey said, "The whole secret of prayer is found in those words, "in the Spirit!"

We are exhorted to pray "in the Holy Ghost." *"But ye, beloved, building up yourselves on your most holy faith, praying in the Holy Ghost"* (Jude 20).

The first lesson you must learn in Christ's School of Prayer, and the key to true power in prayer, is that your prayers must originate from the Holy Spirit.

God is a Spirit not bound by time or space. The only way you can know Him is by His Spirit dwelling in you.

The Holy Spirit ushers you into the Father's Presence. He is the One Who **calls** you to pray, **teaches** you to pray, **guides** you in your prayers, **gives** you faith and **strengthens** you in your prayers.

To become mighty in prayer, you must be willing to go beyond ordinary prayer—beyond the limitations of your natural mind—and develop a total dependence upon the Holy Spirit. Only the Holy Spirit can enable you to know the heartbeat of God, the priority of God, and the will of God so that you can pray and see God's results. **True prayer is the Holy Spirit releasing the mind and will of the Father in us, and then giving the divine unction and utterance to speak the word of faith to accomplish it.**

PRAYER – BEYOND NATURAL LIMITATIONS

The Apostle Paul gives us a clear understanding of the vital role of the Holy Spirit and prayer.

So too the [Holy] Spirit comes to our aid and bears us up in our weakness; for we do not know what prayer to offer nor how to offer it worthily as we ought, but the Spirit Himself goes to meet our supplication and pleads in our behalf with unspeakable yearnings and groanings too deep for utterance. And He Who searches the hearts of men knows what is the mind of the [Holy] Spirit [what His intent is], because the Spirit intercedes and pleads [before God] in behalf of the saints according to and in harmony with God's will.

Romans 8:26-27 AMP

To go beyond ordinary prayer, you must break through every natural barrier so that the Spirit inside you begins to pray.

Paul said we do not even know how or what to pray. We must stop trying to pray according to our natural understanding. The natural mind does not understand the things of the Spirit. *"But the natural man receiveth not the things of the spirit of God: for they are foolishness unto him: neither can he know them, because they are spiritually discerned"* (1 Corinthians 2:14).

When the Spirit of God in you takes over and prays through you, you will always pray the will of God. And, you will always receive the answer!

"If you would pray in faith, be sure to walk every day with God. If you do, He will tell you what to pray for. Be filled with His spirit and He will give you objects enough to pray for. He will give you as much of the spirit of prayer as you have strength of body to bear."
Charles Finney

Prayer prayed in and by the Spirit—that is prayed in the will of God—never goes unanswered!

The Holy Spirit living within us knows our infirmities. In the natural, we don't know how to pray. But, when the Holy Spirit begins to take over, we go beyond ordinary prayer—beyond our capacity—and we enter a new dimension of prayer.

Paul said, "...He Who searches the hearts of men knows what is in the mind of the [Holy] Spirit—what His intent is—because the Spirit intercedes and pleads (before God) in behalf of the saints according to and in harmony with God's will" (Romans 8:27 AMP).

We provide the vessel; the Holy Spirit does the interceding according to the will of God!

As I stated earlier, the Old Testament prophets and saints never prayed to God as their Father. They prayed to Jehovah. But now, because of our relationship with Christ, we are able to call Him our Father. Jesus said, "And when that time comes, you will ask nothing of Me [you will need to ask Me no questions]. I assure you, most solemnly I tell you, that My Father will grant you whatever you ask in My name [presenting all that I AM]" (John 16:23 AMP).

And, because of the Holy Spirit living within us, we have the divine capability to go beyond our natural capacity and the Holy Spirit, Who knows the mind of God, intercedes for us according to the mind and will of God!

We will go more in-depth into the strategic role of the Holy Spirit, and how to pray prayers that are divinely charged and energized by the Spirit in chapter nine.

In your pursuit of learning how to pray in the powerful dimension of prayer Christ intended for His Church, no ordinary praying, you must seek to be filled and under full control of the Holy Spirit. The more you surrender your life to Christ and die to self, the more you give room for the Holy Spirit to work in you and release His power through you.

The Father yearns and is searching for those whom He can use in prayer to accomplish His will in this end-time hour.

Will you respond to the wooing of His Spirit?

Will you empty yourself and allow the Holy Spirit to flow through you in an unprecedented measure?

You can remain at the level of ordinary prayer. Or, you can determine that you will rise to a new level of prayer that goes beyond your ordinary capacity, beyond your natural mind and all the things you have learned, beyond your thoughts and become a vessel that the Holy Spirit can pray through.

When the Holy Spirit prays through you, it is the only time when the answers will be manifested 100% of the time, because it is not ordinary praying.

Only when our prayers are divinely energized by the Holy Spirit do prayer breakthroughs really happen and we take possession of God's promises.

TRUE PRAYER IS BORN OF THE SPIRIT

One of the first things Jesus taught was that God is a Spirit!

As He was traveling through Samaria, He met a Samaritan woman at Jacob's well. In this familiar story is a major key in knowing the secret of how to pray.

Jesus was weary from His journey and sat down at the well. His disciples had gone into the city to buy something to eat.

As He sat there, a Samaritan woman came to the well to draw water. This was not a chance meeting that day but a divine appointment that would forever change her spiritual destiny. Through the encounter this woman would have with Christ, many Samaritans would come to receive Him as their Messiah and Savior.

Jesus said to the woman, "...give me to drink" (John 4:7).

The woman was no doubt shocked that Jesus had even spoken to her. The Samaritans were despised by the Jews. The Jews cursed them by the sacred name of God and by the curse of the upper and lower house of judgment with the law, "That no Israelite eat anything that is a Samaritan's, for it is as if he should eat swine's flesh."

Fixing her eyes on Jesus, the woman asked, "How is that you, a Jew, ask me to give you a drink? I'm a woman of Samaria. The Jews have no dealings with the Samaritans" (see John 4:9).

Sitting before her was the promised Messiah, the Son of God, but she did not even know it.

Jesus replied, "If you only knew who you were talking to, who I am, you would have asked me to give you a drink of living water" (see John 4:10).

The woman still did not understand who Jesus was or what He meant. She was limited by her natural mind. She saw He didn't have a bucket with which to draw water and said, "The well is deep and you don't have anything to draw the water. Where is this living water?" (see John 4:11).

Jesus wasn't talking about natural water, but the living water of the Holy Spirit. He said concerning the natural water in the well, "Whoever drinks of this water will thirst again. But, I have some living water. If you drink of it, you will never thirst again, but it will be in you like an artesian well springing up within you" (see John 4:13-14).

The water Jesus was talking about was the Holy Spirit that He was going to send. The living water of the Holy Spirit would flow out of those who received Him like a mighty river!

What about you?

Are you thirsty?

Do you want a fresh drink of that living water so that you will be able to worship and pray in the power of His Spirit?

This is an hour when the Father is looking for those who are crying out for Him. He is seeking those who will worship Him in Spirit and in truth. By faith, cry out to Him now and allow Him to breathe His Spirit upon you and release a fresh anointing into your life.

How hungry are you for God? How much of a longing do you have inside your being for God?

The best music in the world cannot quench the thirst you have for God. Even reading the Word cannot quench the thirst you have in your soul for more of God.

There is only one thing that quenches the thirst and hunger that you have in your heart. It is when you commune with Him in prayer.

Nothing else satisfies, quenches the thirst and fills the void.

The beautiful song, *"Breathe,"* expresses this hunger so beautifully: "This is the air I breathe, Your Holy Presence living in me. This is my daily bread, your very Word spoken to me. I'm desperate for You...I'm lost without You."

Jesus broke through the outward form and religious barriers concerning worship and communion with the Father. The Samaritan woman, perceiving He was a prophet, wanted to know the correct *place* to worship.

She was concerned with the *outward formalities* of prayer.

Christ was concerned with the *inner workings* of the Spirit in prayer.

The Samaritans worshipped the God of Israel, but had erected a Temple on Mount Gerizim in competition with the Temple God established in Jerusalem. She was bound by tradition. She said, *"Our fathers worshipped in this mountain; and ye say, that in Jerusalem is the place where men ought to worship"* (John 4:20).

Jesus said: *"But an hour is coming, and now is, when the true worshipers shall worship the Father in spirit and truth: for such people the Father seeks to be His worshipers. God is spirit, and those who worship Him must worship in spirit and truth"* (John 4:23-24 NAS).

In other words, the hour had come when no longer would true worship be in the ceremonial observances of the Mosaic Law nor in the importance placed upon the place of worship, but upon worship and communion with the Father in the Spirit!

A DIVINE LINK TO THE FATHER

There are Christians today who pray, but they barely know what they are asking for. They pray earnestly, but receive little. They have not learned how to worship and commune with God in Spirit and in truth.

The only way we will be able to reach the heart of the Father in prayer is by His Spirit. The Father has given us the Holy Spirit which is the Spirit of adoption whereby we are able to cry, "Abba, Father." The Apostle Paul said:

For [the Spirit which] you have now received [is] not a spirit of slavery to put you once more in bondage to fear, but you have received the Spirit of adoption [the Spirit producing sonship] in [the bliss of] which we cry, Abba! [That is] Father! The Spirit Himself [thus] testifies together with our own spirit, [assuring us] that we are children of God.

Romans 8:15-16 AMP

The Spirit of God in us is a divine link between the Father and us. By His Spirit we are able to know Him, to know His heart, to live in continual communion with Him.

In Christ's School of Prayer we must realize that true prayer is not based upon a formula.

It is not based upon the stirring of our emotions or just going through some spiritual exercise.

It involves our spirits reaching up by the power of the Holy Spirit He has placed within us to commune with the Father.

True prayer is not relegated to a specific time or place. It is a way of life and should encompass every area of our lives. It goes beyond all natural limitations and is the highest and holiest work to which man can arise.

"The extent of the abiding is the exact measure of the power of prayer. It is the Spirit dwelling within us that prays, not in words and thoughts always, but in a breathing and a being, deeper than utterance."
Andrew Murray

Through Spirit directed and empowered prayer, we take possession of our spiritual inheritance and have the privilege of working together with the Father to bring His will to pass on the earth.

In chapter two we will continue our journey in the pursuit of learning how to go beyond ordinary prayer into the powerful supernatural dimension of the Spirit to pray prayers that move the hand of God. We will look closely at the single most important aspect of prayer that positions us spiritually to take hold of all that God planned for His Church to receive.

It is my prayer that your heart will begin to beat with greater fervency and passion for the Father.

I pray that you will cry out to Him and wait before Him, in His Presence, until you are so saturated and empowered by His Spirit that your prayers will be fervent, on fire and straight from the Father's heart to fulfill His will.

> *Father, thank you for placing Your Spirit within us giving us divine access to Your Throne. We submit ourselves fully into Your hands. Holy Spirit, have full control in our lives! Teach us to pray! Reveal to us the Father's heart, His will and His vision for our lives, families, cities and nations. Father, impart to us divine ability to pray prayers that will release Your power and anointing to bring salvation, healing and deliverance. Anoint us to pray prayers that will result in Satan's strongholds being destroyed and Your Kingdom and will being established in every nation.*

CHAPTER TWO

A HOLY SUMMONS

This is not a Kindergarten book on prayer.

We are not just focusing on the ABC's.

We are not interested in head knowledge or formulas.

This book is a *summons* to those who have seen in the Spirit the unlimited power and potential of prayer God intends for His people to possess; and, who have a burning passion that cannot be quenched to learn how to operate in that power to fulfill God's will.

Prayer is a spiritual force through which God releases His immeasurable, supernatural power to meet the needs of His people and establish His will and Kingdom upon the earth.

"God has ordained that the power to change things, to restrain evil, to calm human hatred, and to heal the world's wounds is released by the prayer of His people."
Wesley L. Duewel

There are absolutely no limitations, no circumstances, and no adverse circumstances that can hinder God's power from being released in answer to the cries of His children!

God has promised, *"Call unto Me, and I will answer thee, and show thee great and mighty things, which thou knowest not"* (Jeremiah 33:3). He is the Almighty God Who has said, *"Behold, I am the Lord, the God of all flesh: is there any thing too hard for me?"* (Jeremiah 32:27).

God is calling the Church to shake itself out of its complacency!

Although we are witnessing the greatest prayer movement in the history of the Church, with millions of people uniting in prayer with prayer networks, prayer outreaches and national and worldwide prayer initiatives, a great majority of Christians have fallen into a spiritual slumber. They go day after day, week after week without spending time in prayer.

According to a survey conducted in the United States, the average minister today spends less than fifteen minutes a day in any kind of penetrating prayer and the average Christian less than ten minutes!

Many use prayer only as an escape mechanism. They wait until they are in trouble to cry out to God. Others pray only as a last resort. They don't pray until they realize they cannot do it by themselves, until their way doesn't work.

There are Christians today who have so neglected their prayer life, they no longer have a will or desire to pray. There is no real joy in spending time alone with God. When they do pray, it is only from a sense of duty.

There are Christian leaders, pastors, teachers and Christian workers who have become so involved in the work of the ministry: preaching, teaching, making pastoral visits, singing and other church activities, that they fail to take time to pray. Instead of operating upon the power they receive through prayer, they begin to operate in their own strength.

IT IS TIME FOR THE CHURCH OF JESUS CHRIST TO WAKE UP!

Jesus warned that in the days before His coming, people would become so involved in the pursuit of the world and its pleasures, so pressured by the cares of life that His coming would come upon them unaware. He said, *"Watch ye therefore, and pray always, that ye may be accounted worthy to escape all these things that shall come to pass, and to stand before the Son of man"* (Luke 21:36).

"To be too busy with God's work to commune with God, to be busy with doing church work without taking time to talk to God about His work, is the highway to backsliding." E. M. Bounds

Many Christians have become so preoccupied with making a living, taking care of their families and enjoying the pleasures of this life that they are spiritually disabled. They have become too busy to pray. As a result, their spiritual eyes and discernment have grown dim until they cannot discern the signs of Christ's coming. Their spiritual ears have grown dull until they are unable to hear what the Spirit of God is saying. Jesus also warned:

> *But of that day and that hour knoweth no man, no, not the angels which are in heaven, neither the Son, but the Father. Take ye heed, watch and pray: for ye know not when the time is....And what I say unto you I say unto all, Watch.*
>
> Mark 13:32-33, 37

He said, "Watch and pray always!" Jesus warned us to stay spiritually alert through prayer. Watch and Pray must become so ingrained into our spirits until it becomes our heartbeat!

Christ's message to His Church today is:

"Shake yourselves! Rise up out of your sleep! The hour is late and there is no time to sleep or to become careless. This is a time to become vigilant in prayer. It is time to seek My face, to receive My direction, My anointing and My power to equip and prepare you for this hour! Rise up! Come and wait before Me. As you remain in My Presence I will reveal Myself to you. I will speak to you! I will release all that you need to walk in My power and might to accomplish My will."

The word of the Lord for us is "Watch and pray!" We must be continually on the alert, with our spiritual eyes open and our focus set on praying for God's will and purposes to be fulfilled in our lives, our cities and nations.

It is time for us to go beyond the 'bless me' stage in our prayers where we are only focused upon getting our needs met. The Father desires to meet our needs and wants us to bring our needs before Him. However, too many times the major focus of our prayers has become centered upon ourselves and we have become selfish in our prayers.

REACHING INTO HEAVEN AND BRINGING HEAVEN'S RESOURCES TO EARTH

Prayer is the most powerful force upon the earth. We have not even begun to tap into the unlimited power available to us through mighty prevailing prayer!

When Christ ascended into heaven, He intended the Church to be the most powerful force upon the earth. He sent the Holy Spirit, the Third Person of the Trinity, to live within us and to empower us to do the same works He had done, healing the sick, casting out demons, breaking bondages, setting people free and raising the dead. He defeated Satan and gave us power and authority over all the power of the enemy. He gave us the *legal right* to use His Name in prayer to fulfill His will upon earth.

The key to unlocking this unlimited power source in prayer is found in the promise Christ gave us: *And whatsoever ye shall ask in my name, that will I do, that the Father may be glorified in the Son. If ye shall ask anythng in my name, I will do it* (John 14:13-14). It is my prayer that before you finish reading this book, this verse will be indelibly printed upon your heart and it will become a living reality and experience in your prayer life.

"All who call on God in true faith, earnestly from the heart, will certainly be heard and will receive what they have asked and desired." Martin Luther

Jesus said that whatsoever we ask **in His Name** He will do it! The only condition attached to this promise is concerning **how** we ask. In upcoming chapters we will unlock this promise as we look closely at what Christ taught concerning how we are to ask.

Christ's intention for the Church is that through prayer we would reach up into Heaven and bring down His Kingdom upon earth!

He intended that we would use the power and authority in His Name to reach into the very Throne Room of Almighty God and bring Heaven's resources on earth to fulfill His will. He said to pray, *"Thy kingdom come, Thy will be done in earth, as it is in heaven"* (Matthew 6:10).

The Church, as a whole, has been unable to walk in the power Christ intended because of two things: Our failure to pray; and our lack of prevailing prayer.

The Church today is spiritually impotent like the disciples when they were faced with the challenge of casting a demon out of a young boy. When Jesus came down from the Mount of Transfiguration, He found His disciples defeated and confused. A man had brought his demon-possessed boy to them to be healed.

The father knelt down before Jesus and said, *"Lord, have mercy on my son: for he is lunatic, and sore vexed: for ofttimes he falleth into the fire, and oft into the water. And I brought him to thy disciples, and they could not cure him"* (Matthew 17:15-16).

Notice Jesus' response. He did not try to make excuses for His disciples. He did not waste words and there was no doubt as to what He meant. He rebuked His disciples saying, *"O unbelieving and perverted generation, how long shall I be with you? How long shall I put up with you? Bring him here to Me"* (Matthew 17:17 NAS).

The disciples had attempted to cast the demon out of the boy, but failed. They were commissioned and sent forth by Jesus to proclaim the Kingdom of God, heal the sick and cast out devils, but something prevented them that day from casting the demon out of the boy.

Jesus rebuked the demon and the boy was healed instantly!

Later the disciples came to Jesus privately and asked Him, "*Why couldn't we drive it out?*" (Matthew 17:19 NIV).

Look closely at Jesus' answer: "*Because of the littleness of your faith; for truly I say to you, if you have faith as a mustard seed, you shall say to this mountain, 'Move from here to there,' and it shall move; and nothing shall be impossible to you*" (Matthew 17:20 NAS).

Jesus did not sugarcoat the truth. He told His disciples plainly that they were unable to cast the demon out of the boy because of the "littleness" of their faith. He told them if they had faith the size of a small grain of mustard seed, nothing would be impossible to them.

Do you see it? Christ intends for His Church to live in a powerful dimension where nothing is impossible! He intends His power to flow through our lives to meet the desperate needs of this world.

Jesus said the key to operating in the same power He demonstrated in casting out the demon and setting the boy free was prayer and fasting. He said, "*But this kind does not go out except by prayer and fasting*" (Matthew 17:21 AMP).

THE CHURCH IS AT A CROSSROADS!

The great needs in our cities and nations are before us, like this man and his demon-possessed boy who stood before the disciples.

"Never did the Church need more than now those who can raise up everywhere memorials of God's supernatural

power, memorials of answers to prayer, memorials of promises fulfilled." E. M. Bounds

The only hope for the world is for the Church—men and women who have learned at the feet of Jesus how to prevail with God in prayer—to answer the call of the Spirit!

By His Spirit He is calling the Church in this hour to rise up to a new level of prayer. He wants to give you a fresh revelation and experience in prayer so that you will use the power and authority in His Name to see Satan's strongholds demolished; people groups and entire nations reached with the Gospel.

In chapter eleven I will go more in-depth into what Jesus taught concerning praying in His Name, and how you can live in a powerful dimension of prayer whereby you are able to go beyond the natural into the supernatural to take hold of the impossible!

Wesley Duewel, in his book, *Mighty Prevailing Prayer* wrote that the great need of the world is people who know how to prevail in prayer:

We need great answers to prayer, changed lives and situations—answers that bear upon them the stamp of the divine. We need mighty demonstrations of the reality and concern of God and His activity and power, which will force the world to recognize that God is truly God, that God is sovereign, and that God is involved in His world today. We need mighty answers to prayer that will bring new life to the church and new strength, faith, and courage to faint believers; that will silence, dumbfound and convict evil men; and that will thwart, defeat and drive back the assaults of Satan.

We must hear the cry of the Spirit!

The world is in desperate need for a generation of people full of the power and anointing of the Holy Spirit, who know how to pray divinely energized prayers that will shake the gates of hell, loose those bound in chains of darkness and bring about His Kingdom on earth.

PRAYER MUST BE A LIFESTYLE

The Apostle Paul gives us a powerful, comprehensive understanding of the importance and power of prayer and how we are to pray. He included prayer as part of the spiritual arsenal we must have to wage war and defeat the enemy. After listing the various pieces of spiritual armor, he said, *"Praying always with all prayer and supplication in the Spirit, and watching thereunto with all perseverance and supplication for all saints"* (Ephesians 6:18).

In this one verse, Paul stresses six very important things we must remember concerning prayer:

    1. Pray always, at all times, on all occasions.

    2. Pray with all different types of prayer.

    3. Pray in the Spirit.

    4. Watch in prayer.

    5. Persevere in prayer.

    6. Make supplication for all saints.

Paul exhorted believers in the Philippian Church not to be anxious about anything but to pray about **everything**. He said *"Be careful for nothing; but in every thing by prayer and supplication with thanksgiving let your requests be made known unto God"* (Philippians 4:6).

How often we fail to walk in the power and victory in every area of our lives because we do not bring everything to the Lord in prayer. There is a refrain in the old familiar hymn entitled, "What a Friend we Have in Jesus," that is so true: "Oh what peace we often forfeit, oh what needless pain we bear, all because we do not carry everything to God in prayer."

Paul made it very clear that in every thing we do, we are to cover it in prayer. Our entire lives are to be saturated with prayer. We are to pray without ceasing! Paul told the Church in Thessalonica, *"Rejoice evermore. Pray without ceasing. In every thing give thanks: for this is the will of God in Christ Jesus concerning you"* (I Thessalonians 5:16-18).

He urged them to have strong persistent prayer. He said, "*Continue in prayer, and watch in the same with thanksgiving*" (Colossians 4:2).

In writing to Timothy, one of the first things Paul emphasized was the importance of prayer. He said, "*I exhort therefore, that, first of all, supplications, prayers, intercessions, and giving of thanks, be made for all men*" (1 Timothy 2:1).

To pray in the powerful dimension Christ intended prayer must become a **lifestyle.** We must live in continual communion and fellowship with the Father where prayer is as natural as the breath we breathe.

There are many different types of prayer, all of which are vitally important. Paul mentions four in the above verses: prayer, supplications, intercession and thanksgiving. As we study some of the major types of prayer and their purposes, you will receive a fuller revelation of how Christ intends your entire life to be a life of prayer and intercession.

"Here is the secret of a life in prayer. Take time in the inner chamber to bow down and worship; and wait on Him until He unveils Himself, and takes possession of you, and goes out with you to show how a man can live and walk in abiding fellowship with an unseen Lord."
Andrew Murray

The call to prayer is first and foremost a call to a living, vibrant relationship with the Father and with Christ. The desire of the Father's heart is that His children come into His Holy Presence and live there continually in communion and fellowship.

We were created to have fellowship with God! Our entire existence, as sons and daughters of God, revolves around our relationship with Him where we are hearing and responding to His voice. It is based upon listening to His voice and knowing and doing His will.

In the Old Testament we read how the children of Israel stood at the foot of Mount Sinai and trembled in fear at the sound of God's voice. They were unable to come near unto Him.

Today, through the blood of Jesus, we can enjoy intimate communion and fellowship with God where He talks with us and we are able to hear His voice and receive all the blessings of His covenant with us.

There is no longer a barrier separating us from God. We have been brought into the Kingdom of God as His sons and daughters! He has placed His Spirit within us giving us direct access to Him. We can now go boldly into His Presence crying, "Abba…Father!"

In His first dealings with Moses and the children of Israel we see God summoning Moses to come up to the mountain to meet with him. God told Moses, *"Come up to Me on the mountain and remain there…"* (Exodus 24:12 NAS).

"When we pray, we are standing in the palace on the glittering floor of the great King's own reception room and thus, we are placed upon a vantage ground."
Charles Spurgeon

It was there on the mountain, God spoke to Moses. He revealed Himself to Moses and gave him the tables of stone with the Law and commandments for the children of Israel. There God revealed His glory.

It was there on the mountain Moses spent forty days and nights praying, fasting and interceding on behalf of Israel.

It was there he communed and fellowshipped with Almighty God Who had manifested His Presence in a glory cloud that covered the mountain for six days. On the seventh day, Moses heard the voice of God calling him and he went up into the mountain to meet with Him.

The glory of the Lord rested on Mount Sinai, and the cloud covered it six days. On the seventh day God called to Moses out of the midst of the cloud. And the glory of the Lord appeared to the Israelites like devouring fire on the top of the mountain. Moses entered into the midst of the cloud, and went up the mountain, and Moses was on the mountain forty days and nights.

(Exodus 24:16-18 AMP).

WE NEED TO STAY IN THE GLORY CLOUD

What a beautiful picture of the intimate relationship the Father desires to have with His sons and daughters today! Just as Moses entered into the glory cloud where He met with God, the Father desires us to draw near to Him. He wants us to come and wait in His Presence and stay in the glory cloud where He can reveal Himself intimately to us, reveal His love, speak to us and receive our love and worship.

God revealed His desire to commune with man when He directed Moses to build the Mercy Seat, put it on the Ark of the Covenant and place it in the Holy of Holies. God told Moses, *"And there I will meet with thee, and I will commune with thee from above the mercy seat..."* (Exodus 25:22).

He instructed Moses to build an altar and place it at the door of the Tabernacle where continual burnt offerings were to be offered unto Him. He said, *"And there I will meet with the children of Israel, and the tabernacle shall be sanctified by my glory"* (Exodus 29:43).

The word "commune" means to converse or talk together, intimacy; and the word "communion" means "interchange, or sharing thoughts or emotions; intimate communication. In prayer we commune with God first of all, by ministering to Him, showering our love upon Him, waiting silently in worship and adoration for Who He is. God longs for our love and ministry to Him, but too often, we go to Him to receive things from Him and to ask favors from Him.

"One of the great reasons why prayer in the inner chamber does not bring more joy and blessing is that it is too selfish and selfishness is the death of prayer."
Andrew Murray

The Father is interested in a love relationship with you! He is seeking those who will worship Him in Spirit and in truth! He is looking for those who will love Him enough to develop a personal, intimate relationship whereby they are living in unbroken fellowship and communion with Him on a day-by-day, moment by moment basis.

This type of relationship involves more than just reading a short devotional in the morning and saying a 5-minute prayer, or a prayer before you fall asleep at night. It involves communing with God throughout the day, on the job, driving down the freeway, wherever you are. It involves time spent daily when you find a quiet place to commune with God. Jesus taught that when we pray we are to shut ourselves into a secret place where we can be alone with God. He said, *"pray to thy Father which is in secret; and thy Father which seeth in secret shall reward thee openly"* (Matthew 6:6).

The Father wants us to have a relationship with Him whereby we not only give ourselves to Him, but He also gives Himself to us. When we enter into His Presence and begin to pour out our hearts and worship Him, He gives Himself to us. As we begin to worship Him with all our hearts, His Presence overshadows us like the glory cloud that overshadowed Moses on Mt. Sinai.

"Someone has well said, 'The goal of prayer is the ear of God.' This is a goal that can only be reached by patient, continued, and continuous waiting upon Him and

pouring out our heart to Him and permitting Him to speak to us. Only by so doing can we expect to know him." E. M. Bounds

God communes with us as we wait upon Him. He unfolds to us a greater revelation of Himself. As we commune with Him, His very life flows into us! He reveals His heart and releases His strength and anointing into our lives. His power is released as we wait upon Him. So many times we are so busy doing the work of the ministry that we fail to wait upon God and commune with Him. As a result, His power and anointing is missing in our lives. Our priority in prayer must be first, to commune with God and to minister to Him through our worship before we bring our petitions to Him.

THE #1 PRIORITY IN PRAYER

After the children of Israel sinned, God told Moses that He would not go with the people into the land He promised to give them. When the children of Israel heard this, they mourned and tore off their golden ornaments. Moses set up the Tabernacle outside the camp and all those who sought the Lord went out to the Tabernacle. When Moses entered the Tabernacle, *"...the cloudy pillar descended, and stood at the door of the tabernacle, and the Lord talked with Moses"* (Exodus 33:9).

Moses had a divine encounter where God spoke to him *"face to face, as a man speaketh unto his friend"* (Exodus 33:11).

Listen to Moses' prayer: *"...if I have found grace in thy sight, show me now thy way, that I may know thee, that I may find grace in thy sight: and consider that this nation is thy people"* (Exodus 33:13).

God answered, *"...My presence shall go with thee..."* (Exodus 33:14).

Moses replied, *"If your Presence does not go with us, do not send us up from here"* (Exodus 33:15 NIV). Moses understood that it was God's Presence with him and the children of Israel that set them apart from all the other people on earth. Today as sons and daughters of God, His

Holy Presence living in us is what sets us apart from all other people, nations and tribes.

God did not answer Moses' prayers simply because of the words he spoke. Moses didn't follow a "formula" for his prayers. He did not depend on his natural abilities or powers of persuasion to change God's mind.

Moses had a deep, intimate relationship with God. He knew the depth of God's love and mercy. He knew His divine faithfulness. He hungered after God's Presence and would have chosen to stay in the wilderness unless God's Presence went with them. The cry of his heart was, "I must have your Presence with me. I want to know you!"

"Prayer is able to prevail with heaven and bend omnipotence to its desire." Charles Spurgeon

Is this the cry of your heart?

Just as God summoned Moses up to the mountain to commune with Him, He desires you to come into His Presence and to have intimate communion and fellowship with Him.

Are you hungry for more of God's Presence?

Deep inside your innermost being are you crying out to know Christ more intimately?

The basis and foundation for your prayer and intercession is your personal intimate relationship with the Father. It is the key to praying with power and receiving answers to your prayers. As one of His children, born of His Spirit, He knows you intimately by name. He knows your thoughts and everything about you, and He still loves you with an everlasting love. Your greatest priority in prayer should be seeking to know God, to be in His Presence and to pour out your heart to Him. David had an insatiable desire to be in God's Presence.

One thing have I asked of the Lord, that will I seek after, inquire for and (insistently) require, that I may dwell in the house of the Lord (in His presence) all the days of my life, to behold and gaze upon the beauty (the sweet attractiveness and the delightful loveliness) of the Lord, and to meditate, consider and inquire in His temple.

Psalm 27:4 AMP

David said, "*One thing have I asked of the Lord...*" The one thing He desired above all else, and set his spiritual focus on, was to live continually in God's Presence. Listen to his prayer when he was in the wilderness in Judah:

O GOD, you are my God, earnestly I seek you; my soul thirsts for you, my body longs for you, in a dry and weary land where there is no water. I have seen you in the sanctuary and beheld your power and your glory.

Psalm 63:1-2 NIV

David had an intimate relationship with God. He said, "My whole being follows hard after You and clings closely to You." He poured out His love in worship and praise and spent time with Him in the sanctuary enabling him to say, "I have seen you...I have beheld your glory and I am going to passionately pursue you!"

HOW HUNGRY ARE YOU FOR GOD'S PRESENCE?

Communion with God involves passionate desire. From your innermost being there must also arise an insatiable desire to know the Father and live in unbroken communion with Him and with Christ.

The greatest desire of Paul's heart was, "*That I may know him, and the power of his resurrection, and the fellowship of his sufferings, being made conformable unto his death*" (Philippians 3:10).

With every fiber of your being you must cry out, "That I may know you!" You must be willing to shut yourself in with Him and spend time

47

in His Presence, getting to know Him, allowing His words to take root in your heart.

Like Moses you must desire to be shut up in the glory cloud of His Presence.

You must so desire and depend upon His Presence that you, too, will say, "If your Presence doesn't go with me, I don't want to go!"

When you live in this intimate relationship, your prayers will rise to a new level. They will be based not upon carnal, selfish desires but on His desires and His will. You will no longer depend on your own natural understanding to pray. You will pray according to how He directs you by His Spirit living and working in you. Your prayers will be divinely energized!

"He who knows how to overcome with God in prayer has heaven and earth at his disposal." Charles Spurgeon

MOVE FROM THE OUTER COURT INTO THE HOLY OF HOLIES

Because of Christ's blood, which He shed on Calvary for the atonement of man's sin, you have the privilege and *legal right* in prayer to boldly enter into the most holy place…into the Throne Room of God, the very Holy of Holies, where God in all His power and glory dwells.

For fifteen centuries Israel had a sanctuary with a "Holy of Holies," into which, no one except the High Priest could enter under penalty of death. No one could have access into God's Presence.

The priests were not allowed to enter, but ministered outside in the outer court offering up sacrifices to God. Once a year, on the Day of Atonement, the High Priest, after he had consecrated himself, was allowed to enter in and pour out a blood offering upon the Mercy Seat for the sins of himself and the people.

Through His blood, Christ, our great High Priest, *"entered in once into the holy place, having obtained eternal redemption for us"* (Hebrews 9:12).

When He died, the veil in the Temple, separating man from entering into the Holiest and from God's Presence was forever destroyed!

The Holiest of all has been opened to you whereby you can live continually in the fullness of God's Holy Presence. Don't be content with an outer court experience. The Father paid the ultimate price of the sacrifice of His Son, giving you full access, not only to live in His Presence and enjoy intimate communion with Him, but also to partake of all that He has provided for you.

Our great High Priest is there, seated on the right hand of the Father. Nothing else remains to be done. Everything you need has been provided for through His blood. Christ is there interceding before the Father on your behalf and drawing you, by His Spirit, into His Presence and union with Him.

Christ's desire is that you be united with Him and the Father as ONE! In His great High Priestly prayer Jesus prayed:

> *Neither for these alone do I pray – it is not for their sake only that I make this request – but also for those who will ever come to believe in (trust, cling to, rely on) Me through their word and teaching; So that they all may be one [just] as You, Father, are in Me and I in You, that they also may be one in Us, so that the world may believe and be convinced that you have sent Me.*
>
> John 17:20-21 AMP

He said, *"I in them and you in Me..."* (John 17:23 AMP).

In this holy union with Christ and the Father, they have made their dwelling place within your spirit making the closest, most intimate relationship possible.

If a person [really] loves Me, he will keep My word – obey My teaching; and My Father will love him, and We will come to him and make Our home (abode, special dwelling place) with him.

John 14:23 AMP

In this verse Jesus said "We" will come! The Father, Son and Holy Spirit make Their dwelling place in you. Your communion together is made possible by His Spirit. There are no barriers to the depth of the relationship you can have! The desire of the Father and of Christ is that you know Them in all Their fullness. The only limitations are what we place upon Them through our indifference and lack of desire.

In His message to the seven churches, Jesus said, *"Behold, I stand at the door, and knock: if any man hear my voice, and open the door, I will come in to him, and sup with him, and he with me"* (Revelation 3:20).

This scripture is often used in relation to salvation. However, Jesus was not simply talking about the unbeliever accepting Him into his heart. He was talking about the deep fellowship and communion He desires to have with us today. He said, "I want to come in and sup with you." The Greek word, *"sup"* in this verse is *"deipneo"* which refers to taking the chief meal of the day. Christ desires you to draw near to Him so that He can enjoy fellowship with you as a person enjoys talking with close friends and family during a special meal.

Jesus said, "If any man hear my voice…" If you hear His voice and respond, He will come and commune with you. In this relationship Christ wants you to know Him personally. Not just know about Him or have "head knowledge" of Him, but truly know Him through personal experience.

The Father is just waiting and longing for His children to draw near to Him. He is summoning us to leave the outer court and enter into the Holiest, into His holy Presence where we can have intimate face-to-face communion with Him. The Apostle Paul wrote:

Having, therefore, brethren, boldness to enter into the holiest by the blood of Jesus, By a new and living way, which he hath consecrated for us, through the veil, that is to say, his flesh; and having a high priest over the house of God; Let us draw near...

Hebrews 10:19-22

The summons from the Throne of God to you is "Draw Near!"
What an awesome privilege we have to live in communion and fellowship with the Father. God is drawing us to Himself, calling us to a higher dimension of prayer, greater than anything we have ever known. **Let us draw near!**

BECOME CONSUMED WITH A PASSIONATE DESIRE FOR GOD

Set your priority in prayer to first and foremost spend time communing with the Father and with Christ. Set aside time in prayer to seek the Father's face and not just His hand of blessing. As you come into His Presence, acknowledge Him for Who He is. Take time to be silent before Him listening to hear His voice.

"In prayer it is better to have a heart without words than words without a heart."
John Bunyan

Communion in prayer is not a monologue, but a dialogue. So many times when we pray, we spend the majority of our time doing all the talking. True communion involves listening for God's voice to know His will and direction. Jesus said, *"My sheep hear my voice...and they follow me"* (John 10:27). He said, *"I know my sheep, and my sheep know me..."* (John 10:14 NIV). In essence Jesus was saying that He knows all those who truly belong to Him and they know Him. Through their intimacy, they recognize and know His voice. The more you develop intimacy with the Lord the more you will be able to hear and discern His voice.

There in the Holiest—in His awesome Presence—you will receive a divine life flow of His anointing. You will be strengthened and renewed. In His glorious Presence, He will pour out His love upon you!

> **"Prayer is having an audience with the King of kings, that eternal, omnipotent King in comparison with Whom all earthly kings and queens are nothing."**
> **R. A. Torrey**

First and foremost in our prayers we must spend time shut in with the Father, waiting before Him, drawing from His strength and allowing Him to reveal Himself to us. Then, once we have entered this place of communion and fellowship we enter into *power intimacy* where we are positioned and empowered to intercede on behalf of others.

The call of the Spirit today is a call to the Church of Jesus Christ to return to a personal, intimate relationship with the Father and with Christ through prayer. We will be barren, cut off from the divine life flow of God, without a renewed dedication and commitment to intimacy through prayer.

> *I am the vine, ye are the branches: He that abideth in me, and I in him, the same bringeth forth much fruit: for without me ye can do nothing. If a man abide not in me, he is cast forth as a branch, and is withered; and men gather them, and cast them into the fire, and they are burned.*
>
> John 15:5-6

It is through our union and communion with Christ that we are able to ask whatever we will in prayer and it will be done. Jesus said, *"If ye abide in me, and my words abide in you, ye shall ask what ye will, and it shall be done unto you"* (John 15:7).

Become consumed with a passionate desire to know the Father and Christ intimately and live in unbroken communion and fellowship. Then, when you come into this powerful position, you will be able to pray with power and authority and take dominion in the spirit realm.

This beloved, is where you must begin if you are to truly know the power of prayer and be used by God to impact the world through your prayers.

Are you ready to begin today to rise up to this new level of prayer?

Are you ready to receive the holy summons from the Throne?

There are three powerful aspects of prayer that causes Satan and his demons to tremble and run from us in defeat. God wants to give you fresh revelation concerning them. In chapter three you will learn how to ignite these powerful aspects of prayer in your life to enable you to receive greater prayer victories and more answers to prayer than you ever dreamed possible.

Lord, teach us to pray!

Father, thank you for paying the ultimate price giving us divine access into the Holy of Holies...into Your Presence. We have heard the wooing of Your Spirit to draw near to you in a more intimate relationship and we are hungry for your Presence. We long to hear Your voice, to know Your heart, to fellowship with You. Dear Lord, thank you for the blood you shed making it possible for us to come boldly into the Father's Presence. We desire You more than life itself. You are everything we need and all that we desire. Draw us to yourself in a deeper dimension of intimacy, greater than anything we have ever known. Reveal Yourself to us. Open our eyes to see and know You in all Your power and glory. We give ourselves wholly to You.

CHAPTER THREE

BREAK OPEN YOUR ALABASTER BOX

"Praise is the Christian's heavy artillery; praise is more effective in spiritual warfare than is an atom bomb in military battle." Wesley Duewel

Mary quickly ran to her room and over to the tiny chest where she kept her alabaster bottle hidden away. She carefully unwound the cloth she had wrapped around the bottle to protect it from being broken. As she held the fragile, white alabaster bottle in her hands, she fingered it lovingly. Inside the bottle was spikenard, a very rare and expensive perfume she had kept stored away for the future.

She slowly opened the bottle to smell the beautiful fragrance of the perfume. As she looked at the alabaster bottle she remembered all the sacrifices that had been made to buy it. It was her most valuable possession, worth 300 denari, which was the equivalent to a man's wages for an entire year.

Mary thought for a moment about what Martha, Lazarus and the Lord's disciples might think about her and what she planned to do with it. Surely they would think she was foolish, or that she was being too bold or daring.

Jesus had come to Bethany on the way to Jerusalem to celebrate the Passover. Many people had come to the house to see Jesus and also to see her brother Lazarus and hear him tell the story how Jesus had brought him back from the dead. She had helped Martha prepare a special meal for Jesus and his disciples.

After hesitating for a moment, she made her way back to the room where Jesus was sitting as He ate and talked with Lazarus, Peter, James, John and his other close disciples. Ignoring the puzzled look on Martha's face, and the gaze of the disciples, Mary came and knelt at Jesus' feet. She had often sat at His feet to listen and capture every word He spoke. She loved the sound of His voice and just being near Him. Love emanated from His countenance and as He spoke His voice resonated with the power and majesty of a King.

Kneeling before Jesus, without speaking a word, Mary opened the alabaster bottle and began to pour it over His feet. She could sense the eyes of the disciples and people in the room focusing upon her.

They may have been thinking that she was just striving for attention or that she was making a spectacle of herself, but Mary didn't care.

For a long time she had been thinking about how she could show Jesus her love and gratitude. She had also heard Jesus say that He was going to be taken by the Jews and crucified and she couldn't bear the thought of it. Mary's heart was overflowing with love for her Lord and Master. She didn't know when she would have this opportunity again to pour out her love for Him.

Hot tears flowed down Mary's face and mingled with the perfume as she washed His feet. She unwound her long black hair, leaned over and used it to wipe His feet. She loved Jesus more than her own life and this was her way of showing Him how much she loved Him. Nothing the people around her could say or do to her mattered. Everything else was shut out of her heart and mind. The most important thing to her at that moment was showering her love upon Jesus.

As Mary washed and caressed Jesus' feet, the beautiful aroma of the spikenard filled the room.

Judas Iscariot came and stood before Mary and glared at her with a look of disgust. It was obvious that he considered this lavish expression of her love a waste. He wanted Jesus to rebuke her.

"Mary, what are you doing? What is wrong with you? Why wasn't this spikenard sold for 300 denari and given to the poor?"

The room grew quiet as they waited for Jesus' response.

Still sitting at His feet, Mary looked up at Jesus with tears of love and gratitude.

"Let her alone!" Jesus said as He lovingly placed His hand on her shoulder. "What she is doing now is in preparation for the day of my burial. The poor you will have with you always but I will not always be with you."

As Mary listened to Jesus, her heart was filled with joy. Jesus didn't rebuke her. He said that her act of love and worship would be a living memorial to her throughout the ages!

"As you enter the inner chamber, let your first work be to thank God for the unspeakable love that invites you to come to Him and to converse freely with Him."
Andrew Murray

Jesus knew what was in Mary's heart and that she had unreservedly, and with total abandonment, given all that she had in true worship at His feet. He said, *"..., Wheresoever this gospel shall be preached in the whole world, there shall also this, that this woman hath done, be told for a memorial of her"* (Matthew 26:13).

This story is one of the greatest illustrations of true worship in the Bible. Mary sacrificed her most valuable possession in an act of lavish worship. She is an example of the true worshippers God is looking for today.

TRUE WORSHIP VS. SOULISH WORSHIP

Worship is a powerful form of prayer that brings God's glory down and puts the enemy to flight! Yet there is a lack of understanding in the Body of Christ concerning true worship.

Within the Church there is a lot of *soulish* worship. Worship, for the most part, has been relegated to a time designated for corporate worship during church services, conferences and meetings where a choir, worship leader or worship team leads the people in singing a few songs.

In some churches the time allotted for worship is very limited and structured. There is no time allowed for spontaneous worship where the people spend time pouring out their love to God in praise and worship. The songs are rehearsed and timed to fit within a set time frame.

Often there is a formula for the time of worship. The pattern is to start with a couple of upbeat, fast-paced songs and then move to a slower more worshipful song to prepare them for the sermon.

In many churches the worship music has become more entertainment than worship and the singers more performance-oriented than worship- oriented. Most of the time the worship music is designed to stir up the emotions and bring the people to an emotional high. People come to hear the good singing and music to be blessed, instead of coming to *bless God* through their praise and worship.

Many times people respond to the beat or the enthusiasm and energy generated by the music, but they are not truly worshipping God. They may sing, dance, clap their hands and shout; but true worship is not flowing out of their hearts.

God dwells in the praises of His people. He longs to manifest His Presence and to commune with His people. It grieves His heart that there are many churches where Christians have shut Him out through their soulish worship.

Don't misunderstand me. I love to sing, dance, shout and rejoice during worship. All of these forms of worship are wonderful, but they must not become our focal point. Having our emotions stirred is not enough.

Jesus told the Samaritan woman at Jacob's well, "...*an hour is coming, and now is, when the true worshipers shall worship the Father in spirit and truth; for such people the Father seeks to be His worshipers. God is spirit, and those who worship Him must worship in spirit and truth*" (John 4:23-24 NAS).

"Here is one of the greatest values of praise: it decentralizes self. The worship and praise of God demands a shift of center from self to God. One cannot praise God without relinquishing occupation with self."
Paul E. Billheimer

True praise and worship does not originate from the soul: the mind, will and emotions. Our emotions may be stirred, but true worship must originate in the Spirit! With the coming of the Holy Spirit came a new power and ability to commune and worship God. Through the Holy Spirit, living in us, we have a **divine link** whereby our spirits can commune directly with the Father.

Worship is not some dead, dry, formal routine based upon man-made traditions.

It is not an emotional "high" that we must work up.

The praise and worship that reaches the heart of the Father is done in the Spirit. It is an expression of love, praise and adoration from the heart that is *directed to and focused upon God.*

It exalts Him and Him alone.

There is no pre-determined pattern that must be followed or a particular form to use in worshipping God in the Spirit. True praise and worship is not limited or confined to a church gathering or conference. Praise should rise up within God's people continually wherever they are. It should be spontaneous, coming from a heart overflowing with love, like Mary's lavish worship at Jesus' feet.

Mary was a true worshipper and built a memorial to the Lord through her worship.

The Father is looking for true worshippers!

You can be one of them!

A sovereign move of God is coming to the Church whereby He will bring forth a pure stream of worship.

As God's people are set free and enter this new dimension of worship where they are no longer bound by tradition; but are unreservedly worshiping and praising God with all their hearts, God's glory will come down. Bondages will be broken and people will be healed!

The heavens will be opened through praise and worship. And there, in the holy atmosphere of God's Presence, intercessors will be able to boldly stand before the Throne of God and intercede on behalf of people groups and nations.

THE FATHER IS LOOKING FOR TRUE WORSHIPPERS

Worship, praise and thanksgiving are all powerful forms of prayer that bring you before God's Throne and activates God's power on your behalf to defeat the enemy.

"Solomon prevailed much with God in prayer at the dedication of the temple, but it was the voice of praise which brought down the glory that filled the house."
Dwight L. Moody

David, who worshipped God passionately, said to *"come before his presence with singing" (Psalm 100:2); and to "Enter into his gates with thanksgiving, and into his courts with praise: be thankful unto him, and bless his name" (Psalm 100:4).*

True worship, in the Spirit, ushers you into the Holy of Holies—into the very Presence of the Father. It is a *divine encounter* with God!

The Greek word for worship is *"proskyneo"* meaning, "to prostrate oneself, do reverence to." It denotes adoration of God and Christ. Adoration is the act of rendering divine honor, esteem and love. Adoration brings man into the immediate and direct contact with God.

To worship simply means to ascribe worth. When we worship the Father and the Lord Jesus, we pour out our love for Who They are rather than what They have done for us.

Worship centers on Who God is, while praise and thanksgiving involves giving glory to God and thanking Him for what He has done. God has said, *"He who brings an offering of praise and thanksgiving honors and glorifies Me..."* (Psalm 50:23 AMP).

Thanksgiving is an aspect of prayer whereby we recognize and give thanks to God for all His blessings. Like praise, it is a type of prayer that draws the heart away from self and centers it upon God. This is why when we come before God we need to begin by worshipping, thanking and praising Him before we present our needs.

Jesus said that true worshippers would worship in spirit and in truth. In a world of idolatry, where man has turned his back on God to worship power, money, sex and the world's pleasures, God is searching for true worshippers! He desires those who will build a living memorial to Him through worship, like Mary, who poured out lavish worship on the Lord Jesus.

Many Christians in the Church are holding onto idols in their hearts. Many have placed their families, careers and pursuit of worldly pleasures first place in their lives, instead of the Lord and their worship of Him. These things have become their idols.

There are others who have put the work of the Lord and ministry, above the Lord. Ministry has become their god. They have exalted the work of the Lord above the Lord Himself. They have become so busy in their work for the Lord that they have neglected to spend time in His Presence, worshipping Him.

This is spiritual idolatry!

The Father is looking and yearning for those who will worship Him wholeheartedly, who will not just honor Him with their lips and say they love Him, but will truly worship Him.

THE FATHER LONGS FOR TRUE HEART WORSHIP

To gain a clearer understanding of what true worship really is, we need to look at the life and example of Abraham. One of the first recorded instances of the word worship is found in Genesis 22.

God wanted to know Abraham's heart and whether or not he loved Him above everything else. He directed Abraham to sacrifice his beloved son, Isaac. Abraham obeyed God. When he reached the place of sacrifice, where God had directed him to go on Mt. Moriah, he left his servants. He told them, *"Stay here with the donkey while I and the boy go over there. We will worship and then we will come back to you"* (Genesis 22:5 NIV).

Abraham, in obedience to God, was on the way to offer Isaac on an altar as a sacrifice to God. Yet, he said, *"We will worship."* He believed God, who had given him the promise that through Isaac and his seed he would become the father of many nations. He was willing to offer his son in worship on the altar knowing that God was able to raise him from the dead. That is why he told his servants, *"We will worship and then we will come back to you."*

Abraham's worship involved his willingness to give God the thing of greatest value and that was dearest to his heart — his son, Isaac, for whom he had prayed and believed God for. It involved more than just words. He didn't just tell God how much he loved Him. He worshipped God and poured out love through his act of obedience and faith.

"Wherever there is true prayer, there thanksgiving and gratitude stand close by; ready to respond when the answer comes. For as prayer brings the answer, so the answer brings forth gratitude and praise."
E. M. Bounds

When Job lost everything, including all of his children, he worshipped and blessed the name of the Lord! *"Then Job arose, and rent his mantle, and shaved his head, and fell down upon the ground, and worshipped"* (Job 1:20).

His worship of God was not dependent upon his circumstances or his feelings. His heart was heavy with grief. He was in mourning for his children, yet he offered up worship to God. He knew God and trusted Him completely. He said, *"Though he slay me, yet will I trust Him"* (Job 13:15). In essence, Job was saying, "No matter what comes my way, no matter what happens to me, I'm going to love and worship God!"

A close ministry associate recently shared with me the following true story of a woman in Nigeria who sang praises and worshipped God in one of the most devastating circumstances imaginable.

This 45 year-old woman lives in Plateau State where militant Muslims waged jihad against the Christians. She was one of the survivors.

Two men with machetes captured her as she ran in fear. They sliced into her neck and arm with machetes. A portion of her tongue was severed when one of the blows ripped through her right cheek.

In the midst of this attack, she began thanking God for sparing her life. Then she bowed her head and started singing, continuing to thank and praise the Lord!

This woman sang praises even with part of her tongue severed! Although her words may have been distorted because of her injuries, I believe her song was more beautiful to Him than that of any well-trained choir on earth because the words came from the heart of a true worshipper!

True worship involves our verbal expression of adoration and praise as well as our actions. We are directed to offer up to God sacrifices of praise. The Apostle Paul admonished us: *"Through Jesus, therefore, let us continually offer to God a sacrifice of praise – the fruit of lips that confess his name"* (Hebrews 13:15 NIV). When we worship the Lord, we are giving ourselves wholly to Him. Paul said, *"...I urge you, brothers, in view of God's mercy, to offer your bodies as living sacrifices, holy and pleasing to God—this is your spiritual act of worship"* (Romans 12:1 NIV).

As you give yourself as a living sacrifice to God and come before Him, pouring out your love and worshipping Him for Who He is, He receives your worship, and, in turn, gives Himself to you. His glory comes down and His Presence is manifested.

Today, there is a great hunger in the Body of Christ for God's Presence. The Father is saying to us that if we are truly hungry for Him, we need to just shut ourselves away somewhere and wait before Him. As we begin to pour out our love and worship Him, *in the Spirit,* His Presence will fill our homes and churches.

The Father is not withholding Himself from His children. He is just waiting for us to break through all man-made tradition and formalities and come into His Presence and worship.

TRUE WORSHIP RELEASES A DIVINE LIFE FLOW FROM THE THRONE

When Solomon dedicated the Temple, there was a pure stream of worship that ascended to God, and God came down to meet them!

David, who was one of God's true worshippers, knew the importance of worship. He said, *"I will bless the Lord at all times: his praise shall continually be in my mouth"* (Psalm 34:1). He told God, *"Seven times a day do I praise thee because of thy righteous judgments"* (Psalm 119:164).

David commissioned 4,000 of the 38,000 Levites, set apart for the service of the Lord, to serve as singers and musicians in the Temple. He also set apart 288 of this number, of the sons of Asaph, Heman, and Jeduthan to prophesy with harps, psalteries and cymbals.

There was an offering of *continual praise* from the temple lifted up before the Lord. The appointed Levites were instructed to stand every morning and every evening to thank and praise the Lord and to offer the burnt sacrifices unto the Lord (See 1 Chronicles 23:30-31). Today, we are the Temple of the Holy Spirit and continual praise and worship should flow forth out of our hearts. David said, *"From the rising of the sun unto the going down of the same, the Lord's name is to be praised"* (Psalm 113:3).

When Solomon dedicated the Temple, this great choir of 4,000 singers and musicians lifted their voices in worship and played songs of praise unto God upon their instruments.

All the singers and musicians had been consecrated and set apart. They were standing at one end of the altar wearing white linen, holding cymbals, psalteries and harps in their hands. Standing alongside them were 120 priests sounding the trumpets.

As the voices of the singers, musicians and the priests blowing the trumpets blended together as one worshipping God, He manifested His Presence in a glory cloud. The shekinah glory of God so filled the Temple, the priests were unable to stand (See 2 Chronicles 5:13-14).

It is interesting to note that when the Ark was brought into the Temple by the Levites, the glory of God did not come down.

When the sacrifices were offered, the glory of God did not come down.

Solomon stood and lifted His hands toward heaven and prayed. But the glory of God did not come down.

It did not come down when they built the Temple or offered sacrifices. It was when they worshipped and praised God that the glory of the Lord came down!

When we begin to worship and praise God, a *divine life* flow from the Throne of God is released. God accepts our worship and, in turn, ministers to us and through us.

REFUSE TO BOW DOWN AT A COUNTERFEIT ALTAR

God created man to worship Him. The one thing He desires of us is our worship. He did not create us to be servants, only concerned about our work for Him. He desires sons and daughters who will love Him with all their hearts. The Father wants our hearts first. If He gains our hearts in worship, then we will be ready to minister in His power.

One of the major strategies used by Satan throughout the ages in an effort to destroy God's people, and weaken the Church, has been to introduce a perverted substitute worship and draw people away from worshipping the One true and living God.

Satan hates it when people worship God in Spirit and truth because it is so powerful. He knows that he cannot stand against God's people when they begin to worship and praise Him. Paul Billheimer, who wrote, *"Destined For the Throne"* said, "Satan is allergic to praise, so where there is massive triumphant praise, Satan is paralyzed, bound, and banished."

"Let us sing a hymn and spite the devil."
Martin Luther

In His relationship with the children of Israel, God established the commandments, which they were to keep and use as a guideline for their lives. The very first commandment is: *"Thou shalt have no other gods before me"* (Exodus 20:3). Above everything else He wanted their love. *"And thou shalt love the Lord thy God with all thine heart, and with all thy soul, and with all thy might"* (Deuteronomy 6:5).

They were not to make any graven images or to worship any other gods. God told them, "...for I the LORD thy God am a jealous God..." (Exodus 20:5).

Their lives were built around worship of the One true and living God. As long as they loved, worshipped and obeyed God, they were strong and powerful. God fought for them. He delivered their enemies into their hands and they reaped His blessings and supernatural provision.

But the Children of Israel turned away from God and began to intermarry with the heathen nations. They built altars and began to worship and offer sacrifices to other gods. As a result, they were defeated and dispersed throughout the nations.

Even while Moses was on the mountain meeting with God, Aaron led the people into idolatry by building a golden calf for them to worship (See Exodus 32:1-6). Their hearts were turned away from God by a counterfeit substitute for worship inspired by Satan himself. God would have destroyed them all at that time had it not been for Moses' intercession.

King Nebuchadnezzar made an image of gold and made a decree that when the music played all the people were to fall down and worship it. All those who refused to fall down and worship would be cast into a burning fiery furnace.

Among the people of the land there were three true worshippers, Shadrach, Meschach and Abednego, who refused to bow down and worship the golden image. They were not afraid of the king or the fiery furnace. They told King Nebuchadnezzar:

...we do not need to defend ourselves before you in this matter. If we are thrown into the blazing furnace, the God we serve is able to save us from it, and he will rescue us from your hand, O king. But even if he does not, we want you to know, O king, that we will not serve your gods or worship the image of gold you have set up.

Daniel 3:16-18 NIV

The three Hebrew children refused to compromise and give in to this demand to worship at a counterfeit altar. They were willing to die rather than deny God and worship the golden image.

This is the type of worshippers God is looking for – those who refuse to compromise or allow any thing or any one to become a substitute for the true worship of the only true and living God.

In the wilderness Satan tried to tempt Jesus to fall down and worship him. Satan told Jesus, *"If thou therefore wilt worship me, all shall be thine"* (Luke 4:7).

Jesus answered, *"Get thee behind me, Satan: for it is written, Thou shalt worship the Lord thy God, and him only shalt thou serve"* (Luke 4:8).

Satan desires to have the worship and praise that is only intended for God and he will use every possible means today to try to hinder believers from coming before God and worshipping Him.

Satan will try to get you to worship at the altar of wealth and prosperity. Jesus said, *"...Ye cannot serve God and mammon"* (Matthew 6:24).

He will try to cause you to bow down at the altar of worldly possessions and other worldly desires. Don't do it! John wrote, *"Love not the world, neither the things that are in the world. If any man love the world, the love of the Father is not in him"* (1 John 2:15).

Satan will try to deceive you and cause you to bow down at the altar of self – where you are more concerned about your own selfish desires and consumed with your pursuit of fulfilling them, rather than your pursuit of the Lord. Jesus said, *"He that taketh not his cross, and followeth after me, is not worthy of me. He that findeth his life shall lose it: and that loseth his life for my sake shall find it"* (Matthew 10:38-39).

Satan will try to cause you to worship at the altar of family and loved ones. He will try to get you to become so focused upon your husband, wife, children or other loved ones that they actually become idols and take the place God should have in your life. Jesus said, *"He that loveth father or mother more than me is not worthy of me:*

and he that loveth son or daughter more than me is not worthy of me" (Matthew 10:37).

Like the three Hebrew children, refuse to bow down!

IGNITE THE POWERFUL WEAPONS OF WORSHIP, PRAISE AND THANKSGIVING TO DEFEAT SATAN

"Praise opens the door to more grace." John Wesley

Praise and worship in your mouth is a powerful weapon to defeat Satan. We are to face our circumstances and things coming upon the earth before the Lord's return, not with fear and trepidation, but with the "High Praises" of God in our mouths and the two-edged sword of His Word in our hands.

This is an hour when God's people must declare His praises among the nations. God has made us a "royal priesthood" to proclaim His praises to the ends of the earth.

> *But ye are a chosen generation, a royal priesthood, an holy nation, a peculiar people; that ye should shew forth the praises of him who called you out of darkness into his marvelous light.*
>
> 1 Peter 2:9

The people of this world need to see the reality of God's love and power demonstrated through Christians. They need to see Christians rejoicing and singing God's praises in the midst of every adversity and trial we face.

Something happens in the Spirit realm when God's people begin to truly praise, sing and worship Him. There is a release in the Spirit and new freedom comes forth. The shackles of fear, doubt and worry begin to fall off.

"Praise beats back the powers of darkness, scatters the demon opponents, and frustrates Satan's strategies."
Wesley L. Duewel

As worship rises out of the believers' hearts unto the Lord, Satan knows he is defeated and must retreat.

In the familiar story of the battle of Jehoshaphat and the children of Israel against the Ammonites and Moabites, we see the power of worship and praise in defeating the enemy.

The children of Israel were greatly outnumbered and when Jehoshaphat heard the news that the great multitude of the armies of the Ammonites, Moabites and their allied forces were coming to battle against them, he cried out and pleaded their case before the Lord.

As the people of Judah came together, the Lord spoke to them through Jahaziel. God told them, *"Be not afraid nor dismayed by reason of this great multitude; for the battle is not yours but God's"* (2 Chronicles 20:15).

When the people heard the word of the Lord, they all fell on their faces before God and worshipped! The Levites, who had been appointed singers, stood up and began to praise God with a loud voice.

Their praise and worship set in motion their victory!

The following morning, as the army assembled to go out into battle, Jehoshaphat appointed singers to go before the army to sing praises to the Lord (See 2 Chronicles 20:21).

They were tremendously outnumbered by a great multitude that was stationed, armed and ready to attack and destroy them. Yet, they were not in a defensive position, they were in an *offensive* position.

Their weapons: praise and worship!

The moment they began to sing and praise God, something happened in the spiritual realm.

And when they began to sing and to praise, the LORD set ambushments against the children of Ammon, Moab, and mount Seir, which were come against Judah; and they were smitten.

2 Chronicles 20:22

As their praises reached God's Throne, God supernaturally intervened on their behalf and brought confusion into the enemy's camp! In this confusion their enemies began to attack and kill one another. No one escaped!

The people of Judah experienced such a great victory that it was not necessary for them to even lift their swords in battle. God used the praise and worship in their mouths to defeat their enemies.

It took them three whole days to gather the spoils.

Regardless of the circumstances you face in your life or the greatness of your need, as you ignite the powerful weapons of praise, worship and thanksgiving, God will supernaturally intervene and make you victorious.

Don't wait until the battle is won to praise and worship the Lord.

Face Satan and his demon principalities with praise and worship on your lips. As you do, God will fight for you, as He did for Israel. The enemy will hear your worship and know he is defeated!

MAKE PASSIONATE WORSHIP YOUR GREATEST DESIRE

Worship, praise and thanksgiving are vitally linked in prayer. In fact, they are inseparable. The Apostle Paul said, *"Continue in prayer, and watch in the same with thanksgiving"* (Colossians 4:2). Writing to the Thessalonians, he again links prayer and thanksgiving: *"Rejoice evermore. Pray without ceasing. In every thing give thanks: for this is the will of God in Christ Jesus concerning you"* (1 Thessalonians 5:16-18). And to the Philippians he wrote: *"Be careful for nothing; but in every*

71

thing by prayer and supplication with thanksgiving let your requests be made known unto God" (Philippians 4:6).

We are to give thanks in everything! When we come to present our petitions before God, we are to bring them with thanksgiving upon our lips. We need to thank Him for what He has already done, thank Him because He has already heard us and because we know He will answer our prayer!

"Prayer and praise are like the breathing in and out of air and make up that spiritual respiration by which the inner life is instrumentally supported. We take in an inspiration of heavenly air as we pray; we breathe it out again in praise unto God from whom it came."
Charles Spurgeon

Do not be bound by man's traditions and do not limit worship and praise to only the time set aside in church gatherings. Let your worship and praise be spontaneous. God never intended our worship to be limited to the confines of a church or building. He wants you to have a song of praise and worship continually upon your heart. In writing to the Ephesians, Paul said: *"...but be filled with the Spirit; Speaking to yourselves in psalms and hymns and spiritual songs, singing and making melody in your heart to the Lord"* (Ephesians 5:18-19).

Whenever you come before the Father in prayer, remember that by His Spirit in you, you have a *divine link* that enables you to commune and worship Him in the Spirit. You have been given divine access into the Holy of Holies and stand before Him in His awesome Presence.

Begin your time alone with the Father by first worshipping Him for Who He is: The Great "I AM"; Jehovah Jireh; Abba Father; Jehovah Shalom; Jehovah Nissi; Jehovah Rapha; All powerful; Ancient of Days.

Worship the Lord as the King of Kings, Lord of Lords, Savior, Redeemer, Deliverer, Lamb of God, Lion of Judah and soon coming King!

Throughout the Book of Revelation, we are given a glimpse of the worship that will take place before the Throne of God in Heaven. John heard the sound of four angelic beings singing praises to God. Continually rising from the Throne is the sound of these four angelic beings singing, "*...Holy, holy, holy, Lord God Almighty, which was, and is, and is to come*" (Revelation 4:8).

One of the first things to do during worship is to recognize the awesome glory, majesty and holiness of God. He alone is holy! David said, "*Exhalt the Lord our God, and worship at his holy hill: for the Lord our God is holy*" (Psalm 99:9). We are to exalt and praise Him because He is a holy God.

As you come into His Presence, honor and praise Him for His holiness. He is perfect in all His ways. Praise Him for His mercy, His lovingkindness and His faithfulness.

Begin to praise and thank Him for what He has done for you. Throughout the day, wherever you go, praise Him and tell Him how much you love Him.

During your time of worship, shut away with Him, God wants you to abandon yourself in worshipping Him.

The word, "*Halal*" is one of the many original Hebrew root words for praise in the Scriptures. It means, "to be clamourY foolish about the adoration of God." In other words, it means to worship and praise God with a passion, forgetting everything, losing sight of what anyone will say and totally losing ourselves in Him.

Our one consuming desire should be to praise and glorify God with all that we are. This is the kind of praise and worship that David offered up to God as he led a procession of the Levites, priests and singers in bringing the Ark of the Covenant to Jerusalem.

David threw off his robes and began to dance before the Ark of God's Presence. His dance was not rehearsed or choreographed. It was spontaneous.

The great joy welling up within him could not be contained and it exploded into joyous praise and worship. As he danced, he was no doubt circling, whirling, singing, sometimes shouting and jumping for joy.

The key to experiencing the fullness of God's Presence is to humble ourselves before Him, lay aside all pre-conceived ideas and cry out to Him with all our hearts as David did. Just as David worshipped God with unbridled passion, He desires His people to seek Him with all their hearts and to worship Him with total abandonment.

You must be willing to forget everyone and everything and worship Him in spirit and truth.

Cast off your robes of pride and self-sufficiency and begin to sing, shout and dance before Him.

In whatever battle or circumstance you face, wait before the Father in worship. Let Him fill your heart with a new song of praise, worship and thanksgiving. You will feel His loving arms enfolding you and lifting you above the swirling tempest. The enemy will retreat in defeat and you will walk in victory.

Christ has chosen His Church to be the channel through which He releases His power on earth to meet the desperate needs of the world. Before Christ ascended to Heaven, He called His disciples around Him and gave them the key to prayer that brings down God's power upon earth and commissioned them to fulfill His work on earth through that power.

If the Church is going to reach the millions in the world today who have never heard the Gospel and meet the desperate needs of the world, we must have a greater revelation of the awesome responsibility Christ has given us and activate the power of intercession. In chapter four we will look at Christ's mandate of prayer. You will learn how you can be used by God, through intercession, to change the spiritual destiny of nations.

Lord, teach us to pray!

Father, our hearts rejoice to know that You love us with an everlasting love and that You desire our worship and praise. You

alone are worthy of all praise, honor, glory and blessing! We are hungry for You! Our spirits cry out to know You in a greater capacity. We love You and desire You above everything else. You are the only true and living God. You are high and holy and we lift You up and exalt Your holy name. We praise and worship You because You are full of mercy, grace and truth. We desire to know You in Your fullness. With all our hearts we want to worship You in Spirit and truth. Teach us to open our alabaster boxes of true worship and worship You in Spirit and truth.

CHAPTER FOUR

CHRIST'S PRAYER MANDATE

We are at war!

There is no peace in our streets. There is no peace in our schools, shopping centers, subways or on airplanes.

Fear stalks the streets of our cities and plagues our nations.

There is a fierce battle raging which is far greater than World War I, World War II and all the wars ever fought on earth combined.

The magnitude of the fate of untold millions of casualties defies all human understanding.

Every year, millions die and face an eternity without God. They are confined to outer darkness where *"there shall be weeping and gnashing of teeth"* (Matthew 8:12).

With the world's population reaching more than six billion, one-half have still not been reached with the Gospel!

There is war, famine, economic upheaval, and terrorism in the nations on a level never before experienced.

The world is in turmoil – like a woman in travail. World leaders are desperate, seeking solutions to crises and complex problems for which there seems to be no possible solution.

The world, with its desperate needs, awaits deliverance. In its hopelessness and despair, it waits for the only power capable of answering its needs – the intercession of God's people!

"Remember the marks of a true intercessor: a sense of human need, a Christlike love in the heart, a consciousness of personal impotence, faith in the power of prayer, courage to persevere in spite of refusal, and the assurance of an abundant reward." Andrew Murray

Our God, who is merciful and longsuffering, desires to pour out His blessings. He sees the pain and suffering, the sin and despair holding multitudes in bondage and His Father's heart is grieved. He paid the ultimate price to break the chains of sin and death off mankind. He has provided untold blessings and everything man needs, and is ready and willing to release all He has provided.

Christ defeated Satan and destroyed the power of death, and has placed in the hands of His Church the keys to His Kingdom. He is now seated at the right hand of the Father, where He is involved in unceasing intercession for His people. Through the Holy Spirit, Christ has given us power over all the power of Satan.

He has united us with Himself and the Father as one.

He has brought us into divine partnership with Himself and bound Himself to us by His Word.

By His Spirit, He has given us *unlimited divine* access to the Father.

He has given us His delegated power and authority through His Name to preach the Gospel, heal the sick, cast out devils and raise the dead.

And, He has chosen us to be the channel through which He releases His power upon earth through our intercession! John Wesley has well spoken, "God does nothing but in answer to prayer." God has limited His work on earth and made it dependent upon the prayers of His people. The measure of His power and blessing on earth is determined by the measure of intercession arising before His Throne.

Through intercession we pray into being God's will on earth as it is in heaven.

In Christ's Sermon on the Mount, He said this is how we are to pray: "*...Our Father which art in heaven, Hallowed be thy name. Thy kingdom come. Thy will be done in earth, as it is in heaven...*" (Matthew 6:9-10).

Christ has placed in our hands the awesome responsibility and privilege of bringing His kingdom down to earth through intercession. In His final moments with His disciples He said, "*Ye have not chosen me, but I have chosen you, and ordained you, that ye should go and bring forth fruit, and that your fruit should remain: that whatsoever ye shall ask of the Father in my name, he may give it you*" (John 15:16).

Christ, Who is seated at the right hand of the Father, in a position of power and authority over all power and principalities in heaven and on earth, intends to use the prayers of His Church to fulfill His purposes in the nations before He returns. He said, "I have chosen and ordained you!"

He intends to release His power through our intercession into our cities and nations to bring in the great end-time harvest of souls.

❧

> **"*Intercession is the most perfect form of prayer, in that it is the prayer that Christ prays on His throne.*"**
> **Andrew Murray**

He plans to use the anointed prayers of His people to wage war in the heavenlies and tear down and destroy the strongholds of the enemy that are holding entire people groups, cities and nations in bondage.

He has given us His power and authority – all of Heaven is at our disposal – and He has promised *whatever we ask* in the power and authority of His Name, He will do it!

OUR INTERCESSION MUST FLOW FROM THE THRONE THROUGH US TO THE WORLD

Andrew Murray has said, "Intercession is to be the great link between heaven and earth. The intercession of the Son, begun upon earth, continued in heaven, and carried on by His redeemed people upon earth, will bring about the mighty change."

Intercession is standing in the gap on behalf of people, cities and nations; in the position of delegated authority, to plead the promises of God in faith and bring God's kingdom down upon earth with His will being done as it is in heaven.

Intercession goes beyond prayer petitioning God to meet one's own needs. It involves petitioning God on behalf of others. Oftentimes it will also involve weeping, travailing, groaning in the Spirit and spiritual warfare.

An intercessor is "one who stands in the gap; who prays, petitions, or pleads on behalf of another."

This type of intercession is not the "normal" five-minute prayer, where we give God a list of names of people we would like to see saved and delivered out of Satan's hands. "O God, save Aunt Suzie, my bother John...Uncle Joe...deliver my friend Tom."

The type of intercession God is calling us to is much more than that. It involves getting on our faces before God in prayer, mourning, weeping and travailing...waiting before Him in prayer and not letting go until the work has been done. It involves a willingness to stand in the gap on behalf of others, as well as entire nations.

An intercessor is able to plead effectively because he gives his life for others. He has laid aside His own interests and, as much as possible, has taken their place. Intercession is not substitution for sin. There has only been one substitute for a world of sinners...Jesus Christ.

True intercession so identifies the intercessor with the one for whom he is praying that it brings him into a prevailing place with God. In our intercession for others, we must be willing to "sit where they sit". We must identify with their needs and feel their infirmities so that we will gain a position of prayer where we can intercede effectively on their behalf.

The Greek word *"entynchan_"* is used throughout the New Testament to refer to intercession. It means "to approach, pray, plead, intercede." It is the word used when Paul wrote to the Romans referring to Christ's continuing intercession on our behalf.

> *He who did not withhold or spare [even] His own Son but gave Him up for us all, will He not also with Him freely and graciously give us all [other] things?...Who is there to condemn [us]? Will Christ Jesus, (the Messiah), Who died, or rather Who was raised from the dead, Who is at the right hand of God actually pleading as He intercedes for us?*
> Romans 8:32, 34 AMP

Paul wrote concerning Christ's unceasing intercession for us:

> *But He holds His priesthood unchangeably because He lives on forever. Therefore He is able also to save to the uttermost (completely, perfectly, finally, and for all time and eternity) those who come to God through Him, since He is always living to make petition to God and intercede with Him and intervene for them.*
> Hebrews 7:24-25 AMP

To really understand the depth of intercession that Christ intends for His Church to engage in upon earth, we must turn our eyes toward Him. There, in the Presence of the Father, He continues His all-powerful intercession without ceasing. It is His plan and will that His work and ministry of intercession be accomplished on earth through His Church.

"Prayer was never meant to be incidental to the work of God. It is the work...in all work for God, prayer is the working power of all that God would do through His people." Andrew Murray

The ministry of intercession involves joining Him in His intercession, whereby our intercession flows from the Throne through us to the world.

THE COMING OF THE HOLY SPIRIT MARKED A NEW ERA OF POWER FOR THE CHURCH

Christ has entrusted into our hands the responsibility of not only fulfilling His work upon earth, but that we are to do even greater works than He did, in the same power and authority.

How will this be possible?

Prayer is the channel through which we receive His power and authority to do the greater works!

With His disciples gathered around Him, Christ said:

> *...He that believeth on me, the works that I do shall he do also; and greater works than these shall he do; because I go unto my Father. And whatsoever ye shall ask in my name, that will I do, that the Father may be glorified in the Son. If ye shall ask any thing in my name, I will do it.*
>
> John 14:12-14

Christ's ascension to the Father and the coming of the Holy Spirit marked the coming of a new era of power for the Church.

Jesus told His disciples they would do greater works He had done, **"because I go unto my Father."** The Holy Spirit had not yet come. He was returning to the Father and was going to send the Holy Spirit to give them supernatural power and divine capability to do the same works He had done and even greater!

Christ was going to send the Holy Spirit, who is a Spirit of supplication, to release His intercession through them. Man, in his limited natural abilities, is unable to pray effectively. Through the natural mind, we cannot know the mind and will of the Father. *"But the natural man receiveth not the things of the Spirit of God: for they are foolishness unto him: neither can he know them, because they are spiritually discerned"* (1 Corinthians 2:14).

If you truly desire to be an intercessor, you must learn this very important truth. In your natural, limited abilities you do not know how to pray! You must recognize this fact and develop a total dependence upon the Holy Spirit.

> *Likewise the Spirit also helpeth our infirmities: for we know not what we should pray for as we ought: but the Spirit itself maketh intercession for us with groanings which cannot be uttered. And he that searcheth the hearts knoweth what is the mind of the Spirit, because he maketh intercession for the saints according to the will of God.*
>
> Romans 8:26-27

You don't have to worry about your inability to pray. Through the Holy Spirit you will receive a divine capability to pray.

"The life of Christ flowing through us and the words of Christ living in us, these give power to prayer. They breathe the spirit of prayer, and make the body, blood, and bones of prayer." E. M. Bounds

Jesus told the disciples, *"…It is expedient for you that I go away, for if I go not away, the Comforter will not come unto you; but if I depart, I will send him unto you"* (John 16:7).

His final instruction to them after His resurrection was, *"…I send the promise of my Father upon you: but tarry ye in the city of Jerusalem, until ye be endued with power from on high"* (Luke 24:49).

The disciples were going to need something beyond themselves, beyond the limitations of their natural minds to be able to communicate with the Father and see His will established on earth. And, the Church today must have something more than we have if we are going to be able to pray with power that produces results!

Jesus' parting words to the disciples were: *"But ye shall receive power, after that the Holy Ghost is come upon you: and ye shall be witnesses unto me both in Jerusalem, and in all Judaea, and in Samaria, and unto the uttermost part of the earth"* (Acts 1:8).

Jesus, after being on the earth forty days in His resurrected body, giving infallible, undeniable evidence and proof that He was Who He claimed to be, told His disciples, "I'm going to equip you! You are going to receive the same Holy Spirit and the same power and anointing that I have!" He said, "You're going to get what I got!" I have witnessed to the world that I am alive. Now, I'm going back to My Father and I'm commissioning you to carry on my work. You will be witnesses of me and you will have the ability to show the world that I am not in the grave, but that I am alive!"

Christ did not send the Holy Spirit upon the Church so that believers would just be blessed, warm a church pew, listen to a good sermon and be inspired by the worship team. He sent the Holy Spirit to give us an experience whereby we will receive and live, pray and minister by another power…the power of the Holy Spirit!

SOMETHING SUPERNATURAL MUST HAPPEN TO THE CHURCH!

There are six billion people on the earth and one-half of them have never heard the Name of Jesus!

"I question if any believer can have the burden of souls upon him – a passion for souls – and not agonize in prayer." Martin Luther

There is something desperately wrong in the experience of God's people. We cannot just keep reading these passages of Scripture and pass over them. We must get the mask off and enter into an experience of power, into a new strategic level of prayer where we go to the root cause, demolish strongholds, and get the answers we need to change our cities and nations.

The Church cannot continue to deal with just the surface problems: abortion, homosexuality, pornography, drugs and the other major blights plaguing our society. We need men and women to rise up with a powerful prayer anointing and go to the root cause to eliminate the strongholds.

We don't want to have these things cropping up around us again, and again, and again. We want total victory!

God wants to bring His people to a new strategic spiritual warfare level of intercession so that when they pray, answers come, His Name is glorified and His will is done on earth.

There are many people praying. But, there is a big difference in people just praying, and people interceding and getting results.

Do you want to enter into this new level of intercession?

It must start with you! You must change! You must become so spiritually dissatisfied that you refuse to stay where you are. You must enter into an experience where you know that you have the power through prayer that Christ promised.

Jesus said, "*...I give unto you power to tread on serpents and scorpions, and over all the power of the enemy...*" (Luke 10:19). You must not be satisfied until you have an experience where this promise has become a reality in your spiritual life.

When Jesus commissioned His disciples, He gave them power against unclean spirits to cast them out, and to heal all manner of sickness and disease (Matthew 10:1). He made it clear concerning what they were to do and the power He was giving them. He said, "You have power over all the power of the enemy. You will tread on serpents! You will cast out devils! You will heal the sick!"

I'm so tired of preachers standing in the pulpit and saying, "I don't have any power to heal the sick." Preachers, if you don't have any power to heal the sick, quit the ministry! You have no business preaching!

The world is in desperate need. Our cities are bound by the power of the enemy. Souls are dying and going to hell every day! It's time to get the mask off!

We must have a supernatural impartation of a new strategic level of spiritual warfare prayer and intercession! To fulfill God's purposes in this end-time hour, it will take prayer and fasting—intercession—on a new level. All our education, organizations, church denominations, plans and strategies are insufficient for the hour in which we live.

FATHER, BREATHE YOUR SPIRIT UPON US ONCE AGAIN!

God never intended the Church to be as it is today. He raised up a people—the Jews. He called and raised them up for a divine purpose: to use them to show the whole world that the sun, moon, stars, thunder and rain are not God; but that Jehovah is the One true and living God!

Two thousand years ago, He chose another people! He breathed the Holy Spirit upon 120 in the upper room and gave birth to the Church. And the major distinguishing feature of His Church was power!

Look at the Apostle Paul. He lived in Asia two years and it is recorded that every person in Asia—the Jews and the Greeks, all heard the Gospel (Acts 19:10).

Something unusual had to happen or this couldn't have taken place.

Paul didn't have radios or television to preach from.

He didn't even have the Bible available to distribute.

But, through this one man's ministry, all of Asia in the space of two years heard the Gospel!

The reason Paul was able to do this was because he walked in the delegated authority God gave him. God worked special miracles through Paul. Handkerchiefs and aprons, placed upon Paul's body, were brought to the sick and placed upon them. Evil spirits left and all manner of sickness and disease were healed (See Acts 19:11-12).

Compare this with the experience of most of the preachers in our churches today who say, ("I don't have any power to heal the sick. I can't heal the sick.").

The evil spirits recognized the power and authority of God operating through Paul. When the seven sons of Sceva tried to cast out a demon using Jesus' Name, the evil spirit answered, *"...Jesus I know, and Paul I know; but who are you?"* (Acts 19:15). They had used the Name of Jesus saying, *"...We adjure you by Jesus whom Paul preacheth"* (Acts 19:13). But, they were powerless because they didn't have an experience, a relationship with Christ and didn't have God's delegated authority.

The man with the evil spirit jumped on them and they all ran out of the house naked and wounded. The news of what happened spread to the Jews and Greeks throughout Ephesus and revival broke out!

The fear of God came upon the people. They confessed their sins and many of them brought their books on sorcery and witchcraft and burned them in a great bonfire in the streets.

The city of Ephesus was shaken by God's power because Paul walked in the delegated authority He had received.

We can have thousands of churches in our cities, but we will never turn them upside down for the Kingdom of God with the politically correct, sugarcoated, milk toast Christianity being preached. It will take a message preached in a demonstration of power with signs, wonders and miracles taking place in the Name of Jesus.

The only way we will see entire cities and nations transformed and a great harvest of souls in the nations is for something supernatural to occur in the Church. We need God to breathe His Spirit upon us once again and raise up intercessors who have the power, who know what it means to pray and intercede before God with delegated authority!

EXERCISE GOD'S DELEGATED AUTHORITY IN PRAYER

Christ intends for us to exercise the same power and authority He demonstrated on earth through our prayers!

One of the first things Jesus did after spending forty days and nights in the wilderness where He was fasting and praying was to return to Galilee where He taught in the synagogues.

When He left the wilderness, where He had a face-to-face confrontation with Satan, He did not come out in a weakened condition. He came out "in the power of the Spirit!"

When He came to Capernaum, He went into the synagogue to teach. *"And they were astonished at his doctrine: for his word was with power"* (Luke 4:32). A man with an unclean spirit was in the synagogue. The unclean spirit recognized Jesus and knew He had delegated power over him. The spirit cried out, *"...Let us alone; what have we to do with thee, thou Jesus of Nazareth? art thou come to destroy us? I know thee who thou art; the Holy One of God"* (Luke 4:34).

Jesus rebuked the unclean spirit and cast it out of the man. In the midst of the synagogue, the man was thrown down by the unclean spirit. The people looked at the man and then at Jesus with great amazement and said, *"What a word is this! for with authority and power he commandeth the unclean spirits, and they come out"* (Luke 4:36).

The literal translation of what they said is, "What is in this man's mouth?" In essence they were saying: "My God! What is in this man's mouth that when He speaks the demons come out! What's in His mouth?"

The people saw and heard things they had never before witnessed. They had seen people with unclean spirits acting up. But they had never seen anyone face unclean spirits, call them out and see people instantly delivered and set free.

They identified what was in Jesus' mouth with two words: authority and power.

The word "authority" is translated from the Greek word, *"exousia"* which means "the right to exercise". They looked at Jesus and this is what they said, "With what authority—*exousia*—or right to exercise, does this man have in His mouth? What is He exercising?"

The word "power" is translated from the Greek word, *"dunamis"*. The literal translation of *"dunamis"* in this verse means "the miracle working power of God."

What the people were so amazed by was this: "What's in this man's mouth? Where does He get the right to exercise the miracle working power of God?"

Delegated authority!

This is the same type of delegated power and authority Christ has given to His Church that He intends us to exercise when we pray. It is the God-given authority we have through the power of the Holy Spirit.

You have the same power and authority Jesus demonstrated when He walked upon the earth 2,000 years ago! It's yours; it legally belongs to you. It's greater than any other power and authority known to man, and Christ wants you to activate it through your prayers.

ASK– MAKE A DEMAND!

Jesus said, *"If ye abide in me, and my words abide in you, ye shall ask what ye will, and it shall be done unto you"* (John 15:7). The word "ask" in the original Greek means "a demand on that which is due." In the delegated power and authority He has given you, you are to ask—make a demand on that which is due. Why? Because you have *"exousia"*. It's your right! It's been given to you!

"Give me Scotland or I die!" *John Welch*

Over and over in the Word Jesus directs us to "Ask!" *"And whatsoever ye shall ask in my name, that will I do, that the Father may be glorified in* the Son" (John 14:13). *"If ye shall ask any thing in my name, I will do it"* (John 14:14). *"Whatsoever ye shall ask the Father in my name, he will give it you"* (John 16:23). *"...ask and ye shall receive, that your joy may be full"* (John 16:24).

In His final moments with His disciples, Jesus said:

> And in that day ye shall ask me nothing. Verily, verily, I say unto you, Whatsoever ye shall ask the Father in my name, he will give it you. Hitherto have ye asked nothing in my name: ask, and ye shall receive, that your joy may be full.
>
> John 16:23-24

> At that day ye shall ask in my name: and I say not unto you, that I will pray the Father for you: For the Father himself loveth you, because ye have loved me, and have believed that I come out from God.
>
> John 16:26-27

Jesus said, "In that day". He was referring to the time when the Holy Spirit would be outpoured upon them giving them delegated power and authority. Jesus was returning to the Father. In a few short hours He would go to the cross, face Satan and the powers of hell, and defeat him. Through His blood that would be poured out, man would be forever set free from the power of Satan. The bondage of sin would be broken!

On the third day, He would rise from the dead in great triumph. The works of the devil would be destroyed and He would be exalted to a position of power and authority over all powers and principalities in heaven and in hell.

He would be given the Name above every other name!

> ...God exalted him to the highest place and gave him the name that is above every name, that at the name of Jesus every knee should bow, in heaven and on earth and under the earth, and every tongue confess that Jesus Christ is Lord, to the glory of God the Father.
>
> Phil. 2:9-11 NIV

In essence Jesus was saying, "You've never asked anything in My Name before, but now the time has come for your delegated authority. It's time to exercise *"exousia"*—the right to use My Name."

"You've never made a demand on anything due from the Father in My Name. I'm going to My Father and I'm sending the Holy Spirit. You will receive power and whatever you ask the Father—make a demand of something due—in My Name, I will do it!"

"My Name is the most important thing you must have to make a demand of that which is due. The Father has given Me a Name that is above every name—a Name whereby every knee will bow and every tongue shall confess—a Name whereby Satan and every demon principality has been destroyed. Use it! ASK—MAKE A DEMAND!

THREE MAJOR PHASES OF INTERCESSION

Christ has entrusted within the lives of all true believers the same mighty power and authority that resides in His Name. In chapter eleven I will take you deeper into this revelation of asking and exercising power and authority in His Name. When you intercede and pray in the power and authority that is in Jesus' Name, you will be able to ask anything whatsoever you will and He will do it!

As we look at Christ's role as our Great-Intercessor, there are three important phases in intercession:

1. Identification
2. Self-sacrifice
3. Power and authority

PHASE ONE: IDENTIFICATION

True intercession, first of all, involves **identification.** As our High Priest-Intercessor, Christ identified with us by taking upon Himself the form of flesh and blood. He left the glories of Heaven and His glory with the Father and became one of us so that He would be a faithful and merciful High Priest Who feels our infirmities and would be qualified to intercede on our behalf.

In our intercession, we must also first be willing to identify with those for whom we are interceding, **at the point of their need.** We must so identify with them that we take their burdens upon ourselves, feel their pain and sorrow and present their needs before the Father as if they were our own.

It is not enough to simply pray, "Lord, save the lost." As intercessors, we must be willing first of all to identify with the people who are lost in our communities and cities.

There is no way we can possibly pray effectively for the lost and intercede upon their behalf if we are so far removed from them we cannot identify with them at the point of their need.

What has happened within the Church today is that we have separated and isolated ourselves from the lost. We are far removed from their needs and their suffering. For the most part, we stay within the four walls of our comfortable churches. Our hearts have become hardened to the desperate needs of the lost in our cities.

We must be willing to identify with the homeless, the destitute, those bound by drugs or alcohol, the prostitutes and gang members, to the point we feel their infirmities, feel their pain and sorrow and our hearts are moved with compassion upon them. Only then will we be able to stand in the gap before God and effectively intercede upon their behalf and move the hand of God.

This type of identification was manifested in Christ's life. As our High Priest-Intercessor, interceding for a lost world, **He sat where we sit.** He took our nature upon Himself. He learned obedience through the things which He suffered. He was tempted in all points as we are. And He who knew no sin became sin for us (2 Corinthians 5:21). Through His intercession for us, He gained his position of supreme power and authority over all things!

An intercessor is able to plead effectively because he gives his life for others. He has laid aside His own self-interests and, as much as possible, has taken their place. Intercession is not substitution for sin. There has only been one substitute for a world of sinners, Jesus Christ.

True intercession so identifies the intercessor with the one for whom he is praying, that it brings him into a prevailing place with God.

In our intercession for others, we must be willing to "sit where they sit." We must identify with their needs and feel their infirmities so that we will gain a position in prayer where we can intercede effectively on their behalf.

PHASE TWO: SELF-SACRIFICE

Christ, the Great-Intercessor, made the ultimate sacrifice by laying down His life for us. Jesus said, *"Greater love hath no man than this, that a man lay down his life for his friends"* (John 15:13).

In our intercession, we must come to the place where we are willing to lay down our own lives sacrificially on behalf of those for whom we are praying. Self must be crucified! We must be willing to lay aside our own desires and give ourselves sacrificially through prayer and fasting on behalf of the needs of others.

Jesus said, *"...Except a corn of wheat fall into the ground and die, it abideth alone: but if it die, it bringeth forth much fruit"* (John 12:24). Only as we begin to die to our own selfish desires and give ourselves sacrificially through prayer and fasting on behalf of others, will the Holy Spirit be released to flow through us to fulfill His work of intercession.

One of the major ministries of the Holy Spirit upon the earth today is intercession. It is the Holy Spirit who lays a burden upon our hearts for others and calls us to intercede. Only as we are dead to self can He flow freely to intercede **through us.**

There are many Christians today who mistakenly think they are not qualified or do not know how to intercede. The truth is, we become intercessors by reason of the Intercessor who lives within us! The more we die to self and yield ourselves to the Holy Spirit, the more He is able to intercede through us.

When we come to the place where we have fully surrendered our lives, our wills, our desires and our plans and allow the Holy Spirit free reign in our lives, there is absolutely no limit to the depths of intercession and what the Holy Spirit can accomplish on earth through us!

> *...the Spirit also helpeth our infirmities: for we know not what we should pray for as we ought: but the Spirit itself maketh intercession for us with groanings which cannot be uttered. And he that searcheth the hearts knoweth what is the mind of the Spirit, because he maketh intercession for the saints according to the will of God.*
>
> Romans 8:26-27

During intercession, as we fully yield ourselves to the Holy Spirit, He will pray through us. As we begin to pray in the Spirit, in unknown tongues, the Spirit begins to travail and make intercession "with groanings which cannot be uttered."

When we pray in the Spirit, in tongues, we are also building up ourselves and our faith. (Jude 20) The Holy Spirit is released within us to strengthen us in our time of need.

When we face circumstances that seem overwhelming or impossible in the natural realm, and we begin to pray in the Holy Spirit, in tongues, the Holy Spirit intercedes for us. He comes to our aid and releases His power within us to overcome every obstacle and trial we face.

PHASE THREE: POWER AND AUTHORITY

Through Christ's intercession, His identification, His obedience and full surrender to God's will, His willingness to lay down His life as a sacrifice, and His death upon the cross, He obtained His position of supreme authority over all things.

As self begins to die and we allow the Holy Spirit to have full control to pray through us with groanings and gushings of the Spirit, we then enter into that realm of power and authority that is ours in Jesus' Name. We have gained a powerful spiritual position through intercession where we are able to speak the word of deliverance. We are "clothed" with authority by the Holy Spirit; and it is from this position of strength the "greater works" Jesus spoke of are done in His Name! This is true intercession. This is what is meant by going into the spiritual arena of intercession to win the battle first in prayer.

There have been many times on the frontlines of battle, in the nations of the world, when I have prayed in the Spirit, wrestled and travailed on behalf of the needs of that nation for hours and hours and days at a time, until we experienced a full release of the power and anointing of God. The battle was first won through this intercession before we saw the great victory of multiplied thousands accept Christ and a release of His miracle-healing power.

This place of power and authority is not something we can obtain in our own strength. It is a place of intercession that the Holy Spirit will bring us into as we yield ourselves to Him. The Intercessor, Who lives within us, will fulfill His work of intercession upon the earth today through us as we present our bodies a living sacrifice.

This new dimension of power and authority through intercession is where we are able to come before God on behalf of our needs; on behalf of our families and unsaved loved ones: on behalf of the lost and desperate needs in our cities and boldly take hold of all God has provided through His covenant with us.

YOU HAVE A SACRED, HOLY CALLING!

The role of Intercessor is a high and holy calling. Just as Jesus made intercession for the world through His life and death and has reconciled us to God, His Church, (you and I) have been called to intercede and reconcile men to God.

By His Spirit, you have been made a priest, a royal priesthood.

The Apostle Paul said: *"But ye are a chosen generation, a royal priesthood, an holy nation, a peculiar people; that ye should show forth the praises of him who hath called you out of darkness into his marvelous light"* (1 Peter 2:9).

God wants you to become an intercessor. Not only through intercessory prayer, but also through your life, through your actions as well as your words.

As you intercede, remember these vital phases of intercession:

1. IDENTIFICATION

2. SELF-SACRIFICE

3. POWER AND AUTHORIITY

The type of intercession God is calling us to involves getting on our faces before Him in prayer; mourning, weeping and travailing in the Spirit. It involves consecrating and setting ourselves apart for fasting and prayer, waiting before Him and not letting go until the work has been done. It requires us to be willing to stand in the gap on behalf of others, as well as entire nations.

God wants to use you in this end-time hour to fulfill His will.

As we join together in this new, powerful dimension of prayer, we will see greater answers to prayer than we have ever seen! Our intercessory prayers will impact entire nations!

INTERCEDE FROM YOUR POSITION OF DOMINION AUTHORITY!

The only way we will see a supernatural release of God's power that will impact the nations is for God's people to rise up with a new prayer anointing that will change the course of a sinful world.

I want to share with you a true story about Martin Luther, the great Reformer. In 1540 he had an associate by the name of Frederick Marconis. Frederick was Martin's prayer warrior who prayed and interceded on his behalf.

Frederick was at the point of death. When Martin Luther heard he was dying, he wrote him a letter. He said, "Frederick, I command you in Jesus' Name—you will live! You will not die because I have need of you to reform the Church. The Lord will not let me hear that you are dead, but the Lord will permit you to survive me. For this I am praying. This is my will and may my will be done because I speak only to glorify the Name of God."

Death heard the *"exousia"* and was hurled back! Frederick was healed. He died six years later, in 1546, two months after Martin Luther died.

Christ has given you the power and authority to fulfill His will in the nations of the world. He has called, anointed and commissioned you to heal the sick, cast out devils and proclaim the Gospel to the nations in a demonstration of His power.

He is now waiting for you to ASK—to make a demand on what He has already provided.

"We have authority to take from the enemy everything he is holding back. The chief way of taking is by prayer, and by whatever action prayer leads us to. The cry that should be ringing out today is the great cry, 'Take, in Jesus' great Name!' " A. J. Gordon

The time has come when you must pray and intercede from your position of dominion, authority and might, with Christ in the heavenlies, on behalf of the nations now closed to the Gospel, unreached people groups, and a harvest of souls in our cities and nations.

Now, let me ask you some questions:

Are you taking your position of power and authority through prayer?

Are you taking dominion over the evil principalities and powers of darkness over your city through prayer?

How long has it been since you looked at the condition of the lost of your city?

To be able to intercede as Christ taught, you must have a burning, all-consuming passion for the lost. This is not something that can be learned. It can neither be taught nor bought. The Holy Spirit imparts it. You need the Holy Spirit to give you God's heartbeat for the lost.

In 2 Peter 3:9, we read that God is patient toward us (the believers), not willing that any should perish, but that all should come to repentance.

One of the major ministries of the Holy Spirit upon the earth today is intercession. It is the Holy Spirit who lays a burden upon our hearts for others and calls us to intercede. Only as we are dead to self can He flow freely—to intercede through us.

Andrew Murray wrote concerning the vital role of intercession:

> *"We have far too little conception of the place that intercession, as distinguished from prayer for ourselves, ought to have in the Church and the Christian life. In intercession our King upon the throne finds His highest glory. In it we shall find our highest glory too. Through it He continues His saving work and can do nothing without it. Through it alone we can do our work, and nothing avails without it!"*

ACCEPT CHRIST'S PRAYER MANDATE

Christ has given His Church a prayer mandate. He has given us the awesome privilege and responsibility of joining Him in intercession and fulfilling His will in the nations through our prayers. He has also given us the delegated power and authority, through the Holy Spirit to demolish Satan's strongholds, heal the sick, cast out devils and do even greater works than He did, in His Name!

Christ has chosen and ordained you to walk in His power and authority. Jesus said, *"Ye have not chosen me, but I have chosen you, and ordained you..."* (John 15:16). You don't need the ordination papers of a church or denomination. Christ has ordained you! And, He intends for you to continually produce spiritual fruit. He said, *"that ye should go and bring forth fruit, and that your fruit should remain: that whatsoever ye shall ask of the Father in my name, he may give it you"* (John 15:16).

As self begins to die and we allow the Holy Spirit to have full control to pray through us with groans and gushings of the Spirit, we then enter into that realm of power and authority that is ours in Jesus' Name. We have gained a powerful spiritual position through intercession where we are able to speak the word of deliverance. We are "clothed" with authority by the Holy Spirit; and it is from this position of strength the "greater works" Jesus spoke of are done in His Name!

This is true intercession.

This is what is meant by going into the spiritual arena of intercession to win the battle first in prayer.

There have been many times on the frontlines of battle, in the nations of the world, when I have prayed in the Spirit, wrestled and travailed on behalf of the needs of that nation for hours and hours and days at a time, until we experienced a full release of the power and anointing of God. The battle was first won through this intercession before we saw the great victory of multiplied thousands accept Christ and a release of His miracle working power.

This place of delegated power and authority is not something you can obtain in your own strength. It is a place of intercession that the Holy Spirit will bring you into as you yield yourself totally to Him.

The Intercessor, Who lives within you, will fulfill His work of intercession upon the earth today through you as you present your body a living sacrifice.

Through prayer we can move the hand of God, break through all natural limitations and tap into His unlimited power. In chapter five your spiritual eyes will be opened to the unlimited possibilities of prayer. You will be challenged to go beyond your limitations – to believe God for the impossible!

"On earth, as in heaven, intercession is God's chosen, God's only, channel of blessing." Andrew Murray

I urge you to get alone with the Lord. Ask Him to open your eyes to see your position united with Him in intercession from the Throne! Accept Christ's prayer mandate and rise up to a new level of intercession where you are praying with delegated authority to see the people in your city saved, healed and delivered out of Satan's hands. Yield yourself totally to the Holy Spirit and allow Him to pray through you in a dimension you have never experienced.

Lord, teach us to pray!

Father, thank you for the awesome privilege and responsibility you have given us to come before Your Throne and intercede on behalf of lost souls in our cities and nations. Give us Your heartbeat for souls! Open our eyes to see the lost through Your eyes of compassion. Bring us to a new level of strategic intercession where the Holy Spirit is praying through us, travailing and interceding for souls to be won into Your Kingdom. Anoint us, by Your Spirit, to pray with the delegated authority You have given us. Remove every limitation and hindrance that will prevent us from fulfilling our holy calling of intercession before Your Throne. Lord Jesus, we accept Your prayer mandate and the call to pray prayers from Your Throne

in the power and authority of Your Name, to heal the sick, cast out devils and minister to the desperate needs around us with signs, wonders and miracles following.

CHAPTER FIVE

PRAYER THAT TAKES HOLD OF THE IMPOSSIBLE

Prayer is, without a doubt, the most powerful force on earth.

It is unlimited and unsurpassed in its scope and power.

Prayer knows no boundaries and is not limited by time or space.

R. A. Torrey very eloquently and powerfully said concerning the power of prayer: "Prayer can do anything God can do. All that God is and all that God has is at the disposal of prayer."

Through prayer we are transported into the heavenlies where we stand before Almighty God in His glorious majesty, seated upon His Throne.

We are able through prayer, to tap into the unlimited power of God and take hold of the impossible.

The vast, unsearchable resources of Heaven are at our disposal through prayer!

"By His promises, God puts all things He possesses into our hands. Prayer and faith put us in possession of this boundless inheritance." E. M Bounds

God has given us "*...exceeding great and precious promises; that by these ye might be partakers of the divine nature...*" (2 Peter 1:4). There are approximately 37,000 promises in God's Word! From Genesis to Revelation, God has given us His promises, which make provision for every need in every area of our lives to be met.

By His promises, He has placed all things He possesses in our hands. Prayer and faith enable us to take possession of those promises and appropriate them in our lives. We can have all that God has!

Prayer can transcend the laws of nature, invade the realm of the dead and restore life.

Prayer can give instant access to anywhere: into any home, hospital, office, courtroom, prison cell, or any other location desired.

I will never forget when my darling wife, Theresa, was at the point of death. She had been at death's door several times but God healed her. One day in a Partners' Conference a man came up to us and said, "Theresa, honey, is everything all right?" Theresa answered, "Yes, it is now." He said, "Well, on such and such a day God woke me up and for three days I prayed and interceded for you." Those were the three days Theresa had hovered between life and death.

Through prayer, entrance can be gained into nations of the world considered "closed" to the Gospel. Nothing can stop or hinder entrance into communist-controlled areas such as North Korea, Vietnam or remote villages hidden away in the jungles of Africa or South America. God has given us a secret weapon called prayer that gives us access to anywhere in the world!

Your prayers can be used by God to impact cities and nations, bring salvation, healing and deliverance to people in India, Africa, China, Indonesia, Saudi Arabia or any other country.

Through prayer ,angels can be brought down to protect you and your family.

Your prayers can go into a hospital operating room and help guide the surgeon's hands and release a flow of God's healing power into a loved one.

The following is a true story about a minister who was in critical condition in a San Francisco Hospital. For several days he hung between life and death experiencing excruciating pain in his leg. The ministers of his denomination were in a conference and were called to pray for him. In the middle of their session, they knelt as a group and began to pray earnestly for him. At that exact moment, the pain left his body.

A day or two later he lost consciousness and had a vision of heaven. As he talked with Jesus in this vision, he saw two ministers, one standing on each side of him. They were two of his best friends who were in Los Angeles interceding for him at that very moment. Although they were in Los Angeles, physically separated by many miles, through prayer they were at his side.

ABSOLUTELY NOTHING IS IMPOSSIBLE THROUGH PRAYER!

You can live in a dimension of powerful, penetrating prayer where nothing is impossible to you. It may be difficult to understand, but it is true. This is not just an empty statement or spiritual jargon to make one feel good. It is God's promise based upon His word.

Jesus said, "...*If ye have faith as a grain of mustard seed; ye shall say unto this mountain, Remove hence to yonder place; and it shall remove; and nothing shall be impossible to you*" (Matthew 17:20).

Jesus later emphasized this power of doing the impossible when He cursed the fig tree and it dried up according to His Word.

...If you have faith, and do not doubt, you shall not only do what was done to the fig tree, but even if you say to this mountain, 'Be taken up and cast into the sea,' it shall happen. And all things you ask in prayer, believing, you shall receive.

Matthew 21:21-22, NAS

Jesus said that if we have faith and do not doubt, (*"all things you ask in prayer, believing, you shall receive."*) When He said "all", He didn't mean one or two things. He didn't mean 50 percent of the things we ask for. He meant what He said. All means 100 percent!

Six times in His final hours with His disciples, Christ emphasized the unlimited extent of prayer using the all-inclusive words; "all things," "anything," "whatsoever," "all things whatsoever."

These promises are so great and the possibilities of prayer so vast, yet the majority of Christians today have not been able to take hold of them and are living far below what God has provided for them. The Church, as a whole, seems almost unaware of the power God has placed into its hands.

The unlimited possibilities of prayer are linked to the infinite and omnipotent power of God. There is nothing too hard for Him. He has said; *"Behold, I am the LORD, the God of all flesh: is there any thing too hard for me?"* (Jeremiah 32:27).

Christ has promised, *"For everyone that asketh receiveth; and he that seeketh findeth; and to him that knocketh it shall it be opened"* (Matthew 7:8). God has bound Himself to us with His Word and He will not withhold anything from faith and prayer. As our Father, He finds the greatest pleasure in answering and meeting our needs. Jesus said, *"…how much more shall your Father which is in heaven give good things to them that ask him?"* (Matthew 7:11).

"Do not bring before God small petitions and narrow desires and say, 'Lord, do according to these.' Ask for great things, for you are before a great throne."
Charles Spurgeon

God has chosen to place Himself and all He has at our disposal and directs us to ASK. He has said, *"…Ask me of things to come concerning my sons, and concerning the work of my hands command ye me"* (Isaiah 45:11).

God is sovereign, unlimited and all-powerful! He has a master plan and is working upon earth to fulfill that plan. He is in control. He is not sitting in the heavens with His hands folded. He is sovereignly working in the lives of men and nations and, He has ordained prayer as a means whereby He will work though His people to accomplish His will on earth. Prayer is the major force through which He works on earth. Our lack of prayer causes us to forfeit His blessings, divine intervention and provision He would have given had we prayed.

His divine intervention in the circumstances of our lives in meeting the desperate needs in our cities and nations, He has made dependent upon our prayers.

In essence, God is saying to His people: "I have called and ordained you to carry out My work on earth. I have made full provision for all that you need and desire. I am the Creator, the High and Holy One, the great I AM. Whatever you need to fulfill My plan and purposes, ask Me and I will do it. All that you need accomplished, all the provision you need, command Me. I am the Creator of Heaven and Earth and everything in it, ask largely. Do not be slack, negligent or limited in your asking, and I will not be slack or limited in My giving."

THE MASTER KEY TO PRAYER

The master key to prayer is developing a strong relationship with Christ through prayer. To have power with God through prayer, you must live in unbroken fellowship with God. Power in prayer is not a result of man's endeavors, but of the Spirit of the living God! It doesn't matter how loud or how long you pray. It doesn't matter whether you are kneeling, standing, sitting or lying prostrate on your face before God. It doesn't even really matter concerning the words or terminology you use when you pray.

Just the smallest whisper of a prayer spoken in faith will move God on your behalf.

There are many Christians who believe they must go through some type of "spiritual gyrations" of a set formula of prayer for God to release His power in answer to their prayers.

As I have stated many times before, "Power does not travel through words, it travels through relationships!"

The power and effectiveness of your prayers are dependent upon a personal intimate relationship with God. Without a strong relationship that has been built through communion with Him, your prayers are nothing more than mere words. Jesus said, "*If ye abide in me, and my words abide in you, ye shall ask what ye will, and it shall be done unto you*" (John 15:7).

When you have developed a strong relationship with God, where you are living in unbroken fellowship and communion with Him, your prayers become mighty through God to the "pulling down of strongholds."

"The great people of earth are the people who pray. I do not mean those who talk about prayer; nor those who say they believe in prayer; nor yet those who can explain about prayer; but I mean those people who take time to pray."
S. D. Gordon

The Apostle Paul told the Corinthians:

For though we live in a world, we do not wage war as the world does. The weapons we fight with are not the weapons of the world. On the contrary, they have divine power to demolish strongholds.

2 Corinthians 10:3-4 NIV

Prayer is a mighty spiritual weapon that God has given you to demolish Satan's strongholds. But how is it activated?

Elijah was a mighty man of prayer. He prayed and fire came from God out of heaven!

He prayed and the dead were raised!

He prayed and the heavens were shut for 3-1/2 years!

He prayed again and the heavens were opened!

For a moment let us look at the prayers Elijah prayed that resulted in a demonstration of the supernatural power of God.

When the son of the widow woman of Zarapheth died, she brought him to Elijah. This woman had seen the miracle power of God released. The cruse of oil and barrel of meal were supernaturally multiplied to meet her need. But when her son died she was overcome with grief and brought him to Elijah.

Imagine that traumatic scene! No doubt the woman was totally distraught, overcome with emotion, weeping and wailing.

Elijah took the boy in his arms and carried him to the room in the widow's house where he was staying. He laid the boy on his bed. Then he began to cry out to God. *"...O Lord my God, hast thou also brought evil upon the widow with whom I sojourn, by slaying her son?"* (1 Kings 17:20).

At first, Elijah did not understand why God had allowed the boy to die. This prayer wasn't an expression of Elijah's doubt. It was simply his honest heartfelt cry.

Elijah knew God intimately. He knew God's unlimited power. As an act of faith, Elijah stretched himself upon the child three times and cried, *"...O Lord my God, I pray thee, let this child's soul come into him again"* (1 Kings 17:21).

Elijah did not pray a long, drawn-out prayer. His prayer was simple and direct. It was a prayer of faith based upon his personal knowledge of Almighty God.

God responded to Elijah's heartfelt cry and restored the child's life. *"And the Lord heard the voice of Elijah; and the soul of the child came into him again, and he revived"* (1 Kings 17:22).

Look at the prayer Elijah prayed when God sent fire from heaven to consume the sacrifice on the altar. His prayer wasn't to draw attention to himself or to somehow prove he was a man of power. He challenged the prophets of Baal and the children of Israel who had fallen into idolatry and were worshipping Baal. The prophets of Baal and all the people agreed together with him that the God who answered by fire was the one, true, living God.

The power released through Elijah's prayer was the result of his relationship with God. He knew God's power. He knew God had anointed him as his prophet, and he knew God would answer.

When the time came to offer the evening sacrifice, Elijah stood before the altar and began to pray:

> ...Lord God of Abraham, Isaac, and of Israel, let it be known this day that thou art God in Israel, and that I am thy servant, and that I have done all these things at thy word. Hear me, O Lord, hear me, that this people may know that thou art the Lord God, and that thou hast turned their heart back again.
>
> 1 Kings 18:36-37

God heard Elijah's prayer and answered by sending fire from heaven. His prayers broke through all natural limitations!

> Then the fire of the Lord fell, and consumed the burnt sacrifice, and the wood, and the stones, and the dust, and licked up the water that was in the trench.
>
> 1 Kings 18:38

When God directed Elijah to declare a 3-1/2 year famine, Elijah simply declared, *"...As the Lord God of Israel liveth, before whom I stand, there shall not be dew nor rain these years, but according to my word"* (1 Kings 17:1).

According to the word Elijah spoke at God's direction, the heavens were shut up. Elijah's prayer transcended the laws of nature! There was no rain or dew and the famine lasted 3-1/2 years. Later, when he prayed for the heavens to be opened, he again prayed according to what God had directed him to do.

"...the word of the Lord came to Elijah in the third year, saying, Go, shew thyself unto Ahab; and I will send rain upon the earth" (1 Kings 18:1).

Elijah acted in faith upon the word the Lord spoke to him and went to Ahab. He told Ahab, *"...Get thee up, eat and drink, for there is a sound of abundance of rain"* (1 Kings 18:41). Elijah wasn't fearful to approach Ahab. He knew the word the Lord had spoken to him would come to pass.

Then, Elijah went up to Mt. Carmel where he prayed, *"...and he cast himself down upon the earth, and put his face between his knees"* (1 Kings 18:42).

He told his servant to go and look toward the sea to see if there was any sign of rain. The servant went and looked but there was no sign of rain. He returned and told Elijah, "There is nothing."

Elijah sent his servant a second time. Again, he returned with the same report, "There is nothing." Elijah did not stop; he persevered in prayer. He sent his servant again and again, a third, fourth, fifth, sixth and seventh time. On the seventh time the servant returned to Elijah and said, *"...Behold, there ariseth a little cloud out of the sea, like a man's hand"* (1 Kings 18:44).

The heavens were opened after a 3-1/2 year famine and there was a great rain in answer to Elijah's prayer.

ELIJAH DID NOT FOLLOW A FORMULA FOR PRAYER

The key to the release of God's power through Elijah's prayer was not because of a "formula" Elijah followed. It was not because of the words he spoke. It was because of Elijah's relationship with God.

Elijah was not superhuman. He was a man with a nature that was subject to the same feelings, passions and desires you and I have. Following his great victory over the prophets of Baal, when God sent fire from heaven in answer to his prayer, Elijah was fearful, discouraged and asked God to let him die.

> *Elijah was a human being with a nature such as we have [with feelings, affections and a constitution like ourselves] and he prayed earnestly for it not to rain, and no rain fell on the earth for three years and six months. And [then] he prayed again and the heavens supplied rain and the land produced its crops [as usual].*
>
> James 5:17-18 AMP

Elijah prayed, in faith, according to what God directed him to do. He knew God would do exactly what he said. There was no doubt or wavering.

"Only divine praying can operate divine promises or carry out divine purposes." E. M. Bounds

God has planned for you to have this same power through prayer! James said, *"The prayer of faith shall save the sick..."* (James 5:15). He said, *"The earnest, (heartfelt, continued) prayer of a righteous man makes tremendous power available [dynamic in its working]"* (James 5:16 AMP).

There are many Christians who pray, but they are only speaking empty words. They have not developed an intimate relationship with God where they truly know Him and know He will hear and do all he has promised in His Word. Without this intimate relationship there can be no real power.

YOUR RELATIONSHIP WITH CHRIST IS THE FOUNDATION FOR YOUR POWER IN PRAYER

To become a powerful end-time spiritual warrior, you must also come into a position where you know Christ, where you are one with Him, where you are able to "see" and "hear" in the Spirit what He wants you to do and to say.

One of God's purposes for your life is for you to grow and develop until you come into the *"[full and accurate knowledge] of the Son of God..."* (Ephesians 4:13 AMP).

There is only one way that you will be able to do this and that is through prayer!

The only way you will be able to really *know* Christ in all His fullness is by spending time alone with Him in *prayer*.

The only way you will be able to know His will for your life is *through prayer*.

The only way you will be able to *penetrate* into the realm of the Spirit, where you are able to "see" and "hear" what He wants you to do and to say, is *through prayer*.

"Prayer is the key that unlocks all the storehouses of God's infinite grace and power." R. A. Torrey

Just as it was necessary for Jesus, in the form of human flesh, to use prayer as a means of communicating with God and knowing His will, it is necessary for you to use prayer as a means of coming into the "full and accurate knowledge" of Jesus.

There is a decision and commitment you must make. Your knowledge of Christ, your relationship, and your union with Him *through prayer* is the source (the foundation) of your strength. Unless you are willing to discipline your life, as Jesus did, to include consistent times of prayer alone with Him where you are allowing Him to reveal Himself and His will to you, you will not be able to survive.

If you are not willing to make this commitment, if you are not willing to discipline your life, you may as well give up. You are already defeated even before you begin! Unless you have this strong foundation of *knowing* Christ through prayer, you will not be able to use the other spiritual weapons God has given you.

Take a moment right now to think about the time you are spending each day in prayer. Time when you are getting to know Christ more fully and allowing Him to reveal His will to you. I'm not speaking about the type of prayer where you spend five or ten minutes petitioning God for something or for your loved ones. I am speaking about the type of prayer where you are waiting before Him in His Presence and seeking earnestly to know Him, hungering for Him to reveal Himself to you.

Ask yourself, "How much time am I spending in prayer coming into a full and accurate knowledge of Jesus?"

Are you spending one hour, thirty minutes, fifteen, ten, or even five minutes a day?

Whatever your commitment is right now, increase it. I realize the demands on your time are great. You may have a family to care for, a job, commitments that fill almost every waking hour. But, you must not allow any of these things to crowd out your time alone with Christ.

Regardless of how much time you think you have, increase the amount of time you are now spending in prayer building your relationship with Christ.

As you do this, you will be strengthened. You will be prepared to face every attack of the enemy as Jesus did. As Christ begins to reveal Himself and His will to you during these times of prayer, you will come into a greater knowledge of Who He is and who you are as a child of the living God. Jesus said, "*...whatever the Father does the Son also does*" (John 5:19 NIV). As Christ manifests Himself to you and reveals to you all that He is and does through prayer, you will be able to do the same works!

GOD WILL USE YOU TO SHAPE THE FUTURE THROUGH YOUR PRAYERS

God has established a universal principle concerning His actions being dependent upon our prayers. He has bound Himself to act in *response* to our prayers. We see this illustrated at the dedication of the Temple. After Solomon prayed, God appeared to him and said:

I have heard thy prayer, and have chosen this place to myself for an house of sacrifice. If I shut up heaven that there be no rain, or if I command the locusts to devour the land, or if I send pestilence among my people; If my people, which are called by my name, shall humble themselves, and pray, and seek my face, and turn from their wicked ways; then will I hear from heaven, and will forgive their sin, and will heal their land. Now mine eyes shall be open, and mine ears attent unto the prayer that is made in this place.

2 Chronicles 7:12-15

We often quote verse 14 above in relation to prayer and believing God for revival and an outpouring of His Spirit upon our cities and nations. But, there is another powerful principle that God wants us to understand.

God told Solomon that whenever he saw the land plagued by drought, locusts or other pestilences among the people, that through the prayers and repentance of His people, He would *heal the land.* He would open the heavens and pour out refreshing rain once again. He would drive out the locusts plaguing their crops and their crops would once again flourish. He would drive out all pestilence from among the people and they would walk in the fullness of His blessings.

115

God said their prayers would arise to His Throne and He would hear their cries and would answer. Their prayers would bring His divine intervention upon earth into their circumstances.

God is rising up a people today who understand this powerful universal principle He has set in motion making prayer the most powerful force on earth.

He has placed everything at our disposal. Every conceivable blessing for our personal lives, families, cities and nations He has made available and is waiting to release.

"The power of the Church to truly bless rests on intercession; asking and receiving heavenly gifts to carry to man." Andrew Murray

He stands ready to intervene in the crises plaguing our world. He longs to reverse the curse of famine, pestilence, sickness and disease that has come upon the earth through man's sin and disobedience. But, He is waiting on the prayers of His people to act.

He is looking for a generation of men and women – intercessors – who will intercede, weep, groan and travail; who through their prayers will move His hand to intervene upon earth and release His full provision.

God intends you to shape the future through your prayers! The destiny of people and nations are in the hands of His intercessors. God has said, *"And I sought for a man among them, that should make up the hedge, and stand in the gap before me for the land, that I should not destroy it..."* (Ezekiel 22:30).

God is more than ready to pour out the fullness of His power and blessing. He is speaking to us today, *"Ask me of things to come concerning my sons, and concerning the work of my hands command ye me!"* (Isaiah 45:11).

The following is a true story of a woman who believed God and took hold of the impossible. Her husband was in a hospital in Philadelphia in very critical condition. He weighed less than one hundred pounds.

His doctor told the wife he was dead. But she said, "No, he is not dead. He cannot be dead. I have prayed for him for twenty-seven years and God has promised me that he would be saved. Do you think God would let him die now after I have prayed twenty-seven years and God has promised, and he is not saved?"

"Well", the doctor replied, "I don't know anything about that, but I know that he is dead." With that they drew a screen around the bed that in the hospital separates between the living and the dead.

Seven other physicians were brought in to examine her husband and all confirmed that he was dead. The woman continued to kneel at the side of her husband's bed insisting that he was not dead – that if he were dead God would bring him back for He had promised her that he would be saved.

The woman asked the nurse for a pillow for her to place under her knees while kneeling at her husband's bedside.

One hour, two hours, three hours passed as she knelt beside the lifeless body of her husband. Four, five, six, thirteen hours passed as she continued kneeling at his side. When they tried to get her to leave, she refused, insisting that God would bring him back from the dead.

At the end of thirteen hours her husband opened his eyes and told his wife he wanted to go home. Through prayer she saw her husband raised from the dead and saved by the power of God!

GOD HAS LINKED OUR PRAYERS WITH THE FULFILLMENT OF HIS END-TIME PLAN

Another illustration of the awesome power God has placed in the hands of His people through prayer is found in the book of

Revelation. John was given a glimpse of God seated upon His Throne. Around the throne were twenty-four elders and four angelic beings, all worshipping God. The Lion of the Tribe of Judah, who appeared as the Lamb of God who had been slain, came forward and took the scroll from the right hand of God.

And when he had taken the book, the four living creatures and the twenty-four elders fell down before the Lamb, having each one a harp and golden bowls full of incense, which are the prayers of the saints.

Revelation 5:8 NAS

Here we see *before* the seals and the awesome judgments of God begin, the prayers of God's people are offered up with incense. Our prayers here on earth on behalf of the lost, our cries to Him regarding the wickedness and immorality surrounding us and for God's will and purposes to be fulfilled do not disappear into thin air. They are not forgotten. They ascend before God, and are as sweet-smelling incense in His nostrils.

After the last seal is opened, *before* the judgments of God are poured out upon the earth there is total silence in Heaven for one-half hour. All of Heaven waits in hushed silence for what will soon be revealed.

Standing before God's Throne is a strong angel holding in his hand a golden censer. The angel is given incense, which he mixes with the prayers of all saints throughout the ages and offers it as an offering to God on the golden altar before the Throne.

The air is permeated with the beautiful fragrance of the prayers and the cloud of incense surrounds the Throne. "*And the smoke of the incense, which came with the prayers of the saints, ascended up before God out of the angel's hand*" (Revelation 8:4).

In the same way that Aaron, on the Day of Atonement took the censer full of burning coals off the altar and went into the Holy of Holies and offered incense before the Mercy Seat; the angel takes the censer with the incense and prayers, and impregnates the air with this holy offering.

The worship in the Tabernacle was to be a type of the Heavenly worship. The Mercy Seat was where God appeared in a glory cloud. God directed that Aaron, the High Priest, cover the Mercy Seat with a cloud of incense.

> *And he shall put the incense upon the fire before the Lord, that the cloud of the incense may cover the mercy seat that is upon the testimony, that he die not.*
>
> Leviticus 16:13

The cloud of incense covering the Mercy Seat in the Tabernacle was symbolic of the cloud of incense mixed with the prayers of God's people that will be offered to God upon His Throne before His judgments are poured out upon the earth.

This heavenly scene reveals the tremendous significance and value that God places upon our prayers.

But, there is more.

In John's vision, after covering the Throne of God with the cloud of incense and prayers, the angel takes the censer, mixes it with fire from off the altar and casts it down to the earth.

Now, notice the results: "...*There were voices, and thunderings, and lightnings, and an earthquake*" (Revelation 8:5).

What tremendous force is this that has brought God's power down to earth?

The prayers of God's people!

God has given us this glimpse of how prayer is vitally linked with the fulfillment of His end-time plan. It isn't until the prayers of God's people are offered to Him that the angels are released to sound the trumpets. Then God's judgments come upon the wicked. The angels are God's means of administering the victory, but it will be the saints and their prayers that will win the final victory.

INCENSE...THUNDER...LIGHTNING!

I believe this glorious scene also reveals Heaven's perspective of prayer and what our prayers look like in heaven. Our prayers today are like incense rising up before God on His Throne. They are mixed with fire from His altar and flung back to earth – as spiritual thunder, lightning and earthquakes! Our prayers result in God's divine intervention and will being done upon the earth.

David gives us a glimpse of what he saw in the Spirit when he prayed for deliverance in his time of trouble. *"In my distress I called to the Lord; I cried to my God for help. From his temple he heard my voice; my cry came before him, into his ears"* (Psalm 18:6 NIV).

Now notice what happened as a result of his prayers:

> *The earth trembled and quaked, and the foundations of the mountains shook; they trembled because he was angry. He parted the heavens and came down, dark clouds were under his feet. Out of the brightness of His presence clouds advanced, with hailstones, and bolts of lightning. The Lord thundered from heaven; the voice of the Most High resounded.*
>
> Psalm 18: 7, 9, 12-13 NIV

Earthquake! Lightning! Thunder! This is what David saw in the spirit realm as to how God answered his prayer. He gives us another glimpse into the heavenly realm concerning the awesome power God released in answer to prayer.

In response to David's prayer God began to act. The result was that God delivered him out of the snare of his enemies. David testified of God's answer to his prayer;

> *He rescued me from my powerful enemy, from my foes who were too strong for me. They confronted me in the day of my disaster,*

but the Lord was my support. He brought me out into a spacious place;
he rescued me because he delighted in me

Psalm 18:17-19 NIV

A spiritual earthquake, fire and a mighty wind was released as the incense of the prayers of 120 men and women ascended before God upon His Throne. *"These all continued with one accord in prayer and supplication, with the women, and Mary the mother of Jesus, and with his brethren"* (Acts 1:14).

In response to their prayers, the Father sent the Holy Spirit in a demonstration of power.

And suddenly there came a sound from heaven as of a rushing mighty
wind, and it filled all the house where they were sitting. And there
appeared unto them cloven tongues like as of fire, and it sat upon each
of them. And they were all filled with the Holy Ghost, and began to
speak with other tongues, as the Spirit gave them utterance.

Acts 2:2-4

Throughout the history of the Early Church we see that whenever the Church prayed, incense went up before the Father—spiritual earthquakes, lightning, thunder—God's power was released resulting in His will being accomplished on earth.

And they continued steadfastly in the apostles' doctrine and fellowship,
and of breaking of bread, and in prayers. And fear came upon every
soul: and many wonders and signs were done by the apostles.

Acts 2:42-43

Are you beginning to see the awesome power and privilege God has given you to partner with Him to bring His power, glory and will down to earth?

PRAYER THAT BREAKS THROUGH ALL NATURAL LIMITATIONS

Throughout the Word we have an indisputable record of the awesome, unlimited power of prayer. We are surrounded by an innumerable host of witnesses! Let us consider the following that have left a living memorial to God through their answered prayers.

"To Moses it was given by intercession to place his hand upon God's throne. To you, by grace, it is given to sit with Christ on His throne and there to intercede and prevail for His kingdom."
Wesley L. Duewel

Moses and the children of Israel stood on the banks of the Red Sea. Pharoah and his great army with their chariots were behind them in hot pursuit. They cried out to God, and He rolled back the Red Sea.

> *And Moses stretched out his hand over the sea; and the Lord caused the sea to go back by a strong east wind all that night, and made the sea dry land, and the waters were divided. And the children of Israel went into the midst of the sea upon dry ground: and the waters were a wall unto them on their right hand, and on their left.*
>
> Exodus 14:21-22

PRAYER THAT BREAKS THE CHAINS OF DEATH

Prayer knows no boundaries because God is unlimited in power! Prayer can reach into the realm of the dead and break the chains of death!

Elisha's prayers invaded the realm of the dead and raised the Shunamite's son from his deathbed.

> *When Elisha reached the house, there was the boy lying dead on his couch. He went in, shut the door on the two of them and prayed to the Lord. Then he got on the bed and lay upon the boy, mouth to mouth, eyes to eyes, hands to hands. As he stretched himself out upon him, the boy's body grew warm. Elisha turned away and walked back and forth in the room and then got on the bed andstretched out upon him once more. The boy sneezed seven times and opened his eyes.*
>
> 2 Kings 4:32-34 NIV

Peter was summoned to Joppa by the disciples to pray for Dorcas who had died. When he arrived at the house, it was filled with mourners. But, that did not stop Peter. Peter knew what it was to pray with delegated authority!

"*But Peter put them all forth, and kneeled down, and prayed*" (Acts 9:40).

Notice that after he had prayed, Peter acted in faith. He spoke to Dorcas' dead body!

> *And turning him to the body said, Tabitha, arise. And she opened her eyes: and when she saw Peter, she sat up and he gave her his hand, and lifted her up, and when he had called the saints and widows, presented her alive.*
>
> Acts 9:40-41

Consider Smith Wigglesworth, who ministered from the early 1900's to the 1940's. He was called the "Apostle of Faith" because he believed and preached that God could do the impossible. It is reported that during his ministry twenty people were raised from the dead after he prayed for them.

Smith depended wholly on the Holy Spirit to flow through him. He lived in unbroken communion and fellowship with God and was continuously seeking God's Presence. He said that he never went half an hour without praying. He constantly prayed in tongues.

One day a woman lay at the point of death. She had a tumor and her body was wracked with pain. An elder from her church, by the name of Mr. Fisher, brought Smith Wigglesworth to pray for her.

Smith told her, "I know you are very weak, but if you wish to be healed and cannot lift your arm, or move it at all, it might be possible that you can raise your finger."

With all the strength she could muster, she focused on raising her finger. Then suddenly, her body went limp and she died.

Mr. Fisher was panic-stricken. "She's dead. She's dead", he cried. He had brought Wigglesworth, hoping that she might be healed, and now she had died.

Wigglesworth pulled back the covers, reached into the bed and pulled her out. He carried her lifeless body across the room and propped it up against the wall. There was no pulse, no breath. She was dead.

He looked into her face and commanded, "In the Name of Jesus, I rebuke this death!" The woman's whole body began to tremble.

"In the Name of Jesus, I command you to walk." The woman awoke to find herself walking across her bedroom floor. The pain was gone and the tumor had disappeared!

Smith Wigglesworth prayed with delegated authority! This is the powerful dimension of prayer God intends His people to operate in to meet the desperate needs around us today as living proof that He is the one true living God.

PRAYER THAT COMMANDS THE FORCES OF NATURE

Joshua and Isaiah commanded the forces of nature through their prayers!

In the battle against the Amorites for Gibeon, God fought for Israel. He rained hailstones down upon their enemies. Joshua prayed to the Lord and commanded the sun and moon to stand still.

On the day the Lord gave the Amorites over to Israel, Joshua said to the Lord in the presence of Israel: "O sun, stand still over Gibeon, O moon, over the Valley of Aijalon." So the sun stood still, and the moon stopped, till the nation avenged itself on its enemies, as it is written in the Book of Jashar. The sun stopped in the middle of the sky and delayed going down about a full day. There has never been a day like it before or since, a day when the Lord listened to a man. Surely the Lord was fighting for Israel.

Joshua 10:12-14 NIV

What mighty force commanded the forces of nature and they obeyed? It was Joshua's prayer.

God heard his prayer and stopped the sun and moon in their courses until Joshua and the children of Israel had avenged themselves on their enemies.

King Hezekiah was at death's door. He cried out to God and God promised to heal him and add fifteen years to his life. Hezekiah requested a sign from Isaiah that he would be healed. The Lord responded:

This sign shalt thou have of the LORD, that the LORD will do the thing that he hath spoken: shall the shadow go forward ten degrees, or go back ten degrees? And Hezekiah answered, It is a light thing for the shadow to go down ten degrees: nay, but let the shadow return backward ten degrees.

2 Kings 20:9-10

Through his prayer, Isaiah tapped into the unlimited power of God and God turned back time! "*And Isaiah the prophet cried unto the*

LORD: *and he brought the shadow ten degrees backward, by which it had gone down in the dial of Ahaz"* (2 Kings 20:11).

DARE TO RISE UP AND TAKE HOLD OF THE IMPOSSIBLE THROUGH PRAYER

The power of prayer is unlimited just as God is unlimited! The major problem in the Church is that we have limited an unlimited God through our lack of knowledge and experience in prayer and through our unbelief.

The record stands true. God has proven Himself faithful to answer the prayers of His people and supernaturally intervene to deliver them out of the hands of their enemies.

When Paul and Silas were beaten and thrown into prison, God heard their prayers. Their prayers and praise arose as incense before the Father, and He responded by sending an earthquake to break their chains and set them free.

> *And at midnight Paul and Silas prayed, and sang praises unto God: and the prisoners heard them. And suddenly there was a great earthquake, so that the foundations of the prison were shaken: and immediately all the doors were opened, and every one's bands were loosed.*
>
> Acts 16:25-26

What mighty force caused the earth to convulse and the foundations of the prison to shake?

The only force on earth powerful enough to do this – the prayers of God's servants, Paul and Silas. Their prayers moved the hand of God and brought supernatural deliverance.

The record stands! We read about those mighty warriors of faith:

...who through faith subdued kingdoms, wrought righteousness, obtained promises, stopped the mouths of lions, quenched the violence of fire, escaped the edge of the sword, out of weakness were made strong, waxed valiant in flight, turned to flight the armies of the aliens. Women received their dead raised to life again...

Hebrews 11:33-35

What mighty force enabled them to accomplish these great spiritual conquests?

Faith and prayer! Faith and prayer are inseparable. Faith must have a voice to express itself. True prayer is the voice of faith!

From these brief examples, we are able to see the all-encompassing, unlimited power of prayer and how God has committed Himself into the hands of His people who know Him and have learned how to pray.

Lord, teach us to pray!

The unlimited potential of prayer is beyond our natural understanding. But the record remains true. With God all things are possible, and all things are possible to those who know how to prevail with God in prayer.

It is exciting to read about Moses, Elijah, Elisha, Joshua, Peter, Paul and how God's awesome power was unleashed upon earth through their prayers. But, God has not changed! He is the same all-powerful, miracle-working God. He doesn't want us to look back. He wants us to remove every limitation we have placed upon Him through our unbelief. He is raising up an end-time army of intercessors today in every nation, who will pray with a powerful fiery prayer anointing and be used to see cities and nations shaken by His power.

Through their prayers, they will bring God's supernatural power down to earth to meet the desperate needs of the world. They will dare to rise up in faith to take hold of the impossible through prayer.

E. M. Bounds has said concerning the unlimited possibilities of prayer, "How vast are the possibilities of prayer! How wide its reach! It lays its hand on Almighty God and moves Him to do what He would not do if prayer was not offered. Prayer is a wonderful power placed by Almighty God in the hands of His saints, which may be used to accomplish great purposes and to achieve unusual results. The only limits to prayer are the promises of God and His ability to fulfill those promises."

THE DESTINY OF THE WORLD IS IN THE HANDS OF INTERCESSORS

This is an hour unlike any other. As the Church prepares for the Lord's return, we must by faith begin to tap into the unlimited power of God, through prayer, to see a mighty wave of His power and glory sweep across this world.

Throughout history, every great movement of God's power in revival has come as a result of fervent, prevailing prayer.

During the Great Awakening in the United States in 1857, in one year more than one million people were saved. It began with a man of prayer, Jeremiah Lanphier. He and two other men began to pray for revival. They soon opened a daily noon prayer meeting in the upper room of the Dutch Reformed Church in Manhattan and invited others.

At first only six people showed up. The following week there were 14, and then 23. They started meeting every day and soon filled the Dutch Reformed Church, the Methodist Church and every public building in downtown New York.

In New York City, 10,000 people a week were saved. The news concerning the prayer meeting spread to outlying cities and other prayer groups sprang up. After six months, 10,000 businessmen were meeting daily at noon in New York City alone. In eight months, from September until May, 50,000 people in New York City were saved and committed their lives to the Lord.

The move of God spread throughout New England where people would meet to pray three times a day. The revival spread up the Hudson river and down the Mohawk. The fire spread from New York to other cities and then swept over the entire country.

Our whole nation was shaken by the power of God as it had never been shaken before. The revival crossed the Atlantic, broke out in Northern Ireland, Scotland, Wales, England, South Africa and Southern India.

Four men in Northern Ireland united together and met every Saturday night to pray for revival. They spent the whole night in prayer. God heard their prayers and the fire of God fell and revival began to spread across Ireland.

God's power was so strong in some parts of Ireland that courts adjourned because there were no cases to try. Jails were closed because there were no prisoners to incarcerate. Many of the notorious and hardened sinners in the land were converted!

The destiny of cities, nations, people groups and this world is in the hands of intercessors that will begin to see the unlimited power of prayer. It is in the hands of those who will submit themselves into the hands of God to be used, through their prayers, to bring down His power and a move of His Spirit that will result in a worldwide harvest of souls.

In chapter six I will share God's prophetic purpose for prayer and the position God is calling His intercessors to fill.

Will you respond to the call of the Spirit?

Will you rise up and take your position in the great army of intercessors God is mobilizing in this hour to wage war in the heavenlies to bring salvation, healing and deliverance to a dying world?

Lord, teach us to pray!

Dear Father,

Thank you for the awesome power you have made available to us through prayer. Forgive us for limiting You through our unbelief. Open our spiritual eyes to see the unlimited resources You have given us, and how You have chosen to bring Your power and glory down to meet the desperate needs in this world through our prayers. Teach us to pray with new spiritual vision that focuses upon You and Your unlimited power. Break every limitation from our natural minds hindering us from praying prayers that will be used to impact this world and result in a worldwide harvest of souls. We want to

build a living memorial to You through answered prayer that will demonstrate to the world that You are the One true living God.

CHAPTER SIX

BETWEEN THE PORCH AND THE ALTAR

The greatest need of the Church today is not more man-made programs. It is not more Church buildings.

It is not more conferences, seminars and meetings where the same people come time after time, receive God's blessings, but leave unchanged.

The greatest need within the Church is strategic warfare prayer and intercession, where the fire of the Holy Spirit is flowing through us to pray prayers that God will use to push back the powers of darkness over people groups and nations!

As we continue our spiritual journey to learn how to pray in the same powerful dimension Christ taught and demonstrated, we must also have a clear understanding of the prophetic purpose of prayer in this end-time hour.

At the beginning of 1995, God revealed to me that He was going to release a new powerful prayer anointing upon the Church!

The purpose of this prayer anointing is not so that Christians can simply enjoy the blessings of God. The purpose of this last great anointing is to divinely enable the Church to fulfill God's purposes and bring in a great end-time harvest before Christ returns, and to penetrate the last satanic strongholds over closed nations.

After 56 years of ministry, and walking very closely with the Lord, I am convinced there is now a new anointing rising up. It is an energizing, global call to prayer that is coming upon the people of God. As a result, we will see the end-time gathering of the greatest harvest this world has ever known!

This anointing will bring us into a new dimension—a new level of strategic spiritual warfare prayer where we will tap into His unlimited power to push back the forces of darkness, to press the battle in the power of His Spirit until we see His kingdom come in every nation, with every tribe, people and tongue having an end-time witness of the Gospel. (In chapters 14 & 15, I share the revelation God gave me concerning this powerful new level of strategic warfare prayer.)

Knowing that the greatest need of the Church and the only answer for a world in crisis is powerful, penetrating prayer, this year I conducted five Schools of Prayer in our World Prayer Center in San Diego. Major Christian leaders and teachers in the area of intercession joined me during these Schools in bringing forth powerful, cutting-edge teaching and revelation on prayer.

We experienced some of the greatest manifestations of God's power during these schools we have ever experienced in the history of my ministry! There were times when God showed me the heavens opened over us, and angels walking in our midst. There were other times as we were praying when it seemed as if waves of liquid fire were flowing over us and we were literally engulfed in God's power and presence.

God is releasing this end-time prayer anointing! In these Schools and our other meetings worldwide there has been a divine impartation and release of a powerful new dimension of prayer. These life-changing Schools of Prayer were web cast live over the Internet to our Global Prayer Strike Force leaders and intercessors in over 48 nations!

AN END-TIME CALL TO PRAYER

Jesus said,

My house shall be called a house of prayer for all nations!
Mark 11:17 AMP

As God is releasing this prayer anointing, He is bringing His Church back to this purpose.

In this end-time hour, God will use the prayers of His people to shake entire cities for His kingdom! As we intercede, He will release a spirit of repentance and salvation. As the Church wages spiritual warfare against the ruling powers and principalities that are over its cities; spirits of lust, violence, hatred, immorality, drug and alcohol addiction, adultery, sexual perversion, worldliness and other demonic forces that have built strongholds and bondages will begin to break off people, and a spirit of conviction and repentance will be loosed!

Receive this prophecy into your spirit:

God is bringing us into a new dimension of authority in our prayers where our words, spoken with authority, invested in the promises of God, will enable us to confront every stronghold of the enemy!

This end-time call to prayer is not just for pastors, evangelists, ministers or Christian leaders. Throughout Church history God has used the prayers of mighty spiritual warriors. Anna, the prophetess, devoted her life to fasting and prayer. She

> ...served God with fastings and prayers night and day
>
> Luke 2:37.

James, the brother of Jesus spent the latter years of his life praying for the churches God was raising up. When he died and his body was prepared for burial, they discovered that his knees were so calloused from hours and hours of kneeling that they almost resembled the knees of a camel. He became known as "camel knees".

Praise God for David Brainerd, missionary to the American Indians, and his life of prayer and tears. Praise God for Charles Finney, John Knox and other great leaders whose prayers were used to help bring revival and shake nations. Praise God for "Praying John Hyde," who devoted his entire life to prayer for India and was perhaps the greatest prayer warrior in the 20th century.

But this end-time call to prayer is not just to those who are called to the ministry of intercession and devote their entire lives to deep intercession. This is a call to the entire Body of Christ, to businessmen, lawyers, secretaries, housewives, doctors, and Christians of all ages and walks of life.

God is calling every member of the Body of Christ to a higher level of commitment to:

1. Intimate communion and fellowship with Him.

2. Intercession and a new level of strategic warfare prayer for their cities and nations.

Regardless of who you are, your age or your circumstances, God can and will use your prayers in your city and nation. You may think, "I'm just a housewife, how can God use me?" Or, "I'm just a seemingly little, insignificant person living in a remote area, how can my prayers make a difference?"

As Dwight L. Moody began his ministry, God used the prayers of a bedridden woman in London to bring a spiritual breakthrough in one of his first meetings. Moody is considered as one of the greatest evangelists of the nineteenth century. In a 40 year period, he won a million souls to Christ, founded three Christian schools, launched a great Christian publishing business, established a Christian conference center and was used to inspire thousands of preachers to win souls and conduct revivals.

In his early ministry he learned the importance and power of prayer. He was invited to preach in a Congregational church in London. Sunday morning as he preached he had great difficulty. He said, "I had no power, no liberty; it seemed like pulling a heavy train up a steep grade, and as I preached I said to myself, 'What a fool I was to consent to preach. I came here to hear others, and here I am preaching.'"

Moody tried to get permission from those in charge of the meeting to be released from preaching again that evening, but they would not give their consent. He went to the meeting that night with a heavy heart. But, he had not been preaching long when it seemed as if the powers of an unseen world had fallen upon the people. He gave the altar call and 500 people rose to their feet!

Moody later shared the secret to what happened to change the spiritual atmosphere in the meeting resulting in a great harvest of souls.

"There were two sisters in that church, one of whom was bedridden; the other one heard me that Sunday morning. She went home and said to her sister, 'Who do you suppose preached for us this morning?' The sister replied, 'I do not know.' Then she said, 'Guess'. The sister guessed all the men that Mr. Lessey was in the habit of exchanging with, but her sister said, 'No.' Then her sister asked, "Who did preach for us this morning?" And she replied, 'Mr. Moody of Chicago.'

"No sooner had she said it than her sister turned pale as death and said, 'What! Mr. Moody of Chicago! I have read of him in an American paper and I have been praying for God to send him to London, and to send him to our church. If I had known he was to preach this morning I would have eaten no breakfast. I would have spent the whole morning in fasting and prayer."

"Now, sister, go out, lock the door, do not let anyone come to see me. Do not let them send me any dinner. I am going to spend the whole afternoon and evening in fasting and prayer." There in her room, hidden away with the Lord, she prayed and God answered!

The key to the spiritual breakthrough Moody experienced during this meeting in his early ministry was the prayers of a bedridden woman, shut away in her room fasting and praying.

OH GOD, SHAKE US!

The prophetic purpose for prayer in this end-time hour is to fulfill God's purposes in the nations before Christ returns. Just as God used John the Baptist as a forerunner of Christ to prepare the way of the Lord, before Christ's return, He is raising up mighty spiritual warriors in every nation with the prophetic purpose of preparing the way before Him.

Something supernatural must happen within the Church!

Praise God for the revivals we have seen break out in recent years in various parts of the United States. But, we need a sweeping, worldwide, sovereign move and outpouring of God's Spirit within the Church today that crosses all denominational barriers! Only prayer that penetrates the darkness can bring it about.

We need a move of God that will shake the Church out of its complacency, rid us of our compromise, disunity, worldliness and sin that has weakened us.

We need God to so anoint our eyes with spiritual eyesalve that we will see our true condition, repent and allow Him to cleanse and purge out everything that is displeasing to Him.

Jesus is coming for a holy Church that is "without spot or wrinkle."

> *...Christ also loved the church, and gave himself for it; That he might sanctify and cleanse it with the washing of water by the word, That he might present it to himself a glorious church, not having spot or wrinkle, or any such thing; but that it should be holy and without blemish.*
>
> Ephesians 5:25-27

In these final hours before His return Christ has planned for His Church to operate in the fullness of His power, and that power can only be received on our knees through prayer and fasting!

When we look at the example of the power flowing through the Early Church and compare it with what we see in the Church today, there is no doubt or question that something is very wrong.

We are not operating in the same power and anointing that was released and flowed through the Early Church. If we were, our cities would be shaken by God's power. We would see multitudes being saved, healed and delivered as a natural result of God's power flowing through the Church.

The truth is our lack of power is a result of our prayerlessness.

THE KEY TO GOD'S POWER IN THE EARLY CHURCH

As we read the exciting account of the early Church, every chapter contains a triumphant shout of victory. It is a story of perpetual progress and constant victory over all opposing forces and strong persecution. We read,

> *...And the Lord added to the church daily such as should be saved.*
>
> Acts 2:47

> *Howbeit many of them which heard the word believed; and the number of the men was about five thousand.*
>
> Acts 4:4

> *And believers were the more added to the Lord, multitudes both of men and women.*
>
> Acts 5:14

> *And the word of God increased; and the number of the disciples multiplied in Jerusalem greatly; and a great company of the priests were obedient to the faith.*
>
> Acts 6:7

The miracle working power of God flowed with signs and wonders being demonstrated as living proof of the Gospel being preached. We read,

> *And fear came upon every soul: and many wonders and signs were done by the apostles.*
>
> Acts 2:43

And with great power gave the apostles witness of the resurrection of the Lord Jesus: and great grace was upon them all.

Acts 4:33

And the people with one accord gave heed unto those things which Philip spake, hearing and seeing the miracles which he did.

Acts 8:6

And God wrought special miracles by the hands of Paul.

Acts 19:11

The reason why God's power flowed though the Early Church in such a great dimension is very evident.

The Early Church was a praying church! They did not merely pray occasionally,

...they continued stedfastly in the apostles' doctrine and fellowship, and in breaking of bread, and in prayers.

Acts 2:42

They all prayed, not just the Apostles or a select few, but the whole membership of the church prayed with stedfast determination.

There were three time periods designated by the Jews for public worship. The third hour of prayer was between the hours of 6:00 A.M. and 9:00 A.M. The sixth hour was between the hours of 9:00 A.M. and 12:00 noon; the ninth hour between the hours of 12:00 noon and 3:00 P.M. During these times designated for prayer, the disciples and believers prayed in their homes or in the Temple. Peter and John were on their way to the Temple for prayer when Peter saw the lame man lying at the gate of the Temple. He lifted him to his feet and said,

...Silver and gold have I none; but such as I have give I thee: In the name of Jesus Christ of Nazareth rise up and walk.

Acts 3:6

THE DISCIPLES GAVE
THEMSELVES TO PRAYER

The Church of Jesus Christ was born, empowered, sustained, and overcame through prayer!

Prayer was their number one priority. The disciples said,

> *But we will give ourselves continually to prayer, and to the ministry of the word.*
>
> Acts 6:4

Prayer was not secondary to the ministry. It was inseparable from the work of the ministry.

The disciples "gave themselves to prayer." In saying this, they put prayer first. They put fervor, urgency and time into it.

Paul gave himself to prayer for the Church. He said,

> *Night and day praying exceedingly…*
>
> 1 Thessalonians 3:10

To the Romans he wrote,

> *For God is my witness…that without ceasing I make mention of you always in my prayers.*
>
> Romans 1:9

He travailed in prayer for the believers. He said,

> *My little children, of whom I travail in birth again until Christ be formed in you,…*
>
> Galatians 4:19

Prayer was not just an occasional occurrence in the lives of the disciples; it was an integral part of their lives. They knew what a powerful force it was and depended upon its power for everything. When they needed God's direction, they prayed. When they needed God's provision, they prayed. When they needed protection and deliverance, they prayed. When they needed doors to open for the Gospel, they prayed.

The believers prayed from house to house. They prayed in the Temple, in prisons, on mountainsides, on riverbanks and wherever they went. When they faced persecution and death, they prayed in the dark cold catacombs.

PETER'S SUPERNATURAL DELIVERANCE

One example of the power released in answer to the prayers of the Church is that of Peter's deliverance out of prison.

King Herod had already killed James, the brother of John, which pleased the Jews. Herod then arrested the Apostle Peter, with the intention of killing him also.

It was Passover Week, the Holy Week of the Jews. Peter was cast into prison to be kept until the Passover Week was completed and then he was to be executed.

Passover Week was nearly over. It was the last night and the next morning Peter was to be beheaded.

In the natural, Peter's situation was hopeless. He was in a dungeon, an impregnable fortress, guarded by sixteen soldiers and chained by each wrist to soldiers sleeping on either side of him.

When the Christians in Jerusalem heard that Peter was in prison, they did not have a meeting to plan his escape. They did not circulate a petition or march down the streets in protest demanding Peter's release.

They prayed!

> *Peter therefore was kept in prison: but prayer was made without ceasing of the church unto God for him.*
>
> Acts 12:5

On the night of his proposed execution, Peter was sound asleep, chained to soldiers sleeping on either side of him.

Meanwhile, across town the Christians were praying, waging war in the heavenlies on Peter's behalf. I do not believe they were sitting quietly or passively praying. Peter was facing possible execution the next morning. They were fervently and earnestly crying out to God for His divine intervention and deliverance for Peter. I believe they were getting violent in the Spirit. Jesus said,

> *And from the days of John the Baptist until now the kingdom of heaven suffereth violence, and the violent take it by force.*
>
> Matthew 11:12

In Acts 12, the Father heard their prayers and answered by dispatching an angel to deliver Peter out of prison.

Suddenly, a glorious light from heaven shone down into that dark dungeon. The angel hit Peter on the side, awakened him and said, "Get up quickly!"

Instantly, Peter's chains fell from his hands and feet and he stood up.

"*Gird yourself and put on your sandals,*" the angel told him.

Peter obeyed and the angel said, "*Cast your garments about you, and follow me!*"

Peter thought he might have been seeing a vision, but he quickly responded to do all the angel directed him to do.

The soldiers were asleep. Peter continued walking past the first guard unnoticed. He walked on past the second guard and came to the strong iron gate leading into the city.

As Peter and the angel stood there, God reached down and opened the gate. Peter did not need a key to unlock it – God caused it to open. Still accompanied by the angel, Peter walked through the gate and onto the street, a free man, delivered by the hand of Almighty God in response to the prayers of the Church!

When Peter was safe, the angel left him. Suddenly, he came to himself and realized he had not been dreaming. He said to himself,

Now I know without a doubt that the Lord sent his angel and rescued me from Herod's clutches and from everything the Jewish people were anticipating.

Acts 12:11 NIV

I can imagine Peter running through the streets to Mark's home where the Church had gathered to pray for him. He knocked loudly on the door.

Rhoda, the servant girl ran to the door. As Peter spoke she immediately recognized his voice but was so excited she ran back to tell the others without opening the door.

"Peter is at the door," Rhoda exclaimed.

The people did not believe her and said to her, "Rhoda, you are out of your mind!"

Rhoda said, "I am not crazy! I tell you it is Peter. I recognized his voice!"

When she continued to insist it was him they told her, "It must be his angel!"

Peter kept on knocking until they finally opened the door and realized in amazement that it really was Peter and God had supernaturally delivered him in answer to their prayers.

INTENSE, FERVENT, AGONIZING PRAYER

The prayers the Church prayed that night that moved the hand of God to supernaturally deliver Peter out of the hands of Herod were not just ordinary prayers.

...prayer was made without ceasing of the church unto God for him.

Acts 12:5

The King James Version translates this type of prayer "without ceasing." Other translations use the words "fervently" or "earnestly."

The original Greek word is "ekten_s" and it literally means "stretch-out-edly." The King James translators thought of the prayer as stretched out a long-time, unceasing prayer.

But, that is not the actual meaning. This Greek word is never used in that sense anywhere in the New Testament. The word actually represents the soul stretched out in intense earnestness toward God.

The prayers the Church prayed that resulted in Peter's deliverance were intense! They were red-hot, fervent! The believers weren't just going through the motions. They were earnestly pouring out their souls on Peter's behalf.

This same Greek word "ekten_s" is used to describe Christ's prayer in the Garden of Gethsemane.

> *And being in agony he prayed more earnestly: and his sweat was as it were great drops of blood falling down to the ground.*
>
> Luke 22:44

The words "more earnestly" in this verse literally mean "more stretched-out-edly" which describes Christ's entire soul being stretched out in intense, fervent agonizing prayer.

The word agony is translated from the Greek word "agnonia" which is the root of the word translated "strive together."

In the Garden of Gethsemane Jesus was wrestling, striving, with every fiber of His Being in earnest, agonizing prayer.

It is this type of intense, fervent prayer that reaches God's ears and which He answers.

Another example of this type of prayer is found in Romans 15:30 when the Apostle Paul was urging the believers in the Church to pray for him. He said, "Now I beseech you brethren, for the Lord Jesus Christ's sake, and for the love of the Spirit, that ye strive together with me in your prayers to God for me."

Paul said, "strive together with me," which in this verse is *"sunagonizo."* *"Agonizo"* means to "contend" or "strive," "wrestle" or "fight." All of these word describe a level of great intensity.

In the Amplified Version it is translated,

> *...to unite with me in earnest wrestling in prayer to God on my behalf."*
> Romans 15:30 AMP

Paul said, Strive! Contend! Labor! Wrestle! Fight!

PRAYER POWER THAT WILL SHAKE CITIES AND NATIONS!

Is it any wonder that when the disciples and believers united in prayer, God's power came down and the place where they were was shaken!

One of the first things the Early Church faced was persecution. After Peter healed the lame man sitting at the gate, he taught the people and preached about Jesus. As a result, more than five thousand believed!

The next day the High Priests brought Peter and John and the man who had been healed before them. They asked, "By what power or by what name, have ye done this?"

Peter, full of the Holy Ghost, was not intimidated. He did not try to appease the High Priests and religious leaders. He wasn't worried about the repercussions of what he would say.

I can see Peter stand and grab hold of the man who had been healed and draw him to his side. Then he boldly declared, *"Be it known unto you all, and to all the people of Israel, that by the name of Jesus Christ of Nazareth, whom ye crucified, whom God raised from the dead, even by him doth this man stand here before you whole"* (Acts 4:10).

Peter clearly told them, "It is by the power and authority of Jesus' Name that this man is totally healed! You crucified Him. But, He is not in the grave! He is risen! God raised Him from the dead. He is sitting at the right hand of the Father. He has delegated to us His power and authority in His Name and it is by His Name that this man is healed!"

But, Peter did not stop there! He made it clear for everyone to know there is no other name whereby men can be saved. He said, *"Neither is there salvation in any other: for there is none other name under heaven given among men, whereby we must be saved"* (Acts 4:12).

We need this same power and boldness in the Church today. Instead of compromising and trying to be politically correct, we need to boldly proclaim for all to hear: There is no other name – not Buddha – not Mohammed – not Kali or the other Hindu gods – whereby men can be saved! There are not many ways to God. There is only one way! There is only One Name, the Name of Jesus Christ, the Son of the Living God!

You know the story. After the High Priests threatened Peter and John not to preach or teach in Jesus' Name, they released them.

Peter and John did not run away somewhere to hide. They met with the other disciples and believers and prayed. They did not have a pity party. They did not meet together to try to devise a plan to win over the High Priests. They did not even ask God to stop the persecution. They prayed intensely, with great fervency, in one accord:

> *And, now, Lord, behold their threatenings: and grant unto thy servants, that with all boldness they may speak thy word. By stretching forth thine hand to heal; and that signs and wonders may be done by the name of thy holy child Jesus.*
>
> Acts 4:29-30

Their prayer was not focused on the power of the enemy. They did not ask God to change the hearts of the High Priests and religious leaders. Their prayer was very specific. They asked for two things:

1. Boldness to speak the Word.

2. Signs and wonders to be done in Jesus' Name.

God heard their prayer and sent a spiritual earthquake!

And when they had prayed, the place was shaken where they were assembled together; and they were all filled with the Holy Ghost, and they spake the word of God with boldness.

Acts 4:31

They left that place charged with the power of God! They refused to be silenced but continued to boldly proclaim the Gospel and work signs and wonders in the Name of Jesus!

And daily in the Temple, and in every house, they ceased not to teach and preach Jesus Christ.

Acts 5:42

The Apostles flooded Jerusalem with the Gospel. We read that multitudes were added to the Lord. The power of God flowed through them in such a mighty way they carried the sick and placed them in cots along the street so that as Peter passed by his shadow might fall on them and they would be healed.

Talk about a citywide revival! The people gathered up the sick and demon-possessed from the towns surrounding Jerusalem and brought them to the disciples to be healed.

Also the people from the cities in the vicinity of Jerusalem were coming together, bringing people who were sick or afflicted with unclean spirits, and they were all being healed.

Acts 5:16, NAS

The disciples were not acting in their own power and authority. They prayed with delegated authority. They spoke healing and cast out demons in the power and authority of Jesus' Name. In His Name, they took dominion and established the Kingdom of God wherever they went.

WHAT WE MUST HAVE IS PRAYER SET ON FIRE BY THE HOLY SPIRIT!

Under the prayer anointing being released, God intends the Church to pray prayers that are set on fire by the Holy Spirit. Remember the prophecy: God is bringing us into a new dimension of authority in our prayers, where our words, spoken with authority, invested in the promises of God, will enable us to confront every stronghold of the enemy!

The Church of Jesus Christ must have this same priority in prayer, the same holy boldness and the same power to meet the desperate needs we face in our cities and nations!

Never has there been a greater time when the world has needed God's divine intervention in meeting its desperate needs. On every hand we see nations torn apart through political upheaval and war.

The world faces an even greater threat than ever before – terrorism. Suicide bombings occur somewhere in the world on almost a daily basis. There is fear and uncertainty everywhere.

Many nations are living in the throes of economic collapse with millions living in poverty and millions more at the point of starvation.

Our cities are plagued with violence, pornography, prostitution, drugs and crime. Our children have become targets of pedophiles and are unsafe on the school playgrounds, their own back yard or even in their own beds.

Homosexuality is being accepted as an alternate lifestyle and gay marriages are accepted and recognized as legal in many countries. Television boldly and openly portrays homosexual relationships. They openly flaunt their sinful lifestyle in gay parades throughout our cities in America.

There are people all around us; in our neighborhoods, on the job, and in the markets, that are bound by sickness and disease, tormented by fear and oppressed by demons.

147

In a world population of over six billion, half of them are still bound in chains of darkness and have not been reached with the Gospel.

The only way we will be able to see our cities and nations transformed; men and women saved, healed and delivered, bondages of drugs, alcohol and sexual perversion broken, is for a great outpouring of God's Spirit to be released upon the Church.

The only way we will see God-ordained changes in our governments, schools, news and television media is to have an outpouring of God's power and Spirit that will affect every area of our society.

The key to the release of a mighty end-time outpouring of God's Spirit is prayer...prayer that is set on fire by the Holy Spirit! We must strive, contend, fight, and wrestle in fervent, earnest prayer until God begins to pour out His Spirit upon us.

AFTERWARD

God promised through the Prophet Joel that He would pour out His Spirit upon all flesh.

> *And it shall come to pass afterward, that I will pour out my spirit upon all flesh; and your sons and your daughters shall prophesy, your old men shall dream dreams, your young men shall see visions. And also upon the servants and upon the handmaids in those days will I pour out my spirit.*
>
> Joel 2:28-29

The key to the release of this end-time outpouring is found in the word "afterward" in the above verses.

Something must happen first. If we go back in this same chapter to verse twelve, we see that God is first calling His people to repentance and intercession.

Therefore also now, saith the LORD, turn ye even to me with all your heart, and with fasting, and with weeping, and with mourning: And rend your heart, and not your garments, and turn unto the LORD your God: for he is gracious and merciful, slow to anger, and of great kindness, and repenteth him of evil.

Joel 2:12-13

In verses fifteen and sixteen we are called to sanctify a fast and call a solemn assembly.

Blow the trumpet in Zion, sanctify a fast, call a solemn assembly: Gather the people, sanctify the congregation, assemble the elders, gather the children...

Joel 2:15-16

In verse seventeen the priests and ministers are called to weep and cry out on behalf of the people.

Let the priests, the ministers of the LORD, weep between the porch and the altar, and let them say, Spare thy people, O LORD, and give not thine heritage to reproach, that the heathen should rule over them: wherefore should they say among the people, Where is their God?.

Joel 2:17

Notice as a result of this repentance, fasting and weeping and interceding before God.

Then will the LORD be jealous for his land, and pity his people

Joel 2:18

Then will come times of rejoicing (see Joel 2:23). Then will come restoration! (see Joel 2:25). Then will come blessing (see Joel 2:26). And then afterwards will come the promised outpouring! The key is after!

TAKE YOUR POSITION AS AN END-TIME INTERCESSOR!

The Spirit of God is sounding an alarm throughout the earth, gathering together intercessors – men and women – who will sound the alarm and begin to intercede – to weep and cry out to God until they see His power and glory poured out.

Knowing that Christ is coming soon, you must take your position as an end-time intercessor.

Our position is "between the porch and the altar" in prayer – on our faces before God – weeping, groaning, travailing and interceding.

In the Church today we hear very little about in-depth intercession where pastors, ministers and members of the Body of Christ spend hours weeping before God on behalf of the sins of the people and for lost souls.

God is calling us back to the altar where we will weep and cry out for the souls of people in our cities.

It was this type of wrestling in prayer for the souls of men throughout Church history that brought the outpouring of God's Spirit.

In the ministry of Charles Finney, there were two men who would go before him into a city and would find a small room where they would spend days weeping and travailing in prayer.

One of those men was Abel Clary. He had been licensed to preach but he had such a spirit of intercession, and was so burdened for the souls of men that his whole time and strength was devoted to prayer. He didn't go to the meetings but prayed night and day. Sometimes he would so agonize in prayer that he could not even stand on his knees. He would lie prostrate on the floor, weeping and groaning before God.

His prayers, along with the other man, Father Nash, were a great key to revival that sprang up all over the country bringing 100,000 souls to Christ in one year!

The prayers of John Welch were used by God to release a mighty outpouring of His Spirit upon Scotland. He prayed with such intensity on behalf of the lost, he cried, "Give me Scotland, or I die." Most people think that it was John Knox who prayed this prayer but it wasn't. It was John Welch. John Knox, the great Scotch reformer, was his Father-in-law.

John Welch thought the day ill spent if he did not spend eight to ten hours in prayer. In the night he would often get up to pray and his wife would complain when she found him lying on the floor weeping. He would tell her, "O woman, I have the souls of three thousand to answer for, and I know not how it is with many of them."

It is my prayer that God will rekindle this fiery passion in prayer for lost souls within every born-again Christian today.

This is the heartbeat of God and if the Church is going to fulfill the work and commission Christ has given it before He returns, this is where it must begin. Prayer is not an end in itself. Our prayers, anointed and directed by the Holy Spirit will produce results. God's purposes will be accomplished, souls will be saved, healed and delivered!

Jesus said,

> *And this gospel of the kingdom shall be preached in all the world for a witness unto all nations; and then shall the end come.*
>
> Matthew 24:14

The only way to penetrate the last remaining strongholds of Satan in the nations and reach the multiplied millions who have never heard the Gospel is through men and women whose hearts are on fire with a burning passion for the lost, and who are willing to pour out their hearts, weeping and travailing in prayer on their behalf.

I urge you to hear the call of the Spirit and to rise up and take your position as an end-time intercessor, "between the porch and the altar" in prayer for the lost in your city and nation. Humble yourself before God and ask Him to rekindle the fire of passion and give you His heartbeat for souls.

Lord, teach us to pray!

Father, we have heard Your end-time call to prayer and the cry of our heart is, release a new prayer anointing upon us! Shake us out of our complacency! Pour out Your Spirit upon us! Change us! Rekindle the fire of passion and love for lost souls. Give us Your heartbeat! Release Your Spirit within us to weep and travail for the lost. Use our prayers to break the chains of sin, sickness and disease in our cities and nations. We present ourselves to You today to be used as end-time intercessors to fulfill Your will and bring in a worldwide harvest of souls.

CHAPTER SEVEN

CHRIST, THE GREAT INTERCESSOR

To understand the powerful position of prayer and intercession God has called you to, you must have a fresh revelation of Christ as the Great Intercessor.

"Christ is today the interceding Sovereign of the universe. He is on the throne interceding for us and waiting for us to join Him as intercessors." Wesley L. Duewel

It is important for you to understand that your position of prayer and intercession is dependent upon your personal relationship with Christ. It is through your relationship with Him that you have full access to the Father. Jesus said, *"If ye abide in me, and my words abide in you, ye shall ask what ye will, and it shall be done unto you"* (John 15:7).

"We are branches of Christ, the Living Vine. We must simply live like branches – abide in Christ – and then we will ask what we will and it will be done unto us." Andrew Murray

This is the *master key* to prayer and intercession! To have power with God through prayer, we must live in unbroken communion and fellowship with Christ. Jesus said, "IF we abide"...remain in Him and His words *remain in us*, then, we will be able to ask and it will be done!

We must stay in communion with Christ...get the Word deep down into our hearts and make it part of our daily lives by living in accordance with it. Otherwise, our prayers will only be words...vain repetitions.

> *And when you pray, do not (multiply words, repeating the same ones over and over, and) heap up phrases as the Gentiles do, for they think they will be heard for their much speaking.*
>
> Matthew 6:7 AMP

True prayer involves the whole person, coming before God with our whole being, not just repeating hollow words or following a "formula" for prayer.

It is through your relationship with Christ as your High Priest-Intercessor that you have full access and can enter the Holy of Holies, and come into the Presence of Almighty God.

Our full and free access into God's Holy Presence has been made possible through the blood Jesus shed for us on the cross.

"Every act of grace in Christ has been preceded by and owes its power to intercession." Andrew Murray

Jesus' entire life was an act of intercession...He stood in the gap between God and man. Isaiah prophesied concerning Him:

> *...Now the LORD saw, And it was displeasing in His sight that there was no justice. And He saw that there was no man, And was astonished that there was no one to intercede; Then His own arm brought salvation to Him; And His righteousness upheld Him. And He put on righteousness like a breastplate, And a helmet of salvation*

*on His head; And He put on garments of vengeance for clothing
And wrapped Himself with zeal as a mantle.*

Isaiah 59:15-17 NAS

Jesus, seeing there was no intercessor…no one to stand in the gap for
the sins of the world…put on His spiritual armor and came to earth to
bring salvation.

AS OUR INTERCESSOR, JESUS IDENTIFIED WITH MAN

Jesus did not elevate Himself above us, but humbled Himself and
was made in the likeness of men (see Philippians 2:7). In identifying
with us, He was willing to lay down His divine attributes and become
like us…sharing the same human nature and being made like us in
all respects.

*Forasmuch then as the children are partakers of flesh and blood, he
also himself likewise took part of the same; that through death he
might destroy him that had the power of death, that is, the
devil…For verily he took not on him the nature of angels; but he
took on him the seed of Abraham. Wherefore in all things it
behooved him to be made like unto his brethren, that he might be a
merciful and faithful high priest in things pertaining to God, to make
reconciliation for the sins of the people.*

Hebrews 2:14, 16-17

As our Intercessor, He was willing to stand in our stead. As sinners,
we were alienated, separated from God. Man had rebelled and sinned
against God. Man had turned his back on God and chose to follow his
own ways, to follow after his own man-made gods. We were worthy of
death. But, Jesus, our Intercessor, was willing to come to earth and

stand in the gap. He was willing to give His own life to die in our place, that we might be reconciled to God.

Throughout His ministry on earth, He was ever interceding for man...bringing him to the Father...forgiving sins...restoring both body and spirit.

AS OUR INTERCESSOR, JESUS WEPT OVER SIN AND COMING JUDGMENT

As our Intercessor, He wept over the sin and judgment that was coming because the people would not heed His warning. On His triumphal entry into Jerusalem, where He was going to offer Himself as a sacrifice for the sins of the world, Jesus wept.

Can you see Jesus there, amid the cries of "Hosanna; Blessed is he that cometh in the name of the Lord," as He stops on the hillside overlooking Jerusalem? As He looks upon the city, tears begin to pour from His eyes...He begins to sob and cry as if His heart is broken. As He weeps, He cries out for Jerusalem:

> ...If you, even you, had only known on this day what would bring you peace – but now it is hidden from your eyes. The days will come upon you when your enemies will build an embankment against you and encircle you and hem you in on every side. They will dash you to the ground, you and the children within your walls. They will not leave one stone on another, because you did not recognize the time of God's coming to you.
>
> Luke 19:42-44 NIV

Later, after proclaiming the judgments that were coming upon Jerusalem, He cried out in anguish:

> O Jerusalem, Jerusalem, you who kill the prophets and stone those sent to you, how often I have longed to gather your children together,

as a hen gathers her chicks under her wings, but you were not willing. Look, your house is left to you desolate. For I tell you, you will not see me again until you say, 'Blessed is he who comes in the name of the Lord.'

Matthew 23:37-39, NIV

AS OUR INTERCESSOR, JESUS TRAVAILED ON OUR BEHALF

Our salvation was not easily acquired. It cost Jesus everything. It was not easy. In the Garden of Gethsemane Jesus wrestled, struggled and travailed in prayer. Isaiah prophesied concerning His travail:

Yet it pleased the LORD to bruise him; he hath put him to grief: when thou shalt make his soul an offering for sin...He shall see of the travail of his soul, and shall be satisfied...

Isaiah 53:10-11

The word "travail" is taken from a Jewish word which means "to writhe in pain." It is compared with the indescribable pain a woman experiences in the last stages of labor before giving birth to her child.

AS OUR INTERCESSOR, JESUS TOOK OUR PLACE ON THE CROSS

As the Roman soldiers beat Jesus mercilessly, He stood there in our place. Jesus was "standing in the gap" for you and me when they nailed His hands and feet to the cross and placed the cross in the ground. There on the cross He was interceding...reconciling us back to God. He took our shame, our rejection, our pain, and our sins upon Himself.

Therefore will I divide him a portion with the great, he shall divide the spoil with the strong; because he hath poured out his soul unto

death: and he was numbered with the transgressors; and he bare the
sin of many, and made intercession for the transgressors.

Isaiah 53:12

As your intercessor, Jesus ascended into heaven and is now seated at
the right hand of the Father where He is standing in the gap, making
intercession for us. He is aware of all your weaknesses and temptations.
He is aware of your pain and suffering. He sees all your sins. And He
is there, in heaven interceding to the Father on your behalf:

But this man (Jesus), because he continueth ever, hath an
unchangeable priesthood. Wherefore he is able also to save them to
the uttermost that come unto God by him, seeing he ever liveth to
make intercession for them.

Hebrews 7:24-25

Christ lives to make intercession for you!

As our High Priest-Intercessor, Christ *identified* with us so completely
by taking upon Himself the form of flesh and blood, although He was
equal with God, He stripped Himself of His divine attributes and
became a man.

Who, being in the form of God, thought it not robbery to be equal
with God: But made himself of no reputation, and took upon him
the form of a servant, and was made in the likeness of men.

Philippians 2:6-7

Christ, our High Priest-Intercessor, did not remain up in the heavens,
but chose to come to live upon the earth and walk among us.
Although He was God, He identified with the frailty of man. Being in
the form of a man, He felt rejection, pain, sorrow, and death. He was
subject to the limitations of a physical body. He was tempted in every
way in which man is tempted, yet without sin. He experienced all this

so He would know the feeling of our infirmities and could intercede before God on our behalf.

"True prayer is the living experience of the truth of the Holy Trinity. The Spirit's breathing, the Son's intercession, and the Father's will become one in us."
Andrew Murray

He identified with man in taking the form of flesh and blood so through His death He would destroy the devil and set man free from the bondage of sin and the fear of death.

Christ experienced the pain and sorrow and the bitter pangs of death on the cross. He took our place and offered His own body as a sacrifice for the sins of all mankind.

THE FOUNDATION FOR OUR PRAYERS

When we truly know, not just in our heads but in our hearts, that Christ lives to make intercession for us, we are able to come *boldly* before God with the full assurance that Christ is there interceding for us and that we will receive what we need from God.

Our *boldness* is not simply a matter of our own human confidence; it is a God-given right that the blood of Jesus bought for us. Our *boldness* is not in ourselves, but in the power of the blood of Jesus. We have faith that we will receive what we ask, not because of our own merit, but because of Jesus' blood.

Because of Adam and Eve's sin, man forfeited his right to have direct access into the Father's Presence where he could fellowship and commune with Him. From the time of Moses until Christ, man was unable to live in God's Presence. For 15 centuries, Israel had a Temple, which had a Holy of Holies wherein God's holy Presence dwelt. Under penalty of death, no one was allowed entrance. No man could have access into God's Presence.

The priests were not allowed to enter, but ministered outside in the outer court offering up sacrifices to God. Once a year, on the Day of Atonement, the high priest, after he had consecrated himself, was allowed to enter in and pour out a blood offering upon the Mercy Seat for the sins of himself and the people.

Man was denied entrance into God's Presence. He could not live in fellowship with God. Jesus, our High Priest, poured out His own blood on the cross. He ascended into heaven and offered it before the Father as an offering for man's sin. *"Neither by the blood of goats and calves, but by his own blood he entered in once into the holy place, having obtained eternal redemption for us"* (Hebrews 9:12).

Through that one offering of His blood, Jesus forever destroyed Satan, broke the chains of sin, sickness and death; and has provided a full and free salvation where our sins are forgiven, and we have power over sin.

The great veil in the Temple separating man from the Holy of Holies...God's Presence...has been destroyed! Through Jesus' blood, we have boldness to enter and live in the fullness of God's Presence. Paul said, *"Having therefore, brethren, boldness to enter into the holiest by the blood of Jesus..."* (Hebrews 10:19).

Not only do we have boldness and confidence to approach God through the blood of Jesus; we have confidence and faith knowing Jesus, our High Priest, is there NOW in the Presence of God on our behalf. Paul said, *"And having an high priest over the house of God; Let us draw near with a true heart in full assurance of faith..."* (Hebrews 10:21-22).

In these verses, we see very clearly the spiritual position we are to take when we come before God in prayer. Paul said we are to draw near to God with a "true heart". When we enter into God's Presence, we must come with a sincere heart that is set upon God and His Word.

We are also to come to God "in full assurance of faith." We must believe that God hears and answers prayer. When we pray, we must release our faith and take hold of what we need from God.

Prayer is not what saves the sick. It is "the prayer of faith" that saves the sick (see James 5:15).

Knowing Jesus is there in the Father's Presence praying for you, interceding on your behalf, you can come into the Father's Presence knowing He is moved with the feeling of your infirmities. He feels your pain...your heartache...the turmoil you feel...your struggle to win over temptation...and is there ready to give you the grace and strength you need.

THROUGH CHRIST'S BLOOD WE HAVE BOLDNESS TO COME INTO GOD'S PRESENCE

Through Jesus Christ, The Great Intercessor and our High Priest, the work has been done. Through His blood, He has provided a full and free salvation where ALL our needs have been met.

Through His blood, we have been granted access into the Holy of Holies...the living Presence of Almighty God...where we can live in unbroken fellowship with God.

Through His blood, we have boldness to come into God's Presence knowing that He hears us and that He will grant whatever we ask.

There is nothing left for Jesus to do for us. It has all been done...finished once and forever! All we need has been provided and made accessible to us. All that remains for us is to come to God in faith, through prayer, and receive what we need.

Seeing then that we have a great high priest, that is passed into the heavens, Jesus the Son of God, let us hold fast our profession. For we have not an high priest which cannot be touched with the feeling of our infirmities; but was in all points tempted like as we are, yet

without sin. Let us therefore come boldly unto the throne of grace,
that we may obtain mercy, and find grace to help in time of need.

Hebrews 4:14-16

In Christ's intercession in the garden, He fully surrendered His will to God. He agonized in prayer until His sweat became as drops of blood falling to the ground. In His prayer, He completely gave up all claim upon His life, for the sake of all mankind.

And he came out, and went, as he was wont, to the mount of Olives; and his disciples also followed him. And when he was at the place, he said unto them, Pray that ye enter not into temptation. And he was withdrawn from them about a stone's cast, and kneeled down, and prayed, Saying, Father, if thou be willing, remove this cup from me: nevertheless not my will, but thine, be done. And there appeared an angel unto him from heaven, strengthening him. And being in an agony he prayed more earnestly: and his sweat was as it were great drops of blood falling down to the ground. And when he rose up from prayer, and was come to his disciples, he found them sleeping for sorrow, And said unto them, Why sleep ye? rise and pray lest ye enter into temptation.

Luke 22:39-46

The greatest battle of the ages was won that day in prayer!
The victory of the cross, His death and resurrection, was first won in prayer!
Our salvation was won that day in prayer!
God sent angels to His side to strengthen and sustain Him as He travailed and agonized in prayer. Then, having won this great victory, Jesus went to the cross.
As the Roman soldiers beat Him mercilessly, He stood there in our place.

There on the cross, He was interceding...reconciling man back to God. He took your shame, your rejection, your pain, and your sins upon Himself.

Therefore will I divide him a portion with the great, and he shall divide the spoil with the strong; because he hath poured out his soul unto death: and he was numbered with the transgressors; and he bare the sin of many, and made intercession for the transgressors.

Isaiah 53:12

PRAY BOLD PRAYERS BASED UPON GOD'S COVENANT!

As our Intercessor, Jesus entered into the Holy of Holies in heaven and offered His blood upon the Mercy Seat for our redemption from sin. Under the Old Covenant, God appointed Aaron, his sons, and the tribe of Levi to serve as priests. No one was allowed to serve as priest who was not of the tribe of Levi. The people were not allowed to go to God directly for themselves. They were required to approach God through the priests, and the priests alone had access to the Holy of Holies.

Once a year, on the Day of Atonement, the high priest entered into the Holy of Holies where he offered up a sacrifice, first for his own sins, and then for the sins of the people. He sprinkled the blood of the bulls and goats upon the Mercy Seat and upon the altar for the atonement of the sins of the people.

God established this priesthood under the Old Covenant as a foreshadowing of the one Great High Priest that would come to take away their sins. As Jesus took His position as High Priest of the New Covenant, this old order of priesthood was no longer necessary.

Under the Old Covenant, those desiring to be priests were required to be from the tribe of Levi. Jesus became High Priest of the New Covenant:

...not on the basis of a bodily legal requirement [an externally imposed command concerning His physical ancestry] but on the basis of the power of an endless and indestructible Life.

Hebrews 7:16 AMP

Today we have a High Priest Who cannot be destroyed...One Who lives forever...One Who has a permanent priesthood!

Because He has a permanent priesthood, Jesus has become the "Surety"...the guarantee...of the New Covenant God has made with us. He is our guarantee that God will do all that He has promised. He is also the guarantee of our faithfulness to keep the covenant with God.

Jesus, our High Priest-Intercessor entered into the Holy of Holies and poured out His blood upon the altar of God.

But [that appointed time came] when Christ (the Messiah) appeared as a High Priest of the better things that have come and are to come. [Then] through the greater and more perfect tabernacle, not made with [human] hands, that is, not a part of this material creation, He went once for all into the [Holy of] Holies [of Heaven], not by virtue of the blood of goats and calves [by which to make reconciliation between God and man], but His own blood, having found and secured a complete redemption (an everlasting release for us).

Hebrews 9:11-12 AMP

Darkness covered the earth! The earth shook violently and the great veil separating the Holy of Holies was split in two and fell in a heap!

Through that one Sacrifice...His broken body...He removed the veil separating God and man, and has given us direct access into the Holy of Holies whereby we can enter into the very Presence of God!

TAKE YOUR POSITION OF POWER
AND AUTHORITY IN PRAYER!

Through that one Sacrifice, all the sin of mankind was forever erased. There is absolutely nothing that remains to be done to secure this everlasting covenant God has made with us. No further sacrifice is needed. The work has been done!

Whereas this One [Christ], after He had offered a single Sacrifice for our sins [that shall avail] for all time, sat down at the right hand of God, Then to wait until His enemies should be made a stool beneath His feet. For by a single offering He has forever completely cleansed and perfected those who are consecrated and made holy.

Hebrews 10:12-14 AMP

The blood that poured forth that day from Jesus' Body completely abolished the Old Covenant and put into effect the New Covenant with all its provisions of forgiveness, deliverance, freedom, healing and all the covenant promises!

Jesus offered Himself as a blood sacrifice so that we would enter into a blood-covenant relationship with Him. His blood...His life...flows through us! It is through a continual partaking of His flesh and His blood...His life...that we have life in abundance.

Reach out by faith and take the Living Bread. "Eat"...feed upon Christ. Make Him the Source of all your nourishment. Depend upon Him for all your needs. Accept the sacrifice of His broken, bleeding body as being sufficient to meet every need in your life.

Daily appropriate the sacrificial offering of His blood upon the altar of your life, not only for forgiveness, but healing, deliverance, and all your daily provisions. His blood has sealed God's covenant promises to us.

Because of Christ's intercession...His obedience and surrender to God's will...His death upon the cross...He obtained a position of

165

supreme power and authority over all powers and principalities in heaven, on earth, and beneath the earth.

> *And after he had appeared in human form He abased and humbled Himself [still further] and carried His obedience to the extreme of death, even the death of the cross! Therefore [because He stooped so low], God has highly exalted Him and has freely bestowed on Him the name that is above every name, That in (at) the name of Jesus every knee should (must) bow, in heaven and on earth under the earth, And every tongue [frankly and openly] confess and acknowledge that Jesus Christ is Lord, to the glory of God the Father.*
>
> Philippians 2:8-11 AMP

When we come to our Father in prayer, He expects us to come boldly...not wavering in our faith...not vacillating...not hoping...but from this position with Christ.

When you ASK the Father, in the power and authority of His Mighty Name, you will not wonder if God has heard your prayers or if He will answer, you will know you will receive it the moment you ask!

"To live in Him, to dwell there, to be one with Him, to draw all life from Him, to let all life from Him flow through us – this is the attitude of prayer and the ability to pray." E. M. Bounds

Once you have received a revelation of this position of power and authority that you have been given in the Name of Jesus, you will be able to pray boldly with power and authority! (In chapter eleven you will learn more about the legal right and authority Christ has given you and how to pray bold prayers in the power of His Name.)

Jesus said, *"What things soever ye desire, when ye pray, believe that ye receive them, and ye shall have them"* (Mark 11:24). When we come into God's Presence and ask Him for the things we need, we must believe that we have received them when we pray...not after we have received them.

There are many Christians who expect to see a physical manifestation of the answer to their prayers before they will believe and, as a result, they do not receive what they have asked because of their unbelief.

Knowing He is seated at the right hand of God the Father as our High Priest-Intercessor is the foundation and basis for our prayers and intercession.

Knowing Christ has secured entrance into the Holy of Holies...in God's Presence.

Knowing He is a faithful and merciful High Priest-Intercessor Who feels our pain and sorrow and is ever interceding to the Father on our behalf, we do not come fearfully or timidly before God...but boldly with full assurance of faith that in Jesus' Name He will hear and answer our prayers!

PRAY BOLD PRAYERS ON BEHALF OF YOUR CITY AND NATION!

The time has come when we must become bold in our prayers! Time is short...Jesus is coming and we do not have time to offer up half-hearted prayers or to pray weak, ineffective prayers that are not prayed in faith, nor in accordance with God's Word. Nor do we have time to continue to pray as a matter of routine, where we follow man-made traditions and formulas for prayers.

If the Church of Jesus Christ is going to fulfill the work God has called us to do in this end-time hour, we must begin to focus our prayers and rise up in the power and authority of the Holy Spirit, to

167

boldly take hold of the victories God has already provided for us in every area of our lives.

"We need God the Father to pray to; we need Jesus Christ the Son to pray through; and we need the Holy Spirit to pray in." R. A. Torrey

This is a time when we must move into a new dimension of prayer, where we are praying bold prayers, based upon God's covenant with us. Victories are ours through the blood of Jesus. Knowing all He has provided for us, we must enter into His Presence boldly on behalf of our own personal needs, on behalf of our unsaved loved ones, on behalf of the lost in our cities, on behalf of the needs of our nations, and on behalf of the work God has called us to do.

"God is bringing us into a new dimension of authority in our prayers where our words, spoken with authority, invested in the promises of God, will enable us to confront every stronghold of the enemy!"

Boldly come before the throne of God through prayer and intercession and ask God, not for just a touch, but for complete healing in your body!

Pray bold prayers upon behalf of your family and unsaved loved ones! Ask and believe God to save every member of your family and deliver them from every bondage of the enemy.

Look around in your community and city, and begin to pray bold prayers for the lost...the destitute...the homeless...those who are bound by drugs or alcohol...the prostitutes...the gang members. Through prayer and fasting, come boldly before God and believe Him to break the bondages off people, deliver them from drugs and alcohol, save them, and heal their bodies.

"We must never forget that God has put the conquering, inheriting, and expanding forces of Christ's cause in prayer. 'Ask of me, and I shall give thee the heathen for thine inheritance, and the uttermost parts of the earth for thy possession!' "

Come boldly before God and cry out, "Lord, give me this city for Your kingdom!" "Lord, give me this nation...save...heal...deliver by Your awesome power!" Be bold in asking God for a mighty end-time move of His Spirit in your home, in your church, in your city and nation! Get on your face before God and begin to weep...to cry out...to travail as Jesus travailed. Give yourself sacrificially in times of prayer and fasting. Cry out to God on behalf of the lost around you. Weep and mourn for the sin and corruption around you. Cry out to God for His mercy.

This is the way God would have you to prepare for the coming Day of the Lord. Hear what the Spirit of God is saying and respond. Do not hesitate. One of Satan's strategies is to do everything He can to stop you from praying. He will try to keep you so busy with other things that you will not have time to pray.

Resist every attempt of the enemy to hinder you from answering this call of the Spirit to intercede. As we join together in establishing a global prayer covering over the world, believe that we will impact entire nations and multitudes will be won into the Kingdom of God!

In chapter eight we will go even deeper into this revelation. Not only has Christ given us unlimited access to the Throne where we can come boldly and present our needs knowing He will answer, but, there is much more! As your Great High Priest, Christ invites you to join Him on His Throne in His intercession.

Lord, teach us to pray!

Lord, You are the Great Intercessor! How we praise You for living a life of intercession and laying down Your life for our sakes so that we could be set free from the power of sin. Thank You for taking our sins upon Yourself and shedding Your blood thereby giving us access into the Holy of Holies. We draw near to You and come boldly before the Throne. Teach us by Your Spirit all that You have provided for us and how to live a life of intercession that You will use to fulfill

Your will upon this earth. We yield ourselves fully to you. Teach us to pray as You pray!

CHAPTER EIGHT

THRONE ROOM INTERCESSION

We have a High Priest, now seated on the Throne of God at the Father's right hand who lives in continuous intercession for us!

Not only is He there interceding *for us*, He calls us to join Him in His intercession.

"The man whom God speaks to face to face becomes partaker of that same power of intercession that there is in Him who is at God's right hand and 'ever liveth to make intercession' " (Hebrews 7:25).
Andrew Murray

Through the power of His blood, He has given us full access into the Holy of Holies to live and dwell in the Presence of the Father.

He has placed all the power of Heaven at our disposal.

He has placed the Holy Spirit within us giving us the power to pray.

He has given us delegated power and authority through His Name.

Once you get a glimpse of Him as *your* great High Priest and see Him there in all His power and glory…

Once you understand fully all that He has provided for you…

Once you understand the reality of your position of being seated with Christ on His Throne…

You will know how to come boldly before the Throne and take hold of His provision for all your needs. You will also be able to intercede with greater power and authority on behalf of the needs in your family, church, city and nation.

The Father wants to bring you into a new powerful dimension of prayer, where you are seeing more answers to prayer in your life than you have ever experienced. In chapter seven you were given a glimpse of Christ as the Great Intercessor and how that as our High Priest He made it possible for us, through the power of His blood, to have full access into the Holy of Holies…into God's Presence. We know that He has a permanent, unchangeable Priesthood and that He is a faithful and merciful High Priest Who continually takes our petitions before the Father and intercedes for us.

Let us delve deeper into this rich revelation to see the position Christ has provided for us with Him in Throne Room Intercession.

It is my prayer that the eyes of your understanding will be opened to see the glorious privilege and birthright you have been given to approach the Throne of God and enter into the Presence of the Father as one of His children. I want you to see by faith how Christ has made it possible for you to sit with Him on His Throne to intercede with Him. I don't want you to just have head knowledge, but a revelation that will go down deep into your spirit.

THE POWER OF AN ENDLESS LIFE

For a moment, let us focus our eyes upon Christ, our Great High Priest seated upon the Throne. He is seated there in a position of the highest honor and supreme power and authority at the right hand of the Father. "*…We have such an high priest, who is set on the right hand of the throne of the Majesty in the heavens*" (Hebrews 8:1).

His ministry on the Throne is one of continuous intercession on our behalf. His priesthood is not like that of earthly priests, but He is "*…a priest for ever after the order of Melchizedek*" (Hebrews 7:17). He is our eternal High Priest. In Him there is no change or ageing. He is from everlasting to everlasting!

This not only means that His priesthood will never cease, but that He ministers to us in "...*the power of an endless life*" (Hebrews 7:16). Christ lives and works continuously, in the power of the divine life. Every act of His holy priesthood and His work in our lives is done in the power of an endless life. There is not a more powerful or significant expression in the entire Book of Hebrews.

Christ, our High Priest, breathes His own life into us. He brings us into intimate fellowship and communion with the Father, fulfills His will and releases all the benefits of redemption in the power of an endless life!

He abides forever – an eternal – ever living – ever working – High Priest. Everything He does for us as our High Priest in heaven He does it in the power of an endless life!

God confirmed Christ's eternal priesthood with His oath. "...*The Lord sware and will not repent himself, Thou are a priest for ever...*" (Hebrews 7:21). God's oath is proof of His unchangeable purposes concerning something which He binds Himself faithfully to perform. His oath seals it! There is nothing that can or will change His purpose.

"Jesus is our eternal High Priest. He is prevailing today on heaven's throne – not only by His Presence and because of His wounds at Calvary, but through His continuing holy pleading; His intercession."
Wesley L. Duewel

Aaron was made a priest without an oath. His priesthood was only temporary, a foreshadow of what was to come. God swore by Himself with an oath concerning Christ's eternal priesthood so that we would know without any possible doubt that Christ will fulfill every promise and impart all that God has provided in our lives.

God has made an oath...one that is impossible to break...establishing Jesus as a permanent High Priest of His covenant with us. His oath is forever settled. It is unchangeable! This oath becomes our confidence. It becomes our strength!

Because Christ is our eternal High Priest, He has an unchangeable priesthood. *"But this man, because he continueth ever, hath an unchangeable priesthood"* (Hebrews 7:24). In the Aaronic priesthood, there was a continual succession of priests. When one died, another would take his place. But, Christ's priesthood is unchangeable! The life and the power, which He ministers, are also unchangeable.

Do you realize what this means to you? There is never a moment in which His ministry as your High Priest is not in full operation.

And because Christ has an eternal, unchangeable priesthood, He is able to save completely – totally – for all time because there is never a moment when He isn't interceding on your behalf.

Therefore He is able to save to the uttermost – completely, perfectly, finally and for all time and eternity – those who come to God through Him, since He is always living to make petition to God and intercede with Him and intervene for them.
Hebrews 7:25 AMP

SEE YOUR FAITHFUL
HIGH PRIEST UPON THE THRONE

Christ, as our Great High Priest is *"A minister of the sanctuary, and of the true tabernacle, which the Lord pitched, and not man"* (Hebrews 8:2). In the tabernacle God directed Moses to set up, the priests served for the service of God according to His will. As representatives of the people, they offered the sacrifices; they received the assurance of God's favor, and pronounced God's blessings upon the people.

Jesus is the Minister of the heavenly sanctuary. As our High Priest, He represents us there before the Throne. He welcomes us and ushers us into the Presence of the Father by His Spirit. He ministers to us from the Throne, releasing God's power and blessings in the power of an endless life.

Beloved, turn your eyes and gaze upon the glory and majesty of Christ, your Great High Priest. There, seated upon the throne, He is interceding for you. Whatever problems or needs you have you can bring boldly to the Father knowing He is your faithful High Priest.

> *So it is evident that it was essential that He be made like His brethren in every respect, in order that He might become a merciful (sympathetic) and faithful High Priest in the things related to God, to make atonement and propitiation for the people's sins. For because He Himself [in His humanity] has suffered in being tempted (tested and tried), He is able [immediately] to run to the cry of (assist, relieve) those who are being tempted and tested and tried [and who therefore are being exposed to suffering.*
>
> Hebrews 2:17-18 AMP

Christ is not far removed from you and your needs. He is your faithful High Priest. He feels your pain and is touched and moved by your infirmities, weaknesses and needs.

Knowing He is there on the Throne interceding on your behalf, do not hesitate. Do not doubt or waver in unbelief. Run to Him in faith. Pour out your heart to Him and receive the help and answers you need. Go boldly into the Father's Presence knowing you will not be denied because your Great High Priest is there.

HE PAID THE SUPREME PRICE FOR US WITH HIS BLOOD

Look upon Christ your High Priest! He is seated on the Throne in a position of supreme power and authority over all power, authority and dominion in heaven or in earth. When you know, that you know, that you know there is no greater power, and know the position He has given you seated with Him on His Throne, you will never be defeated in your prayers!

⸎

"Through the Spirit, Christ's prayers become ours and ours are made His. We ask for what we desire and it is given to us." Andrew Murray

Through the power of His blood shed on the cross, Christ defeated Satan, and broke the power of sin, sickness and death and is now seated in this highest position of power and authority.

To pray with power and boldness knowing your prayers have reached the Throne of God, you need to know the power of the blood of Jesus and apply it to your life.

- **Through the blood of Jesus you are redeemed!** *"Forasmuch as ye know that ye were not redeemed with corruptible things, as silver and gold, from your vain conversation received by tradition from your fathers; But with the precious blood of Christ, as of a lamb without blemish and without spot"* (1 Peter 1:18-19).

- **Through the blood of Jesus you are reconciled to the Father. The blood of Jesus met the demands of a Holy God and provided atonement for your sins. Through His blood you stand acquitted before God. Your sins have been blotted out and there is nothing to prevent you from approaching God.** *"Being justified freely by His grace through the redemption that is in Christ Jesus, whom God set forth to be a propitiation by His blood through faith"*... (Romans 3:24-25).

176

- **Through His blood, you are cleansed from all sin.** *"But if we walk in the light, as he is in the light, we have fellowship one with another, and the blood of Jesus Christ his Son cleanseth us from all sin"* (1 John 1:7).

- **Through the blood you have boldness to enter the Holy of Holies and approach the Throne of God.** *"Having therefore, brethren, boldness to enter into the Holiest by the blood of Jesus"* (Hebrews 10:19).

- **Through the blood you are sanctified.** *"Jesus also, that He might sanctify the people with His own blood, suffered without the gate"* (Hebrews 13:12).

- **Through the blood you are made a king and priest unto God. You not only have the legal right to live in God's Presence and enjoy intimate fellowship with Him, but also to approach Him and obtain His blessings for others.** *"…with your blood you purchased men for God from every tribe and language and people and nation. You have made them to be a kingdom and priests to serve our God, and they will reign on earth"* (Revelation 5:9-10 NIV).

- **Through the blood you have victory over Satan and all his principalities.** *"And they overcame him by the blood of the Lamb, and by the word of their testimony; and they loved not their lives to the death"* (Revelation 12:11).

The blood that Jesus shed is sufficient for all your needs and the needs of mankind! Knowing the power of the blood will give you a boldness and confidence so that when you pray you will not be denied!

NO GREATER POWER!

It was the blood of Jesus that defeated Satan! Jesus came into this world with a divine purpose – to destroy the works of the devil. *"For this purpose the Son of God was manifested, that he might destroy the works of the devil"* (1 John 3:8).

The blood that poured forth from His body destroyed Satan! *"Forasmuch then as the children are partakers of flesh and blood, he also himself likewise took part of the same; that through death he might destroy him that had the power of death, that is, the devil"* (Hebrews 2:14).

Our Great High Priest ascended into heaven where He entered into the Holy of Holies and offered His blood upon the altar of God. *"Neither by the blood of goats and calves, but by his own blood he entered in once into the Holy place, having obtained eternal redemption for us"* (Hebrews 9:12).

The Father accepted the blood as the One all-sufficient sacrifice to redeem man from His sins.   I can almost hear the cry ring out throughout the heavens, "The blood of the Lamb is sufficient! Satan is defeated! Man is redeemed – set free from Satan's power!"

"You are not to tremble before Satan, but are to confront him from the throne." Wesley L. Duewel

Having redeemed man and purchased the Church by His blood, our Great High Priest descends into the unseen world where He proclaims His complete triumph over Satan.

> *For Christ died for sins once for all, the righteous for the unrighteous, to bring you to God. He was put to death in the body but made alive by the Spirit, through whom also he went and preached to the spirits in prison... 1 Peter 3:18-19 NIV.*

See Him in great triumph as He ascends into the heavens leading behind Him a trail of vanquished foes: Satan, sin and death. *"When He ascended on high, He led captivity captive [He led a train of vanquished foes] and He bestowed gifts on men"* (Ephesians 4:8 AMP).

In a bold display, Satan and his principalities were defeated! *"[God] disarmed the principalities and powers were ranged against us and made a bold display and public example of them, in triumphing over them in Him and in it [the cross]"* (Colossians 2:15 AMP).

Today, He is enthroned and seated at the right hand of the Father in a position of highest honor and majesty. The Father exalted Him and gave Him the Name that is above every other name.

Wherefore God also hath highly exalted him, and given him a name which is above every name: That at the name of Jesus every knee should bow, of things in heaven, and things in earth, and things under the earth; And that every tongue should confess that Jesus Christ is Lord, to the glory of God the Father.

Philippians 2:9-11

Almighty God has placed all powers and principalities under Christ's feet and has made Him the Head of the Church.

...He raised Him from the dead and seated Him at His [own] right hand in the heavenly [places], Far above all rule and authority and power and dominion, and every name that is named [above every title that can be conferred] not only in this age and in this world, but also in the age and the world which are to come.

Ephesians 1:20-21 AMP

All power, authority and dominion, not only in this world, but in the world to come are subject to Him.

There is no greater power!

Satan and all his demonic principalities are defeated!

UNITED WITH HIM ON THE THRONE

Christ, our Great High Priest reigns! He is Sovereign of this Universe!

From this exalted position on the Throne, His ongoing ministry is one of intercession. As the Head of His Church He directs and releases His intercession through us.

"We are partakers of Christ's life, His righteousness, and His work. We share in His intercession too. He cannot do it without us." Andrew Murray

Not only has Christ given you legal access to the Throne where you can enjoy intimate communion and fellowship with Him, He has given you the privilege of joining with Him in intercession from the Throne.

Through the power of His Spirit, He has elevated you to a position where you are now spiritually seated with Him on His Throne. By the same Spirit that raised Christ from the dead, He has made you alive with Christ, and in your union with Him you are with Him on the Throne.

The Apostle Paul wrote:

> *And He raised us up together with Him and made us sit down together [giving us joint seating with Him] in the heavenly sphere [by virtue of our being] in Christ Jesus, the Messiah, the Anointed One. He did this that He might clearly demonstrate through the ages to come the immeasurable (limitless, surpassing) riches of His free grace (His unmerited favor) in kindness and goodness of heart toward us in Christ Jesus.*
>
> Ephesians 2:6-7 AMP

Stop for a moment and allow the reality of this great truth to go deep into your spirit. This is not just an ethereal concept. It is a living reality to those who will take hold of it by faith.

You are today seated with Christ on His Throne. And, because all things are under His feet, all things are under your feet! He has given you power over all the power of the enemy (See Luke 10:19).

Satan and all his demonic forces are under your feet!

Seated from your position with Christ on His Throne, you look down from the Throne in spiritual vision at Satan.

In yourself you are weak. You have no power or authority of your own. But, in Christ you are seated beside Him in His position of supreme power and authority.

Christ has delegated to you the privilege of praying in the power and authority of His Name.

Through the Holy Spirit, He has given you His power and authority to not only resist, but to confront Satan and force his retreat.

This is the solid foundation of prayer that will enable you to pray with power and authority to break every yoke of bondage and see God's will fulfilled in your life, family, city and nation.

FROM THE THRONE WE ENFORCE CHRIST'S VICTORY

"It is the sight of Jesus in His intercession that gives us power to pray in His Name. All right and power of prayer is Christ's; He makes us share in His intercession." Andrew Murray

Jesus Christ, our Great High Priest calls us to join Him in Throne Room Intercession.

This is beyond ordinary prayer.

In Throne Room Intercession, we are no longer praying from our limited, earthly position or in our limited strength. In our union with Christ, our High Priest, we are praying prayers *from the Throne!* Prayers that are directed by Him, in His Name, in the power and authority He now has on the Throne which He releases through us!

In Throne Room Intercession, Satan or his demonic forces no longer intimidate us, nor do we face him from our earthly position. We confront him from the Throne. We are no longer facing him from a defensive position. We are initiating prayer attacks *from the Throne* on Satan's strongholds, commanding him to loose his hold and set his captives free.

In Throne Room Intercession we are dealing with cancer, heart disease, diabetes, arthritis and other sicknesses and diseases from our position of power and authority with Christ on His Throne!

No longer do we face our desperate circumstances from an earthly perspective, but we see them from our position seated with Christ on His Throne. We pray prayers and speak the word of faith into our circumstances knowing that we will receive whatever we ask in Jesus' Name.

When we see strongholds of the enemy in our cities and nations, we are no longer limited by our natural abilities and do not pray from our earthly position. In our union with Christ, on His Throne, He reveals His will and releases His Spirit to pray through us prayers that will effect changes according to His will. There is no margin for failure!

In Throne Room Intercession we are not waiting to win the victory.

Christ has already won the victory!

Satan is already defeated!

From our position of power and authority we command Satan to leave. We enforce Christ's victory and bind Satan and his principalities using the power of Jesus' Name.

TAKE YOUR POSITION WITH CHRIST ON HIS THRONE!

Christ intends for us to join Him in His High-Priestly work of intercession and exercise our delegated authority to minister to the needs of others. He has made us kings and priests unto God (see Revelation 1:6). The Apostle Peter said, *"But ye are a chosen generation, a royal priesthood..."* (1 Peter 2:9).

In Israel the priests mediated between God and the children of Israel. They carried the sins and needs of the people into the Presence of God. There, in God's Presence, they obtained the power to declare the pardon of their sins and to release God's blessing upon the people.

As we unite with Christ in His intercession, we are empowered to intercede and minister on His behalf. As His priest-intercessors, we come before the Throne, enter into His Presence and bring the needs of our families, the lost in our cities and the desperate circumstances in our countries before Him in deep intercession.

"The life of Christ flowing through us and the words of Christ living in us, these give power to prayer. They breathe the spirit of prayer and make the body, blood, and bones of prayer." E. M. Bounds

We join Him in Throne Room Intercession. As we begin to cry out, weep and travail before Him, the Holy Spirit begins to reveal the mind and will of God to us regarding the needs. Then as we yield ourselves to the Holy Spirit, He begins to pray through us with deep groanings and gushings of the Spirit.

Knowing that Christ has already paid the price and won the victory, we are able to pray with dominion authority seated with Christ on His Throne.

As we intercede, we are able to tear down Satan's strongholds, bind his power and see God's will accomplished in bringing salvation, healing and deliverance in His Name.

"It is the unfolding of the Word by the Spirit's light, guidance, and teaching that enables us to perform the great office of intercessors on earth in harmony with the great intercession of Jesus Christ at the Father's right hand in heaven." E. M. Bounds

This is a high and holy calling. What a privilege we have been given to join our Great High Priest on the Throne in His ministry of intercession! The key to living in this new dimension of Throne Room Intercession is your union with Christ. In His High Priestly prayer, Jesus prayed, *"That they all may be one; as thou, Father, art in me, and I in thee, that they also may be one in us..."* (John 17:21). He said, *"I in them, and thou in me, that they may be made perfect in one..."* (John 17:23).

The power in prayer that will bring God's divine intervention into our lives and upon this earth is dependent upon us living in a relationship with Christ where we are one with Him. Jesus said, *"If you live in Me [abide vitally united to Me] and My words remain in you and continue to live in your hearts, ask whatever you will and it shall be done for you"* (John 15:7 AMP).

Christ intends for us to reign in this life now!

> *For if, by the trespass of the one man, death reigned through that one man, how much more will those who receive God's abundant provision of grace and of the gift of righteousness reign in life through the one man, Jesus Christ.*
>
> Romans 5:17 NIV

We are called to rule and reign with Him through Throne Room Intercession. This is our birthright and made possible by His Spirit.

It is my prayer that God will so imprint this powerful truth into your spirit that you will, in reality, take your position seated at His side as one of His High Priest Intercessors.

Not only has Christ made it possible for you to join Him on His Throne in intercession, He has given you a Divine Enabler that will take you beyond your natural capability to pray prayers that are divinely energized and 100% effective 100% of the time!

In chapter nine you will learn more about this Divine Enabler.

Lord, teach us to pray!

Dear Jesus, we have been given a glimpse of You as our Great High Priest and all that you have provided for us through Your blood. Our hearts are overwhelmed with the knowledge of the awesome price you paid to redeem us and bring us into fellowship with the Father. To know that You have given us the blessed privilege of joining You in intercession from the Throne is beyond our comprehension. Anoint our eyes and give us a fresh revelation to see our position with you seated on the Throne and the ministry of intercession you have called us to. As Your ministry on the Throne is one of continuous intercession, unite our prayers with Yours. Lord, teach us to pray. Bring us into true union with You where Your life is flowing through us. Teach us to live our lives knowing we are in You and You are in us. May our lives be so joined with Yours that your intercession will pour through us to bring Your blessing and accomplish Your will on earth.

CHAPTER NINE

OUR DIVINE ENABLER

In our holy pursuit of learning how to pray in the same powerful dimension of prayer as Jesus taught and demonstrated, we have an infallible, Divine Teacher. The Third Person of the Trinity...The Holy Spirit!

"The Holy Spirit breathes the spirit of prayer within you; power in prayer comes from His empowering within."
Wesley Duewel

The blessed Holy Spirit...

- **Implants the desire to pray!**
  The Holy Spirit is a "Spirit of supplication" God promised to pour out. *"And I will pour out...upon the inhabitants of Jerusalem, the Spirit of grace and supplication..."* (Zechariah 12:10). Because He is a Spirit of supplication and He is the Master Intercessor living in us, it is He Who releases the desire in us to pray.

- **Calls us to pray!**
  The Holy Spirit is the Spirit of Adoption whereby we are able to cry, "Abba, Father." *"...But ye have received the Spirit of adoption, whereby we cry, Abba, Father"* (Romans 8:15). Through the indwelling of the Holy Spirit and our union with Christ, the Holy Spirit reveals the heart of the Father, reveals urgent prayer needs and gives us holy promptings to pray.

- **Unfolds the depths and blessings concerning prayer!**
  Jesus said, *"But the Comforter, which is the Holy Ghost, whom the Father will send in my name, he shall teach you all things…"* (John 14:26). The Holy Spirit dwelling in us is the One Who opens our understanding, reveals the depths of intercession and teaches us how to pray.

- **Grants us access to the Father!**
  "For through him we both have access by one Spirit unto the Father" (Ephesians 2:18).

- **Directs us in our prayers!**
  "…but the Spirit itself maketh intercession for us with groanings which cannot be uttered" (Romans 8:26).

- **Gives spiritual vision and discernment!**
  "…for the Spirit searcheth all things, yea the deep things of God "…Now we have received, not the spirit of the world, but the spirit which is of God; that we might know the things that are freely given to us of God" (1 Corinthians 2:10, 12). *"But ye have an unction from the Holy One, and ye know all things"* (1 John 2:20).

- **Releases faith as we pray!**
  "But ye, beloved, building up yourselves on your most holy faith, praying in the Holy Ghost" (Jude 20).

- **Gives boldness in our prayers!**
  "And when they had prayed, the place was shaken where they were assembled together; and they were all filled with the Holy Ghost, and they spake the word of God with boldness" (Acts 4:31).

- **Strengthens and adds perseverance to our prayers!**
  "So too the [Holy] Spirit comes to our aid and bears us up in our weakness…" (Romans 8:26 AMP).

- **Gives us intensity to pray fervently!**
  "But ye shall receive power, after that the Holy Ghost is come upon you" (Acts 1:8). *"He that believeth on me, as the scripture hath said, out of*

his belly shall flow rivers of living water, (But this spake he of the Holy Spirit..." (John 7:38-39).

- **Reveals God's will and prays God's will through us!**
  "And he that searcheth the hearts knoweth what is the mind of the Spirit, because he maketh intercession for the saints according to the will of God" (Romans 8:27). *"Howbeit when he, the Spirit of truth, is come, he will guide you into all truth: for he shall not speak of himself; but whatsoever he shall hear, that shall he speak: and he will shew you things to come...All things that the Father hath are mine: therefore said I, that he shall take of mine, and shall shew it unto you"* (John 16:13, 15).

- **Teaches us to pray in the Spirit and the language of prayer!**
  "...we speak, not in words taught us by human wisdom but in words taught by the Spirit" (1 Corinthians 2:13 NIV). *"For he that speaketh in an unknown tongue speaketh not unto men, but unto God: for no man understandeth him; howbeit in the spirit he speaketh mysteries"* (1 Corinthians 14:2).

- **Anoints us to wage war in the Spirit!**
  "For the weapons of our warfare are not carnal, but mighty through God to the pulling down of strong holds" (2 Corinthians 10:4). *"Put on the whole armour of God, that ye may be able to stand against the wiles of the devil...Praying always with all prayer and supplication in the Spirit..."* (Ephesians 6:11, 18).

Not only is He the Master Teacher of true prayer...
The Holy Spirit is the *Divine Enabler* of prayer!
He releases God's *dunamis*, miracle-working power in us to pray through us with delegated authority.
There are many Christians who do not pray because they feel they do not know how to pray effectively. They do not understand that the

Holy Spirit has been given to enable them to pray with power and that the key is being full of the Holy Spirit. There must be a revelation of the vital role of the Holy Spirit and His ministry of intercession.

"Prayer itself is an art that only the Holy Spirit can teach us. He is the giver of all prayer. Pray for prayer. Pray until you can pray." Charles Spurgeon

There are many prayers being prayed that are totally ineffective and do not get any higher than the ceiling because they are not being prayed in the Spirit. God is a Spirit and the only way we can reach Him is by His Spirit!

Our prayers can be eloquent, emotionally charged and forceful but still be vain and utterly useless if we are praying according to our natural man instead of praying in the Spirit.

"The Holy Spirit as the Spirit of life ends our deadness in prayer...as the Spirit of wisdom delivers us from ignorance in this holy art of prayer...as the Spirit of fire delivers us from coldness in prayer...as the Spirit of might comes to our aid in our weakness as we pray." Leonard Ravenhill

One of the most important lessons you must learn in Christ's School of Prayer is to be filled with the Holy Spirit and to have a total dependence upon Him to pray through you. True prayer originates from the Holy Spirit and the only way you will be able to pray with power and receive the answers you need will be to pray in the Spirit.

The Apostle Paul, Apostle of prayer and one of the mighty prayer warriors of all time, very clearly and emphatically declared, we do not know how to pray as we should. But, he did not stop there.

Likewise the Spirit also helpeth our infirmities: for we know not what we should pray for as we ought: but the Spirit itself maketh intercession for us with groanings which cannot be uttered. And he that searcheth the hearts knoweth what is the mind of the Spirit because he maketh intercession for the saints according to the will of God.

Romans 8:26-27

We are utterly helpless and void of any real power without the presence and power of the Holy Spirit in our lives! When you really begin to realize this and totally depend on the Holy Spirit to teach you to pray and to release His power in you to pray, nothing will be able to stand in the way of your taking hold of all that God has provided for you.

PRAYER BEYOND OUR NATURAL CAPABILITIES

Christ never intended for us to depend upon our limited natural abilities, wisdom, knowledge or strength to pray. Gathered together with His disciples during His final hours upon earth Jesus said, *"And I will pray the Father, and he shall give you another Comforter, that he may abide with you for ever"* (John 14:16).

"We are saved because He died, but that salvation is brought home and secured to us because He sits at the right hand of God and continually makes intercession for us."
Charles Spurgeon

These final moments with His disciples were, without a doubt, the most crucial Jesus ever spent with them. Every word and action was filled with great purpose and deep meaning.

Jesus knew that He was returning to the Father, and in just a few short hours their entire lives would be turned upside down. He knew that Peter would deny Him three times. He had told Peter, "...*Satan hath desired to have you, that he may sift you as wheat: But I have prayed for thee: that thy faith fail not...*" (Luke 22:31-32).

Jesus knew the disciples would all turn away from Him and be scattered. He also knew their human weaknesses and limitations. There was no possible way they would be able to face the onslaught of Satan, imprisonment, persecution and death, and still fulfill the work He had called them to do in their natural strength.

Jesus had told them, "...*It is expedient for you that I go away: for if I go not away, the Comforter will not come unto you; but if I depart, I will send him unto you*" (John 16:7).

Jesus knew that they needed something more than what they possessed within themselves. He told them He was going back to the Father, but in His place He was going to send the Holy Spirit Who would not only remain with them, but would be in them (John 14:17).

Jesus was returning to the Father and would be taking His position at the Father's right hand. There He would continue His ministry as the Great Intercessor interceding for them from the Throne. But, He was sending the Holy Spirit to live within them Who would divinely enable them to carry out His intercession on earth.

In preparing them for the work He had called them to do and for the satanic onslaught they would face, Jesus explained how they would be able to pray with a power they had never yet experienced.

A NEW LEVEL OF PRAYER

It was a moment of great intimacy. The disciples fixed their eyes upon Him and clung to every word. Jesus called them His friends with whom He had no secrets.

I no longer call you servants, because a servant does not know his master's business. Instead, I have called you friends, for everything that I learned from my Father I have made known to you.

John 15:15 NIV

Jesus told them about the Holy Spirit Whom He was going to send and the important role He would have in their lives as their Helper, Comforter, Teacher, Guide and Intercessor. Then He said:

...In that day ye shall ask me nothing. Verily, verily, I say unto you, Whatsoever ye shall ask the Father in my name, he will give it you. Hitherto have ye asked nothing in my name: ask, and ye shall receive that your joy may be full.

John 16:23-24

When Jesus said, "In that day..." He was referring to the outpouring of the Holy Spirit when the Spirit would be released to come and live within them. He was leaving them, but the Holy Spirit was coming to live and dwell in them releasing a power in prayer that, up until that time, was unknown to them.

When the Holy Spirit – the Divine Enabler – came, they would be able to ask – to pray in the power and authority of His Name and obtain "whatsoever" they asked.

In that day *after* He had offered His blood on the Mercy Seat before the Father and had been glorified, He was sending the Holy Spirit to enable them to pray...to fulfill the work He had called them to do in the same power and authority He had.

"I believe that the greatest need of the Church of Jesus Christ in America today and the Church of Jesus Christ throughout the world is men and women who pray in the Holy Spirit with the intense earnestness that He gives and He alone gives." **R. A. Torrey**

The Holy Spirit was not given until Christ was glorified (see John 7:39). At Pentecost the Holy Spirit descended and took up His dwelling place within the lives of the disciples releasing a new power greater than anything they had ever experienced!

Through the Name of Jesus they were able to approach the Father and ask knowing that whatever they asked in the power and authority of His Name, the Father would give it to them. Jesus told them, *"At that day ye shall ask in my name: and I say not unto you, that I will pray the Father for you: For the Father Himself loveth you..."* (John 16:26-27).

With the coming of the Holy Spirit came not only a divine power to work the works of God, but also a new power to pray strong, powerful, bold prayers breathed by the Holy Spirit.

One of the first things we see Peter doing after the Day of Pentecost, is lifting the lame man to his feet and saying, *"...In the name of Jesus Christ of Nazareth rise up and walk!"* (Acts 3:6).

What the Church of Jesus Christ needs and must have today in order to pray prayers that will break every yoke of bondage and result in God's power flowing through us to the nations, is to be baptized and full of the Holy Spirit! We must live in the Spirit, with our actions and lives controlled by Him, to be able to pray in the Spirit.

SPIRIT-BREATHED PRAYER

The Holy Spirit is your Divine Enabler! He is the Master Intercessor Who is the spirit of supplication God promised to pour out (see

Zechariah 12:10). The Holy Spirit makes intercession for us and through us. He is your Teacher. But, unlike earthly teachers who teach the lessons and leave the students on their own, the Divine Enabler stays within us and imparts the ability to put into practice what He has taught us.

The Holy Spirit is the one who imparts spiritual vision and teaches the depths and language of prayer. These are things, which cannot be taught by human wisdom or received through the natural mind. Paul told the Corinthians, *"…we speak, not in words taught us by human wisdom but in words taught by the Spirit…"* (1 Corinthians 2:13 NIV).

There are depths of intercession that can only be reached through the Holy Spirit. Paul said, *"the Spirit itself maketh intercession for us with groanings which cannot be uttered."* There are two Greek words used in this translation, *stenagmois alaletois*. The word *"alaletois"* describes the groanings or sighs as being inarticulate, not able to be expressed in understandable words.

There is a language of prayer that goes beyond our limited natural vocabulary. There are times as we go into deep intercession that the Holy Spirit takes over and begins to pray through us in deep cries, groanings and other utterances that our natural mind does not understand. But, we know by the Spirit that we are touching the very heart of God. It is the language of the Holy Spirit, flowing directly from Him through us to the Father – Spirit to Spirit. And, it transcends our human limitations!

We are unable to adequately express in human words the depths of the heart cry of the Spirit within us. It is too deep for words. The Spirit expresses these deep longings through groanings and other utterances we are unable to otherwise express.

Charles Finney, used mightily by God to bring one of the world's greatest revivals in the mid-1800's, would go off secretly into the woods to pray. When the Spirit began to pray through him, he would be in such depths of intercession with groanings and moanings he would roll in the leaves.

As he traveled from meeting to meeting, he was accompanied by Father Clay and Gather Nash. When he went to Britain for several weeks of special meetings, these two men went also. They rented a dark, damp basement room for twenty-five cents a week and stayed there on their knees lying prostrate before God in deep intercession. Their groaning and agonizing before God was so strong, the woman renting them the room thought they were deathly sick and went to Charles Finney to alert him about their situation and see if anything should be done to help them. Finney assured her there was nothing wrong with them but they were travailing in the Spirit.

Charles Finney would walk down the street and people would fall under the power and anointing of God! When he went into the factories to minister during the lunch hour, the workers would be so under the anointing they wouldn't be able to go back to their machines. They closed the bars and movie theaters. When he left a city you could not find a bar or "honky tonk" open.

PRAYER DIVINELY ENERGIZED BY THE HOLY SPIRIT

Jesus told His disciples, *"But the Comforter, which is the Holy Ghost, whom the Father will send in my name, he shall teach you all things..."* (John 14:26). The Greek word used in this verse to describe the Holy Spirit as Teacher is *paracletos*, meaning paraclete.

A "paraclete" is one who went into the courtroom during a trial and served as a helper or counselor. He stood beside the person giving him courage. The defendant was not alone. His paraclete was with him. The paraclete helped the defendant understand the issues before him, helped him understand what he needed to say and do and was constantly available at his side.

The Holy Spirit is your paraclete – Divine Enabler – when you pray. He is both by your side and *within you*. He is your Helper and Counselor. He pleads within and through you. He reveals the will of the Father and enables you to pray according to His will, knowing that the Father has heard you and that you will receive what you have asked.

Before Pentecost the disciples really did not know how to pray. Nor, did they have the divine power and ability to pray because the Holy Spirit had not yet come. It wasn't until after the Holy Spirit came upon them in the Upper Room that their prayers were divinely energized and charged by the power of Almighty God.

After the Holy Spirit came upon them they became mighty prayer warriors. We see Peter praying and commanding life to come back into a corpse.

> *But Peter put them all forth, and kneeled down, and prayed; and turning him to the body said, Tabitha, arise. And she opened her eyes: and when she saw Peter, she sat up.*
>
> Acts 9:40

We see the Church uniting together in prayer and the place being shaken by a Holy Ghost earthquake!

> *And when they had prayed, the place was shaken where they were assembled together; and they were all filled with the Holy Ghost, and they spake the word of God with boldness.*
>
> Acts 4:31

We see Paul commanding evil spirits to leave the girl possessed by a spirit of divination.

> *...But Paul, being grieved, turned and said to the spirit, I command thee in the name of Jesus Christ to come out of her. And he came out the same hour.*
>
> Acts 16:18

The reason the disciples in the Early Church could pray with such power and authority and see supernatural results is because the Holy Spirit was praying through them.

197

PRAYER BEYOND ALL NATURAL LIMITATIONS!

Prayers that are prayed only in our limited natural strength cannot get the job done!

Weak, ineffective, timid prayers will not get the job done!

Don't think for a moment that the spiritual forces of darkness keeping untold thousands in your city in bondage to sin, drugs, alcohol, sexual perversion and every other form of sin will lose their hold as a result of prayers prayed in man's natural strength.

Our prayers must be directed by the Holy Spirit, divinely energized and empowered by the Holy Spirit!

Christ wants you to be so full of the Holy Spirit and yielded to Him that the Holy Spirit will pray prayers through you that are directed and empowered to pierce through the spiritual forces of darkness and destroy the enemy strongholds.

Regardless of who you are, if you are full of the Holy Spirit and yielded completely to Him, you can stand toe-to-toe with the enemy!

Through the power and anointing of the Holy Spirit, you are transformed into a mighty spiritual warrior. You are no longer limited to praying in your natural understanding. The Holy Spirit *enables* you to go beyond your spiritual capacity.

What Christ is looking for today are people who are so fully yielded and controlled by the Holy Spirit, that they provide Him a vessel and the Spirit, inside them, takes over. When this happens, the Holy Spirit comes to their aid and begins to pray in a new dimension.

The Holy Spirit knows our limitations. *"Likewise the Spirit also helpeth our infirmities: for we know not what we should pray for as we ought..."* (Romans 8:26). He knows we do not know how or what to pray as we should. He comes to our aid and begins to release wisdom and revelation, anoints and directs our prayers and prays through us in an unusual intensity. You may find yourself saying and doing things that look foolish in the natural. In the natural, you would say, "I would never do that. That is not my nature."

The Holy Spirit...our Divine Enabler...Who is One with the Father and Son...knows the mind of God. He searches the deep things of God, reveals God's will and enables you to pray under an anointing you never knew before.

We provide the vessel; the Holy Spirit does the interceding.

The Holy Spirit takes your petitions and requests and intercedes on your behalf before God with deep groanings, which are too deep for words. *"...but the Spirit itself maketh intercession for us with groanings which cannot be uttered"* (Romans 8:26). The Father hears the groanings of the Spirit and releases the answer because it is in accordance with His will.

It is the Holy Spirit who reveals to us all that God has prepared for us and has given to us.

> *...The Spirit searches all things, even the deep things of God. For who among men knows the thoughts of a man except the man's spirit within him? In the same way no one knows the thoughts of God except the Spirit of God. We have not received the spirit of the world but the Spirit who is from God, that we may understand what God has freely given us.*
>
> 1 Corinthians 2:10-12 NIV

When we pray in the Spirit, we are no longer limited by our natural understanding. Not only does the Holy Spirit reveal to us how to pray, he reveals the things God has prepared for us so that we can ask -- make a demand on God's promises – and receive what we need and desire from Him.

NO MORE UNANSWERED PRAYER!

Unless your prayers are divinely energized by the Holy Spirit, supernatural answers to your prayers cannot occur. But, when they are divinely energized by the Spirit, God has taken over in you and your prayers cannot go unanswered!

"It is only as we give ourselves to the Spirit living and praying in us that the glory of the prayer-hearing God and the ever blessed and most effective mediation of the Son can be known by us in their power."
Andrew Murray

When the Spirit of God takes over and prays through us we will always pray in the will of God because the Spirit, who is in us, knows the will of the Father and intercedes for us according to His will. And we will always receive the answer!

It is the only time prayer cannot be denied and where the answer will be manifested 100% of the time.

We can know beyond any doubt that when the Holy Spirit releases His power in us and prays through us that our prayers are answered because they are prayed according to the will of God. *"...the Spirit intercedes and pleads [before God] in behalf of the saints according to and in harmony with God's will"* (Romans 8:27 AMP).

One of the major keys to getting our prayers answered is to pray according to the will of God. When we know that we are praying according to His will, we can come boldly before the Father knowing not only that He has heard us, but that we have received what we have asked.

Look closely at what John wrote in his first epistle:

And this is the confidence – the assurance, the [privilege of] boldness – which we have in Him: [we are sure] that if we ask anything (make any request) according to His will (in agreement with His own plan), He listens to and hears us. And if (since) we [positively] know that He listens to us in whatever we ask, we also know [with settled and absolute knowledge] that we have [granted us as our present possessions] the requests made of Him.

1 John 15:14-15 AMP

When we pray according to His will, there is no doubt, no question; only boldness and total confidence that we will receive what we have asked!

There are many people whose prayers are unanswered because they are praying according to their own will and according to their desires. When we pray with wrong motives, we will not receive. James wrote: *"You ask and do not receive, because you ask with wrong motives, so that you may spend it on your pleasures"* (James 4:3 NAS).

There are others who fail to ask because they are unsure concerning whether or not their request is according to God's will. That is why when they pray they do not come boldly, in faith, before the Father believing He will hear and answer their prayers.

> *But without faith it is impossible to please him: for he that cometh to God must believe that he is, and that he is a rewarder of them that diligently seek him.*

Hebrews 11:6

Your position of faith and boldness before God's Throne is based upon knowing that what you are asking is in conformity to His will.

You may ask, "How is it possible to know if what I am praying is according to God's will?"

There are some circumstances we face that are so complex it is difficult to know the mind and will of God so we will know how to pray. If we depend upon our natural wisdom and understanding we cannot know God's will and we will not be able to pray according to His will and receive the answers we need.

When we allow the Holy Spirit full control to pray through us, we can know 100 percent of the time He is praying according to God's will and we have what we asked.

"When we quietly believe that, in the midst of all our weakness, the Holy Spirit as a Spirit of supplication is dwelling within us, for the very purpose of enabling us to pray in the manner and measure that God desires, our hearts will be filled with hope." Andrew Murray

We may not see the manifestation of the answer to our request with our physical eyes, but we have already received it as our present possession! We know it when we pray!

No more unanswered prayer!

When you learn this powerful truth and allow the Holy Spirit to divinely direct and energize your prayers, you can know, beyond doubt, that you will receive the answers to your prayers.

ALLOW THE HOLY SPIRIT FULL CONTROL TO PRAY THROUGH YOU

"We listen to His voice, respond to His touch of power, and offer ourselves in total surrender to His active lordship, so that, He may indwell us, infill us, and pray through us." Wesley L. Duewel

There is an awesome power released as we pray in "unknown tongues." The Apostle Paul wrote, *"For he that speaketh in an unknown tongue speaketh not unto men, but unto God: for no man understandeth him; howbeit in the spirit he speaketh mysteries"* (1 Corinthians 14:2).

He said, *"I will pray with the spirit, and I will pray with the understanding also..."* (1 Corinthians 14:15). As we pray in the Spirit, in unknown tongues, our prayers are divinely supercharged and energized. They supercede human limitations! They penetrate into the spirit realm and God's power is released to work and accomplish His will!

I pray in tongues regularly for hours at a time. As I pray, my spirit is praying directly to the heart of God. The Holy Spirit is empowering me and I know things are changing in the spirit realm. Hindrances are being removed! Demons are bound! The power of God is being released and the will of God is being accomplished!

How do I know this? Because the Holy Spirit within me is making intercession before the Father according to His will!

When you pray in the Spirit or pray words directed by the Holy Spirit, your words are like mighty swords that enable you to wage war against Satan and his evil principalities. Don't be silent or pray in your mind. There are many conservative people who pray silently. They believe because they have a quiet and reserved personality that they should be very quiet and reserved when they pray.

The prayers that move the hand of God are not directed by our personalities, but by the Spirit of God living within us. We are told to come boldly before the throne of God to receive help in our time of need (see Hebrews 4:16). Jesus said, *"And from the days of John the Baptist until now the kingdom of heaven suffereth violence, and the violent take it by force"* (Matthew 11:12).

I have never seen anyone become spiritually violent in prayer by praying silently or conservatively. When we allow the Holy Spirit within us full freedom to pray through us, we are no longer limited by the type of personality or natural disposition we may have, but we pray according to the power of the Spirit within us! We must allow the Holy Spirit to have full expression through us.

Pray in the Spirit! Pray in unknown tongues! And as you pray, the Holy Spirit prayers through you to execute judgment against the powers of darkness and they must go! The work of the enemy will be exposed!

The Holy Spirit will not only reveal the demonic forces that must be bound; He will also reveal the enemy's strategies and give you a divine, foolproof strategy to defeat the enemy!

As this end-time prayer anointing is being released, if you will accept by faith the prophetic word God is releasing and submit yourself fully to the Holy Spirit, He will anoint your mouth. As the Holy Spirit is released in your life in a greater dimension than you have ever experienced, you will pray prayers that will break through the enemy's resistance. Your prayers will be divinely directed and anointed by the Holy Spirit.

When you pray for your personal needs, your family, city and nation, don't pray according to what you see in the natural. Do not rely on your natural understanding. Rely on the Holy Spirit – your Divine Enabler. Pray in the Spirit – in unknown tongues. Jesus said that the Holy Spirit will flow out of our innermost beings like rivers of living water (see John 7:38). Allow the Holy Spirit to flow out of you like a mighty river bursting through a dam.

"We pray not by the truth the Holy Spirit reveals to us, but we pray by the actual presence of the Holy Spirit. Our prayers are taken up by Him and energized and sanctified by His intercession." E. M. Bounds

You can continue on the level where you have been all your life, or you can determine that you will rise up to a new level of prayer.

Beyond ordinary prayer!

Beyond your ordinary capacity!

Beyond your natural mind!

Beyond all the things you have learned!

You must decide that you will become a yielded vessel for the Holy Spirit to pray prayers through you that are directed and empowered by Him.

Regardless of your current experience in your prayer life, God will transform you into a mighty prayer warrior who will be used to pray Holy Spirit energized and directed prayers!

It is up to you. If you have not been baptized by the Holy Spirit, humble yourself before the Father and ask Him to pour out His Spirit upon you until you are overflowing. Jesus said, *"If ye then, being evil, know how to give good gifts unto your children: how much more shall your heavenly Father give the Holy Spirit to them that ask him?"* (Luke 11:13).

In your pursuit of learning how to pray in the powerful dimension Christ taught and demonstrated, you must first make an absolute total surrender of yourself and allow the Holy Spirit full control of your prayer life.

Yield yourself to Him and cry out "Lord, teach me to pray! Ignite the fire of Your Spirit in me. I yield myself to you. Anoint me to pray prayers that are directed and energized by Your Spirit!"

Lord, teach us to pray!
Father, how we praise You for the priceless gift of the Holy Spirit You have given to us! Thank You for sending Him to live within us, giving us the power and authority to pray prayers that are directed and anointed by You to accomplish Your will. Dear Jesus, teach us to go beyond our natural capacity and to so completely yield our lives to You that the Holy Spirit will have total freedom to pray through us. We submit ourselves to You now and ask You to pour out Your Spirit upon us. Anoint our lips, our minds and spirits with the fire of the Holy Spirit. Release a new prayer anointing upon us and make us mighty spiritual warriors to fulfill Your will in this end-time hour. The cry of our heart is, Lord, teach us to pray! Holy Spirit have full control and pray through us!

CHAPTER TEN

PRAYER COMMAND OF FAITH

Jesus taught and demonstrated a dimension of prayer so vast, so unlimited, so all comprehensive and so powerful that it goes beyond the limitations of our natural minds.

As we cry out, "Lord, teach us to pray!" we must ask the Lord to not only open our spiritual eyes and give us a revelation of this powerful, supernatural prayer dimension; but also that He will enable us to live in it.

We must not be satisfied with head knowledge! We need the reality of what Christ taught manifested in our lives.

Christ intended for His Church to know no limitations! He planned that we would be invincible and that His power would flow through us to fulfill His will and purposes on earth: proclaiming the Gospel, healing the sick, casting out demons, bringing in a worldwide harvest of souls and establishing His Kingdom on earth.

As we look closely at the powerful, life-changing truths Christ gave us, and the power of prayer He demonstrated, you need to understand that this is the powerful dimension of prayer He intends for you to live in!

"Many prayers fail to achieve their purpose because there is no faith behind them. Prayers that are filled with doubt are requests for refusal." **Charles Spurgeon**

Remove every limitation you may have placed upon yourself or upon God. As you see the unlimited potential of prayer, let faith rise up within you.

The great victories Jesus experienced as He ministered to the needs of the people; opening blind eyes, unstopping deaf ears, healing all manner of diseases and raising the dead, were not automatic.

Although He was the Son of God, Jesus did not win these victories in his own strength. He had stripped Himself of His divine abilities.

Who, although being essentially one with God and in the form of God [possessing the fullness of the attributes which make God God], did not think this equality with God was a thing to be eagerly grasped or retained. But stripped Himself [of all privileges and rightful dignity], so as to assume the guise of a servant (slave), in that He became like men and was born a human being.

Philippians 2:6-7 AMP

He did absolutely nothing independent of the Father. Jesus said, *"...The Son can do nothing of himself, but what he seeth the Father do"* (John 5:19); *"...the words that I speak unto you I speak not of myself: but the Father that dwelleth in me, he doeth the works"* (John 14:10).

Jesus ministered to the needs of the people and fulfilled the work He had been called to do through the power of the Holy Spirit. *"...God anointed Jesus of Nazareth with the Holy Ghost and with power: who went about doing good, and healing all that were oppressed of the devil; for God was with him"* (Acts 10:38).

Everything He did was a result of what the Father had revealed to Him while He was in His Presence in prayer and by the power of the Holy Spirit.

Out among the people, Jesus did not pray for the sick. There is only one instance recorded where Jesus openly called upon the Father before healing someone.

Jesus did not pray a long drawn out prayer begging and pleading with God to heal the sick and meet the needs of the people. He spent time alone with God in prayer; but when He ministered to the people, He spoke the *prayer command of faith* and the work was accomplished.

"Hours and hours of praying do not eliminate the need for faith. They may help you to arrive at the position of faith, but without the dynamic of faith, prayer does not prevail." Wesley L. Duewel

Through prayer the power of God was released in His life and whatever He spoke came to pass. He spoke to the impossible circumstances in peoples' lives and they were changed, healed, delivered and set free!

To the leper Jesus spoke the prayer command of faith, "Be clean!" and immediately he was cleansed and made whole.

Jesus spoke the prayer command of faith to the man at the Pool of Bethesda who had been paralyzed 38 years, *"...Rise, take up thy bed, and walk. And immediately the man...took up his bed, and walked"* (John 5:8-9).

To the woman bowed over with a spirit of infirmity for 18 years, Jesus spoke the prayer command of faith, *"...Woman, thou art loosed from thine infirmity. And he laid his hands on her: and immediately she was made straight..."* Luke 13:12-13).

Jesus said to the blind beggar, *"...Receive thy sight:...And immediately he received his sight..."* (Luke 18:42-43).

To the widow's son who had died and was carried away to be buried, Jesus spoke the prayer command of faith, *"...Young man, I say unto thee, Arise. And he that was dead sat up, and began to speak..."* (Luke 7:14-15).

The miracle power of God was released into these impossible situations as He spoke because He had won the victories first in prayer.

Jesus spent time in prayer alone with the Father and then went out and spoke the prayer command of faith in the power and authority He received during His communion with the Father.

FAITH AND PRAYER ARE INSEPARABLE!

"Nothing honors the Father like the faith that is assured that He will do what He has said in giving us whatever we ask." Andrew Murray

One of the reasons we are not living in this powerful dimension of prayer; where we are able to speak the prayer command of faith and see blind eyes opened, the deaf hear and the lame walk, is because we have not first shut ourselves in with the Father receiving His direction and drawing upon His strength.

As a result, our faith is weak.

Regardless of how long, how loud, or how fervent the prayer, there is no power behind it unless it is prayed in faith.

One of the most important lessons you must learn in Christ's School of Prayer is that true prayer is absolutely dependent upon faith. Faith is the one inseparable condition of prayer. *"But without faith it is impossible to please him: for he that cometh to God must believe that he is, and that he is a rewarder of them that diligently seek him"* (Hebrews 11:6).

"We constantly need to be reminded that faith is the one inseparable condition of successful praying. There are other considerations entering into the exercise, but faith is the final, indispensable condition of true praying."
E. M. Bounds

Faith is the one ingredient we must have in our prayers. Paul said that without faith it is impossible to please God. If you do not come before the Father and present your petitions believing that He will answer and give you what you ask, don't waste your breath!

The Father responds to your faith! Faith believes that He is a "rewarder". Jesus said, *"...when thou prayest, enter into thy closet, and when thou hast shut thy door, pray to thy Father which is in secret; and thy Father which seeth in secret shall reward thee openly"* (Matthew 6:6).

Our Father is a Rewarder!

I like what E. M. Bounds has said, "Faith rests its case on diligent prayer, and gives assurance and encouragement to diligent seekers after God, for it is they alone who are richly rewarded when they pray."

Faith is the life and power of prayer!

Without faith we cannot please God and we will not receive anything from Him. *"But let him ask in faith, nothing wavering. For he that wavereth is like a wave of the sea driven with the wind and tossed. For let not that man think that he shall receive any thing of the Lord"* (James 1:6-7).

Only by faith can we know God, receive Christ, live the Christian life and take hold of His full provision for our needs.

If you are going to live in the same powerful dimension of prayer Christ demonstrated, you must live your life and pray in faith!

ONLY WHEN YOU SEE INTO THE INVISIBLE WILL YOU DARE TO TAKE HOLD OF THE IMPOSSIBLE!

In order for our prayers to be full of faith we must no longer focus our eyes upon the visible but upon the invisible! The Apostle Paul said, *"We walk by faith, not by sight"* (2 Corinthians 5:7).

Paul said, *"...we look not at the things which are seen, but at the things which are not seen: for the things which are seen are temporal; but the things which are not seen are eternal"* (2 Corinthians 4:18).

Christ lived and operated in a powerful dimension of prayer where His eyes were not focused upon the circumstances and situations in the natural world, but upon the invisible, eternal, Almighty God with Whom nothing is impossible!

To take hold of the prayer victories you need in the circumstances you face, you must begin to pray with your spiritual focus set and your faith firmly fixed upon a faithful God Who has bound Himself to you with His Word and believe He will answer your prayers.

When you pray, you must take hold of His promises by faith that is securely rooted and grounded upon the divine faithfulness of Almighty God.

Now faith is the assurance (the confirmation, the title-deed) of the things [we] hope for, being the proof of things, [we] do not see and the conviction of their reality [faith perceiving as real fact what is not revealed to the senses].

Hebrews 11:1 AMP

Faith is the assurance, a firm persuasion and expectation that God will do all that He has promised. When you pray in faith, you do not wonder or hope you will receive what you have asked from God. There is a deep inner knowing in your spirit that cannot be shaken.

Faith is the evidence – the proof – of the things we are unable to see with our natural eyes. It reveals to our spirits the *reality* of the things we are praying and believing God for and enables us to take possession of them even *before* they are manifested to our natural senses.

Andrew Murray defined faith this way: "Faith is very far from being a mere conviction of the truth of God's Word or a conclusion drawn from certain premises. It is the ear, which has heard God say what He will do and the eye, which has seen Him doing it. Therefore, where there is true faith, it is impossible for the answer not to come."

Faith is not a natural function of our natural man. It is a supernatural life force given to us by God!

When you go to the Father and present your petitions, it is not enough for you to simply "claim" God's promises. Faith in the promises God has given you is not enough!

The type of faith we are talking about is one that is backed up by deeds and actions. Faith is a fact, but faith is an act!

There is a vast difference between the type of faith the majority of professing Christians have today and the faith Jesus taught that was able to move mountains – where nothing is impossible!

One type of faith ends in talk –

True faith is manifested in deeds.

One crumbles under trials and afflictions –

True faith withstands all opposition and every trial.

One is inoperative – producing no results –

True faith is active and powerful!

The supernatural faith of God is like Christ, who is the *"...author and finisher of our faith"* (Hebrews 12:2).

It is a living faith!

It is an incorruptible faith!

And, it cannot be conquered by the devil.

It is a faith that perseveres – that overcomes every obstacle and endures to the end!

This is the type of faith Jesus demonstrated when He prayed, and it is the type of faith we must have when we come before the Father in prayer.

PRAYER IS THE VOICE OF FAITH!

One of the greatest incidences in Christ's life illustrates the powerful dimension of prayer that He taught, took place on the mountainside, just outside Bethany.

Mary and Martha stood by the bedside of Lazarus. He had become sick and his condition had grown steadily worse. Now, he was at a critical point and each day they grew more concerned.

"If only Jesus were here. He would lay His hands on Lazarus and heal him." Martha sighed.

Mary looked at Martha with a worried look on her face. "Martha, Lazarus is lying here at the point of death! We've got to get a message to Jesus. When He hears that Lazarus is sick, I'm sure He will come. He is our only hope!"

Mary and Martha called a messenger to their house. They told him where he would find Jesus and His disciples and instructed him to tell Jesus, "Lord, the one whom you love is sick!"

"Don't waste one minute! This is a matter of life and death! Don't stop until you find Jesus and give Him this message!" Martha told the messenger.

When the messenger reached Jesus with the news that Lazarus was sick, He told His disciples, "...*This sickness is not unto death, but for the glory of God, that the Son of God may be glorified thereby*" (John 11:4, NAS).

Although Jesus loved Mary, Martha and Lazarus; He remained in the city where He was ministering two more days. At that point Jesus already knew what was going to happen. He saw beyond the natural circumstances into the invisible!

Meanwhile, back in Bethany, I can imagine Mary and Martha anxiously waiting and looking for Jesus to come and heal Lazarus.

"It has already been two days since we sent the message. Why isn't Jesus here?" Martha said to Mary with tears in her eyes.

"I don't know, Martha. Surely He will be here soon. He loves Lazarus and I'm sure He will come," Mary replied.

"But, if He doesn't get here soon, it will be too late! Lazarus is growing weaker by the moment. His breathing is labored and he doesn't respond anymore when we speak to him," Martha answered as she glanced toward the room where Lazarus lay unconscious.

"Go check on him and stay by his bedside while I run to the hillside outside Bethany to look for any sign of Jesus," Mary said to Martha as she headed toward the door.

Mary had just reached the top of the hill overlooking Bethany, when one of their friends came running toward her shouting, "Mary, come quickly! Lazarus is dying!"

Mary ran as fast as she could back to her house, pushed her way through family members and friends who were weeping and fell on her knees at Lazarus' bedside. Martha was there weeping uncontrollably.

"It's too late, Mary! Lazarus is dead!" Martha cried out.

Mary looked at Lazarus's eyes now closed in death. She took his hand in hers and leaned over to kiss his forehead. Then she placed her face on the bed and began to weep.

After the two days had passed, Jesus told His disciples, *"Let us go to Judea again"* (John 11:7, NAS). The disciples were amazed that He wanted to go there because it hadn't been too long since the Jews had wanted to stone Him. But He told them, "Our friend Lazarus has fallen asleep; but I go, that I may awaken him out of sleep" (John 11:11, NAS).

The disciples did not understand that Jesus was talking about Lazarus' death until He told them plainly, *"...Lazarus is dead, and I am glad for your sakes that I was not there, so that you may believe; but let us go to him"* (John 11:14-15, NAS).

Jesus saw beyond the natural circumstances. He loved Lazarus, Mary and Martha. But, He had not gone when they had called Him because He knew He was going to raise him from the dead. As a result, many people would believe in Him and God would be glorified.

When Jesus arrived, Lazarus had been dead four days. All hope in Mary and Martha's hearts was gone. They had buried Lazarus and were surrounded by mourners. They were not looking to Christ, expecting Him to bring Lazarus back to life. Their eyes were still on their circumstances and had limited the power of God. They had resigned themselves to the fact that Lazarus was dead.

The first thing both Mary and Martha said to Jesus was, *"Lord, if you had been here, my brother would not have died"* (John 11:21 AMP). They could not understand why Jesus had waited so long. Why didn't He come when they sent for Him? Why didn't He answer their cry for help?

EVEN DEATH MUST OBEY THE VOICE OF FAITH!

Many Christians today are like Mary and Martha. When they face desperate circumstances, they pray and cry out to the Father. But, when they don't see the answer right away, or their circumstances do not change, they wonder why their prayers are not answered. Their faith begins to waver and they lose hope.

When you pray, do not focus your eyes on the things you see with your natural eyes, the obstacles, and the impossibilities you face. Focus your faith on God, believing and expecting that He will fulfill His Word and answer your prayer.

As you wait for the answer to your prayers, do not waver or become discouraged.

Don't question or doubt God's faithfulness by thinking, "I wonder if God really hears me. I wonder if God meant what He said." Don't question the promises He has given you in His Word.

When you pray, focus your faith on God's faithfulness to you, His power and ability to perform His Word, upon His unfailing record and the infallibility of His Word.

When you do, you will break through the barrier of fear and unbelief!

You will be able to look beyond your impossibilities!

You will stop struggling!

You will stop questioning!

You will be able to pray and persevere in faith until you see the full manifestation of the answer you need.

"The prayer of faith is a prayer that reaches through, consciously touches God's throne, and then rests unshakably in the assurance that the answer will come in God's time." Wesley L. Duewel

Jesus was deeply grieved because of their unbelief. When He saw Mary weeping along with the Jews who were with her, *"...he groaned in the spirit, and was troubled"* (John 11:33).

The Jews with Mary were also full of unbelief. They said, *"Could not he who opened the eyes of the blind man have kept this man from dying?"* (John 11:37 NIV). At this unbelief, Jesus again groaned in the spirit, but this did not stop Him. When He arrived at the cave where Lazarus was buried, He said, *"Take away the stone!"* (John 11:38 NIV).

Martha still had her eyes focused on the natural circumstances instead of the power of Almighty God. She said, *"Lord, he's been there four days and by now his body stinks!"* (paraphrase)

Jesus told her, *"Did I not tell you that if you believed, you would see the glory of God?"* (John 11:40 NIV).

As the disciples, Mary, Martha and the mourners watched, they rolled the stone away from the entrance to the cave.

Then Jesus prayed. He lifted up His eyes toward heaven and said: *"Father, I thank you that you have heard me. I knew that you always hear me, but I said this for the benefit of the people standing here, that they might believe that you sent me"* (John 11:41-42 NIV).

There is a powerful truth in this prayer. Being fully assured that the Father had already heard Him, Jesus accepted the answer and thanked the Father even before He saw a visible manifestation. He said, "Father, I thank you that you have heard me."

When we pray, we are to come to God this same way, in faith and complete assurance. We are to pray, knowing that He always hears us and thank Him in advance, believing we have received the answer before we see a visible manifestation.

After Jesus had prayed this prayer, He spoke a prayer command of faith that penetrated the grave. He spoke to what seemed to be an impossible situation. He spoke to a dead, putrefying body that had been in the grave four days!

With a loud voice He commanded, "Lazarus, come forth!"

At that moment the supernatural power of God was released. At the prayer command of faith, death had to loose its hold! Lazarus' spirit returned to his body. His body was totally healed and restored and he walked out of the cave bound hand and foot with grave clothes. Jesus told them, "...Loose him, and let him go" (John 11:44).

"Only God can move mountains, but faith and prayer moves God." E. M. Bounds

SPEAK THE PRAYER COMMAND OF FAITH INTO YOUR CIRCUMSTANCES!

This story is an example of the powerful dimension of prayer in which Christ intends for us live and operate, to fulfill His will upon the earth.

After Jesus cursed the fig tree and it dried up overnight from the roots, Jesus taught the disciples about this powerful dimension of prayer.

> *...Have faith in God. For verily I say unto you, That whosoever shall say unto this mountain, Be thou removed, and be thou cast into the sea; and shall not doubt in his heart, but shall believe that those things which he saith shall come to pass; he shall have whatsoever he saith.*

Mark 11:22-23

Are you ready to rise up to this new dimension of prayer where you are praying in faith and commanding the mountains...obstacles... difficulties and seeming impossibilities...to move out of your way?

What are the mountains standing between you and the fulfillment of God's will, His purpose and plan for you and your family?

What are the obstacles hindering the progress of Gospel and the kingdom of God in your city and nation?

* An incurable or fatal disease?

* Physical handicaps, paralysis, deafness, blindness?

* Bankruptcy?

* Lack of income or a mountain of debt?

* A marriage torn apart through separation or divorce?

* Loved ones bound by drugs or alcohol?

* Persecution and opposition to the Word of God?

* Satanic strongholds holding people in bondage?

Get ready to speak the prayer command of faith into your circumstances and see those mountains move in Jesus' Name!

The key is in these verses: Jesus said, "*...and shall not doubt in his heart but believe...*" We must stop being double-minded in our praying! Most Christians believe that God answers prayer. But, how often do we pray and not really expect God to answer?

We know God can do all things. But, if we are totally honest with ourselves, how often do we pray, but we are not really sure God will answer the need for which we pray?

Now, look closely at what Jesus was teaching. This next verse summarizes the unlimited potential we have in prayer. Jesus continued by saying: "*Therefore I say unto you, what things soever ye desire, when ye pray, believe that ye receive them, and ye shall have them*" (Mark 11:24).

There is one thing we must do when we pray: Believe that we have received!

When did Jesus say you are to believe that you have received the things you have asked in prayer?

After you have received them?

No!

He said "*when ye pray; believe that ye receive them...*"

You may not actually see the answer manifested until later. But, without having seen it in the natural, you are to believe that the Father has already given it to you!

When we accept forgiveness and Christ into our hearts, it is by faith. In the same way when we pray asking God for things that are in accordance with His will, we must believe it is ours and accept it *when* we pray.

"WHATSOEVER YOU ASK!"

Jesus said, "*All things whatsoever.*" This promise is so all comprehensive; our natural minds immediately begin to place limitations on it. We begin to doubt and say, "This can't possibly be literally true."

Jesus carefully chose His words and used the strongest expression He could find to explain the unlimited potential of prayer.

On many different occasions Jesus repeated this powerful truth: He said, "*If thou canst believe, all things are possible to him that believeth*" (Mark 9:23). "*...If ye have faith as a grain of mustard seed...nothing shall be impossible to you*" (Matthew 17:20).

Six times during His final moments with His disciples He emphasized this all-inclusive promise concerning prayer. In these promises we see heaven open and the Father offering to give us whatever we ask in faith.

Jesus said, "*And whatsoever ye shall ask in my name, that will I do, that the Father may be glorified in the Son*" (John 14:13); "*If ye shall ask anything in my name, I will do it*" (John 14:14); "*...ye shall ask what ye* *will, and it shall be done unto you"* (John 15:7); *"...whatsoever ye shall ask of the Father in my name, he may give it you"* (John 15:16); *"...whatsoever ye ask the Father in my name, he will give it you"* (John 16:23); *"...Ask, and ye shall receive, that your joy may be full"* (John 16:24).

When we pray in faith, we need our requests to be specific. Jesus said, *"...and shall not doubt in his heart, but shall believe those things which he saith shall come to pass; he shall have whatsoever he saith"* (Mark 11:23).

"...Whatsoever he saith!"

This promise is unlimited, in quality and quantity. God is ready to fully supply all your requests of faith and prayer. When we present our petitions to God, they need to be clear, specific and definite. We must believe and expect – not a substitute, not something that looks like it, but the exact things for which we ask.

Smith Wigglesworth, referred to as an apostle of faith because of his strong conviction that with God all things are possible, lived in a powerful dimension of prayer. There were many times he would simply give the prayer command of faith and people were healed and the dead rose.

Wigglesworth's wife, Polly, fell dead at the door of the mission where she had been ministering. The word reached Smith as he was on his way to minister at some meetings.

"Polly's dead, Smith. She fell dead at the mission door."

In the natural, Smith was heartbroken and devastated. But, his eyes were not on the natural circumstances. He began to speak in tongues and praise the Lord, laughing in the Spirit.

Her body was brought to their home. At Smith's instruction, they took her upstairs and laid her lifeless body on the bed.

They told Smith, "She's dead, and we can do no more." He just smiled. He knew differently.

After asking everyone to please leave the room, he closed the door. He turned and walked over to her bed. He knew she was with the Lord but he could not stand the thought of being separated from her.

"In the name of Jesus, death, give her up!" Smith commanded.

Polly opened her eyes and looked at Smith.

"Polly, I need you!" He said.

She answered, "Smith, the Lord wants me."

A great struggle waged within him. He wanted her to be with him and didn't know what he would do without her. But, the Lord spoke to him and said, "She's mine. Her work is done."

With tears streaming down his face Smith told her, "My darling, if the Lord wants you, I will not hold you." He kissed her cheek tenderly. Then he said, "Good-bye for the present."

Polly closed her eyes and went to be with the Lord.

This is just one example of the powerful prayer dimension that Christ has made possible for us to live in. The key is getting rid of doubt and unbelief and releasing our faith in prayer.

GOD IS A REWARDER!

Faith and prayer are inseparable!

We must remember, *"...he that cometh to God must believe that he is, and that he is a rewarder of them that diligently seek him"* (Hebrews 11:6).

Christ wants you to live in this same powerful dimension of prayer that He demonstrated throughout His life. He expects you to believe Him for the impossible. He wants you to pray with faith believing Him to change the very course of nature if necessary to answer your prayers.

"Prayer is simply faith, claiming its natural, yet marvelous prerogatives – faith taking possession of its illimitable inheritance in Christ." E. M. Bounds

Christ has entrusted into your hands the power to take possession of whatever you need through the prayer of faith and in the power and authority of His Name. In chapter eleven I will share this powerful key of taking possession of whatsoever you ask in Jesus' Name.

He wants you to use the prayer command of faith to speak to the obstacles and problems you face believing He will supernaturally intervene and move them.

The Apostle Paul saw a man crippled from birth and spoke the prayer command of faith, *"Stand up on your feet!"* And the man was instantly healed (see Acts 14:10).

At Phillipi, he turned to the girl possessed with a spirit of divination and spoke to the evil spirit in her the prayer command of faith, "In the name of Jesus Christ, I command you to come out of her!" The demon obeyed and she was set free.

When we pray the prayer command of faith we are taking our position with Christ on the Throne, and speaking into the circumstances with all of heaven backing us! We speak in the power and authority of His Name as Christ did.

We say to the blind, "See, in the Name of Jesus!"

We say to cancers and tumors, "Die, in the Name of Jesus!"

We speak the prayer command of faith in Jesus' Name and command Satan to loose his hold on our sons and daughters bound by drugs or alcohol.

As you pray, focus your faith upon God's unfailing record. You can stake your life on it.

It doesn't matter how impossible your circumstances may seem or how long you have waited for an answer to your prayers. As you pray, focus your faith until you are fully persuaded...until you are filled with expectation and are praising God for answering your prayers, even before you see the visible manifestation!

Lord, teach us to pray!

Father, open our eyes to see the unlimited power You have given us in prayer. Forgive our unbelief. Open our eyes to see with eyes of faith all that You have prepared and have waiting for us in answer to our cry of faith. Dear Lord, take us beyond our natural limitations. Teach us how to live in this powerful dimension of prayer where we dare to believe for the impossible. Release your faith in us! Use us to speak the prayer command of faith to remove every obstacle and opposing force standing between us and the fulfillment of Your will in our lives. Use us to speak the prayer command of faith to do the same works You did, healing the sick, casting out demons and setting the captives free. Use us to speak the prayer command of faith in our cities and nations to see deliverance and healing in Your Name!

CHAPTER ELEVEN

BEYOND BASIC TRAINING

As Christ began His ministry, He taught on prayer. In His Sermon on the Mount, His teaching was directed to disciples and followers who knew very little about prayer.

In Christ's School of Prayer it was basic training.

Jesus broke through the traditional barriers and taught them the basics in prayer of approaching God, in childlike faith, as their Father. He said, "...*when ye pray, say, Our Father which art in heaven...*" (Luke 11:2).

In this basic training, He taught them to find a secret place to pray to the Father, who would reward them openly. (see Matthew 6:6) He also taught them how to pray and trust the Father for their basic needs and how to set their priority in prayer. "*But seek ye first the kingdom of God, and his righteousness; and all these things shall be added unto you*" (Matthew 6:33).

In His final meeting with His disciples in the upper room, Christ again taught on prayer. But, it was no longer basic training. It was on a much higher level. He was no longer addressing beginners, but those who had walked closely with Him and had learned at His side.

It was graduation time!

Jesus now calls His disciples His friends. He told them, "*I no longer call you servants, because a servant does not know his master's business. Instead, I have called you friends, for everything that I learned from my Father I have made known to you*" (John 15:15 NIV).

This was a level of deep intimacy and spiritual training where Jesus had drawn this inner circle of "friends" into close fellowship with Him. He had not withheld anything from them, but had revealed all that He had learned from the Father.

In His great intercessory prayer for the Church, as He was preparing to lay down His life in obedience to His Father's will, Jesus told the Father, *"I have manifested thy name unto the men which thou gavest me out of the world..."* (John 17:6); "I made Your Name known to them and revealed Your character and Your very Self, and I will continue to make [You] known..." (John 17:26 AMP).

Jesus said, "I have manifested your name." During His lifetime on earth, Jesus, in the form of human flesh, manifested God's Name to the disciples and to the world. The word "manifested" means to reveal; to make visible; to make known.

Jesus was not referring simply to preaching or teaching about God's Name. It is one thing for an individual to teach about a person or particular subject, but another thing altogether to demonstrate that knowledge from a firsthand experience.

Through His words and actions, Jesus revealed God's Name...Jehovah Elohim, the self-existent Creator; El Shaddai, the Almighty God; Jehovah-Jireh, our divine Provider; Jehovah-Repheka, the Healer; Jehovah-Nissi, the Lord our Conqueror.

Jesus was a visible representation of all that God's Name means!

In the same way, He wants the Church to manifest, (to reveal) and make known His Name!

THE KEY TO UNLOCKING HEAVEN'S RESOURCES

In His final moments with His disciples, Jesus' teaching on prayer was directed to those into whose hands He was now going to place the future of the Kingdom of God upon earth.

Verily, verily, I say unto you, He that believeth on me, the works that I do shall he do also; and greater works than these shall he do; because I go unto my Father. And whatsoever ye shall ask in my name, that will I do, that the Father may be glorified in the Son. If ye shall ask any thing in my name, I will do it.

John 14:12-14

As His Body on earth, the disciples were to not only carry on the work He had done, but to do even greater works in the power and authority of His Name!

Prayer was to be the channel through which the power to do these greater works was received!

"To pray in the name of Jesus, we must pray as He prayed on earth, as He taught us to pray, in union with Him, as He now prays in heaven."
Andrew Murray

Jesus revealed two major reasons they would be able to do the greater works.

1. He was going to the Father to receive all power.

2. They would be able to ask for and receive that power in His Name.

Jesus said, "Because I go to the Father, whatever you ask I will do" (paraphrase). The disciples would be able to ask for and receive everything in His Name and, therefore, would do the greater works.

In these final, parting words with His disciples, Jesus gives us an important and vital truth concerning prayer. In your pursuit of learning how to pray in the powerful dimension Jesus taught, you must learn this lesson:

The only way you will be able to take hold of God's power to do the greater works Christ promised is when you have a full revelation

of the power in Jesus' Name and begin to pray in the power and authority of that Name!

Christ has placed in our hands the awesome, unlimited power that He has on the Throne, seated at the right hand of the Father, and the legal right to exercise that power in His Name; to do the works of God, and even greater works than He did!

In His parting words, He stresses again and again this power of prayer He gives us to ask in His Name. It was as if He wanted this great truth to be indelibly imprinted upon our hearts. Jesus said:

> *And whatsoever ye shall ask in my name, that will I do...If ye shall ask anything in my name, I will do it...that whatsoever ye shall ask of the Father in my name, he may give it you...Verily, verily, I say unto you, Whatsoever ye shall ask the Father in may name, he will give it you...Hitherto have ye asked nothing in my name: ask and ye shall receive...At that day ye shall ask in my name.*

John 14:13-14; 15:16; 16:23-24, 26

Jesus said, "*Ask in My Name!*"

After Jesus had defeated Satan on the cross and was resurrected in great power, His parting words to the disciples before He ascended into Heaven were:

> *And these signs shall follow them that believe; In my name shall they cast out devils; they shall speak with new tongues; They shall take up serpents, and if they drink any deadly thing, it shall not hurt them; they shall lay hands on the sick, and they shall recover.*

Mark 16:17-18

Jesus said, "*In My Name!*"

Jesus has placed all of Heaven at our disposal and has given us the key to unlocking its unlimited resources: prayer in His Name!

THE NAME ABOVE EVERY NAME

"Praying in Jesus' Name means to stand in His stead, to bear His nature, to stand for all which He stood – righteousness, truth, holiness, and zeal." E. M. Bounds

He said, "Whatsoever you shall ask in My Name I will do it!" To take hold of this great promise we must first answer this question:

What does it really mean to pray; to ask in Jesus' Name?

Praying in the Name of Jesus is much more than just simply using the words, "In Jesus' Name" at the end of your prayer. When you know what is behind the Name, what the Name represents, the power that resides in that Name, and the legal right and authority you have to use the Name of Jesus, you will ask whatever you will and it will be done!

When Jesus ascended into Heaven, the Father exalted Him to the highest possible position and gave Him the Name that is above every name.

And after He had appeared in human form, He abased and humbled Himself [still further] and carried His obedience to the extreme of death, even the death of [the] cross! Therefore [because He stooped so low], God has highly exalted Him and has freely bestowed on Him the name that is above every name, That in [at] the name of Jesus every knee should [must] bow, in heaven and on earth and under the earth, And every tongue [frankly and openly] confess and acknowledge that Jesus Christ is Lord, to the glory of God the Father.

Philippians 2:8-11 AMP

Jesus was not exalted and given the Name that is above every name simply because He was the Son of God. He earned it! He paid the supreme price. He carried the sins of the world to the cross. He hung on the cross in shame and disgrace and became the supreme sacrifice to redeem man from sin.

Jesus obtained that Name that is above every name because He was willing to humble Himself and become obedient unto death. Considering the great price that He paid before He was given that Name, we must never take His Name lightly.

We must cherish that Name!

There is power in that Name!

Demons tremble at the mention of His Name!

Just a small faint whisper of the Name of Jesus from the lips of a humble child of God can send a legion of demons on the run!

The following is a true story, told by a missionary in Africa, that illustrates the power of Jesus' Name in time of grave danger. Two African preachers were walking to a village where they were going to preach Sunday morning. They suddenly felt they were being followed. When they turned around, they saw a large lion stalking them. There were no trees to climb and they were terrified. One of them prayed, "Oh God, protect us as You did Daniel in the lions' den." Coming to a fork in the path, they stopped. So did the lion.

"In the name of Jesus, we command you to go the other way!" one of them yelled. The lion growled angrily and pawed the ground while they hurried on their way. Looking back, they saw the lion going down the other path they had commanded it to go in Jesus' Name!

ALL POWER AND AUTHORITY IN HEAVEN AND EARTH ARE IN HIS NAME!

In ancient times, names were very significant because they represented the individual. All that Jesus is and all the power and authority He has now, seated at the right hand of the Father, is in His Name.

Jesus is seated, *"Far above all rule and authority and power and dominion, and every name that is named above every title that can be conferred - not only in this age and in this world, but also in the age and the world which are to come"* (Ephesians 1:21 AMP).

For years, the Church has emphasized that during the consummation of the ages, at Christ's second coming, every knee will bow and every tongue confess that Jesus is Lord. This will happen (see Revelation 5:13).

But, what we have failed to realize is the fact that not only will this happen as the Apostle Paul said in the world that is to come, but everything in heaven, earth and hell must bow and obey the Name of Jesus now, in this world!

"To pray in Jesus' name is to pray in harmony with His character. It is to pray in the fullest oneness and identity with Him." Wesley L. Duewel

We must have a fresh revelation of Christ, as He is today, seated in power and majesty on the Throne.

He is there, on the Throne as the Creator of all things!

He is the image of the invisible God, the firstborn over all creation. For by him all things were created: things in heaven and on earth, visible and invisible, whether thrones or powers or rulers or authorities; all things were created by him and for him.

Colossians 1:15-16 NIV

Jesus is seated on the Throne as the pre-existent Son of God by whom all things are held together! *"And He Himself existed before all things and in Him all things consist cohere, are held together"* (Colossians 1:17 AMP).

He is seated there as the Head of the Church, the Beginning, the Firstborn among the dead, occupying the position of supremacy over all!

He also is the Head of (His) body, the Church; seeing He is the Beginning, the Firstborn from among the dead, so that He alone in everything and in every respect might occupy the chief place [stand first and be pre-eminent].

Colossians 1:18 AMP

All things are under His feet! *"And He has put all things under His feet and has appointed Him the universal and supreme Head of the Church..."* (Ephesians 1:22 AMP).

Think about Christ and the power that He possesses:

• He is above all rule, authority, dominion, and every name that is named.

• All things are in subjection to Him.

• Everything in heaven, on earth, and beneath the earth must obey Him!

Are you ready for this?

All that Jesus is and all the power and authority that He possesses is in His Name!

All the fullness of the Godhead...

Creative power...

Supreme power and authority over all things...

Salvation...

Healing...

Deliverance...

Supernatural provision...

Power over all principalities and powers...is in His Name!

As His representative here on earth, when you pray in the Name of Jesus, you invoke – put into operation – all the power and authority in that Name to manifest the healing, deliverance or whatever you need.

WE MUST TAKE DOMINION IN THE NAME OF JESUS!

Everything in heaven: angels, all the principalities of heaven, the stars, moon, sun, and planets must bow at that mighty Name!

Everything on earth: all creation, every living creature, the elements of nature, men, and governments must bow at that all-powerful Name!

Everything under the earth: Satan and all his evil principalities, the rulers and powers of the darkness of this world, are in subjection and must obey the Name of Jesus!

Satan and all the powers, principalities and rulers of darkness that we wrestle against in this world are not in control!

Governments and heads of state are not in control!

Jesus Christ, the Son of the living God, is the Supreme Authority over all things and He is in control!

Satan hates the Name of Jesus. He knows the day the Church rises up in the power and authority of Jesus' Name, that he will have to retreat. He would like nothing better than for you to be ignorant of the power and authority that belongs to you in Jesus' Name.

Satan knows that he does not have the power, we do!

Jesus' Name is all-powerful, indestructible, and unchangeable!

It legally belongs to us. But, unless we reach out by faith and begin to pray and speak the prayer command of faith, in Jesus' Name, that power will never be realized. In this end-time hour, unless the Church rises up with a full revelation of the power that is in Jesus' Name, we will not be able to operate in the power that God intended.

We are facing an enemy that has already been defeated!

Satan has been operating illegally. Jesus defeated Him and stripped him of his power over us. We have been given power *over all the power of the enemy*" (Luke 10:19). Yet, because we have failed to exercise the power and authority that belongs to us in Jesus' Name, he has continued to attack us with every form of sickness and disease. He has continued to attack our homes and loved ones.

We have allowed Satan to take too much territory. We cannot continue to sit back and allow Satan to gain control of our governments through ungodly leaders!

We cannot allow him to gain control of our school systems!

We cannot allow him to fill our cities with every form of sin, crime, pornography, and destroy people's lives through drugs and alcohol!

We must go forward into battle, in the power and authority of His Name and drive him out and take dominion of the earth.

BE CLOTHED IN A MANTLE OF POWER AND AUTHORITY

To pray in the Name of Jesus means to pray in union with Him, to pray with His mind, His perspective, His motives and with His power and authority. It unites your prayer with His intercession at the right hand of the Father. It is as if you are placing one hand in Christ's hand and touching the needs of the world with your other hand.

"To know fully what it is to pray in His name, we must know Him, too, in His heavenly intercession."
Andrew Murray

In His final hours with His disciples, Christ made them His representatives on earth and commissioned them to go forth in the power and authority of His Name.

They were clothed with a mantle of power and authority in His Name!

Let us look closely at John 16:23. Let these words go deep down into your spirit. Jesus said, *"In that day ye shall ask me nothing. Verily, verily, I say unto you, whatsoever ye shall ask the Father in my name, he will give it you."*

Jesus said, *"In that day..."* Again, I want to emphasize that He was referring to the day when the Holy Spirit would be poured out. Up until that time they had not asked anything in Jesus' Name. Jesus said, *"Hitherto have ye asked nothing in my name..."* (John 16:24). But, He told them, "In that day"...after the Holy Spirit came upon them they would be able to ask...to pray in the power and authority of His Name and receive whatever they asked.

In that day...after He had defeated Satan!

In that day...after He had risen from the grave in great triumph!

In that day...after He had ascended to the Father and offered His blood on the Mercy Seat!

In that day...after He was given all power and authority in heaven, on earth and beneath the earth!

In that day...after He sent the Comforter...the Holy Spirit...the Master Intercessor to live within them!

This is that day!

Christ has commissioned His Body on earth to fulfill His work on earth, heal the sick, cast out devils, make disciples in the nations and bring in a harvest of souls in the power and authority in His Name.

When a person is baptized in the Holy Spirit, he is clothed with a mantle of power and authority in Jesus' Name! And when he prays in His Name, all the power and authority in Heaven backs him!

Just as Jesus fulfilled the will of the Father, in power and authority of the Father's Name, He intends us to fulfill His will in the power and authority of His Name.

Jesus said, *"I have not come on My own authority and of My own accord...I have come in My Father's name"* (John 7:28; 5:43 AMP). When Jesus stretched forth His hand to heal the sick, He knew He was doing it in the power and authority of His Father's Name.

When He spoke to the wind and sea, "Peace, be still"...

When He rebuked the legion of demons and cast them out of the man of Gadara...

When He spoke the word of healing for the Roman Centurion's servant...

When He cried, "Lazarus, come forth," and raised Lazarus from the dead...

He knew He was doing it in the power and authority of His Father's Name.

There was no doubt...not a moment's hesitation...no thought of failure. As He acted in His Father's Name, Almighty God and the host of heaven responded to bring it to pass.

WHAT WE NEED IS A DEMONSTRATION OF THE POWER OF JESUS' NAME

Peter was there among the disciples in the upper room when Jesus taught them this powerful dimension of prayer. We see him after the Holy Spirit came upon him, ministering under the mantle of power and authority in Jesus' Name.

When Peter saw the lame man sitting at the gate near the Temple begging alms, he did not wonder whether or not it was God's will to heal him. There was no hesitation...no doubt. He had a revelation of the power and authority that was in Jesus' Name.

"Prayer in the name of Jesus Christ prevails with God. No other prayer does. There is no other approach to God for any man or woman except through Jesus Christ."
R. A. Torrey

He remembered the words Jesus had spoken that night in the upper room, *"And whatsoever ye shall ask in my name, that will I do, that the Father may be glorified in the Son"* (John 14:13). He remembered that Jesus said they would do even greater works than He had done, in His Name.

Peter knew that as he spoke in the Name of Jesus, he was putting into operation the power that was in Jesus' Name to manifest the healing. He seized the man by the right hand and raised him to his feet saying, *"I do not possess silver and gold, but what I do have I give to you: In the name of Jesus Christ the Nazarene – walk!"* (Acts 3:6 NAS)

Immediately, the man's feet and ankles were strengthened and he began to walk and leap and praise God.

When the people saw and realized what had happened, they ran together and crowded around Peter and John. They had seen Jesus perform many miracles such as this, but they had watched Jesus die on the cross. They were amazed and wondered how these ordinary men would be able to heal the sick.

Peter did not hesitate to tell them that it was faith in Jesus' Name that the man was healed. He told them:

> *The God of Abraham, Isaac, and Jacob, the God of our fathers, has glorified His servant Jesus...And on the basis of faith in His name, it is the name of Jesus which has strengthened this man whom you see and know.*
>
> Acts 3:13, 16 NAS

The following day the rulers, elders and teachers of the law brought Peter and John before them, along with the man who had been healed. They asked, *"...By what power, or in what name, have you done this?"* (Acts 4:7 NAS)

Peter again boldly declared, "the power is in Jesus' Name!" He said:

> *...Let it be known and understood by all of you, and by the whole house of Israel, that in the name and through the power and authority of Jesus Christ of Nazareth, Whom you crucified, [but] whom God raised from the dead, in Him and by means of Him this man is standing here before you well and sound in body*
>
> Acts 4:10 AMP

Miracles in the early Church were normal occurrences. The power wasn't in Peter or the other disciples. They were there manifesting Jesus' Name to the world. As they spoke, healing and casting out demons in the power and authority of Jesus' Name, Jesus was there in the midst of them working with them and setting the people free from Satan's hands (see Mark 16:20).

In the power of Jesus' Name they took dominion and established the Kingdom of God wherever they went. Multitudes of men and women were added to the number of believers daily.

This is a true picture of the Church as God intended it to be. They were not on the defensive. They were not fearful...they were the militant Church. They did not compromise the Word to gain favor with the people, they preached Jesus and *demonstrated* the power of His Name. Today, we have a lot of preaching and teaching, but very little demonstration of power in Jesus' Name.

IT'S GRADUATION TIME!

If we are going to reach this world and bring in a harvest of souls before Christ returns, we must go beyond basic training concerning prayer! It's graduation time!

Christ intends for us to be clothed with a mantle of power and authority that is ours in Jesus' Name. He has given us the legal right – a Power of Attorney to use His Name.

A Power of Attorney is a legal instrument authorizing one to act as the attorney or agent of the grantor. A Power of Attorney legally appoints an individual to act in another's name and place. It gives the individual who has been appointed full power and authority over all personal property and interests belonging to the one granting the Power of Attorney. It authorizes the individual named to act on another person's behalf, as they might or could do if they were personally present.

A Power of Attorney gives an individual the power and authority to take whatever action is required or necessary in maintaining all the personal property and interests of the one granting the Power of Attorney. They are given the power and authority to determine, at their discretion, the purpose and manner in which they will exercise the power, which has been delegated to them.

When we pray in Jesus' Name we are activating our Power of Attorney to act as a representative of Christ on His behalf, in the same manner as He would act if He were actually present here on earth.

Christ is calling the Church today into a higher dimension of prayer greater than what we have ever experienced. He has given us His Name that enables us to take hold of all that we need to push back the powers of darkness in our cities and set the captives free.

As we come together in corporate prayer meetings and unite in prayer, in His Name, His Presence and power is manifested in our midst. Jesus said:

> *Again I say unto you, that if two of you shall agree on earth as touching any thing that they shall ask, it shall be done for them of my Father which is in heaven. For where two or three are gathered together in my name, there am I in the midst of them.*
>
> Matthew 18:19-20

The power to receive whatever we need is in His mighty Name! As we unite in a prayer of agreement and pray in the power and authority of His Name, absolutely nothing is impossible to us.

"Heaven's authority backs any prayer that you truly pray in Jesus' name – not because you use those words, but because you and the prayer are truly in His name."
Wesley L. Duewel

The time has come when we must begin to take hold of the power and authority in that all-powerful Name, that is above every other name, to take dominion and establish the Kingdom of God everywhere we go. We must no longer rely on our own natural abilities, but go forth in our cities and nations, in the Name of Jesus, to proclaim the Gospel in a demonstration of His power.

One of the greatest warfare prayers recorded is the prayer of King Asa. As King Asa and the people of Judah prepared to go out into battle against Zerah the Ethiopian and an army of one million, he prayed:

> *Lord, it is nothing with thee to help, whether with many, or with them that have no power: help us, O Lord our God; for we rest on thee, and in thy name we go against this multitude. O Lord, thou art our God; let not man prevail against thee.*
>
> 2 Chronicles 14:11

King Asa's confidence, as they faced the great army of one million strong, was in the fact they were going into battle in the Name of Almighty God. He said, "in thy name we go against this multitude." As he prayed, God's supernatural power was released. God fought for them, "*So the Lord smote the Ethiopians before Asa, and before Judah...*" (2 Chronicles 14:12). Their enemies were destroyed and they carried away great riches as the spoils of war.

The key to this great victory is that they faced the enemy in the Name of the One true and living God, not in their own natural strength. And, in His Name, there was no possible margin for defeat!

NO MARGIN FOR DEFEAT!

Christ has defeated Satan and has given us the ultimate advantage over him – His all-powerful, indestructible, unchangeable Name. There is absolutely no margin for defeat! When we pray or act in the power and authority of His Name, all of Heaven is backing us and we cannot fail!

You may be struggling under a heavy financial burden.

Your husband or wife may be unsaved.

Your marriage relationship may be deteriorating.

You may have unsaved loved ones, friends or family members hooked on drugs or alcohol.

Whatever the circumstance or problem you face, release your faith and begin to pray in the power and authority of Jesus' Name. Take authority over Satan and his evil principalities and command them to take their hands off your body, off your family and finances. Use the Name of Jesus as a weapon in prayer to bind the demonic forces attacking you, knowing that at the Name of Jesus, they must stop!

Remember, Jesus has appointed you as His legal representative to act in His place and on His behalf. When you pray in the power and authority of His Name, you are praying according to His will, His purposes, His desires and at His direction.

Sickness and disease are the work of the enemy. You do not need to pray to determine whether it is God's will to heal your body, your loved ones or other people in need of healing. Jesus paid the price. The war has been won. He has destroyed the power of sickness and has authorized you to go and heal the sick in the power and authority of His Name.

Exercise your Power of Attorney! Remember, that all Christ is and all His power is in His Name!

It's graduation time!

Christ does not want you to stay at the same level in your prayer life. It is time to move to a new level of praying in the power and authority of His Name!

You may not be called as a pastor, evangelist or missionary, but you are called and chosen by God as a minister in your home and community.

Seize every opportunity to proclaim and manifest the power that is in Jesus' Name in your prayers, through the prayer command of faith and acting in the power and authority of His Name to heal the sick and set the captives free!

"The power to do greater works than Christ did lies in the faith that can grasp His name truly and true praying." E. M. Bounds

There is no other name under heaven given among men, whereby men can be saved!

There is no greater Name!

Ask the Father to take you beyond head knowledge, to give you a fresh revelation and to clothe you with a mantle of power and authority in His Name.

Then, speak His Name!

Pray in His Name!

Proclaim His Name!

Work the works of God in His Name!

Fulfill the will of God in your city and nation in His Name!

Jesus taught a powerful dynamic of the Spirit that will enable you to press through every obstacle to obtain the answers you need in prayer. There are many Christians who have resigned themselves to defeat and are living with unanswered prayer because they have not learned this great truth.

In chapter twelve you will learn about this dynamic of the Spirit and how to put it into practice in your prayer life to receive more answers to prayer than you have ever experienced.

Lord, teach us to pray!

Lord, thank You for the awesome price You paid to obtain the Name that is above every Name. We exalt and glorify Your Name. We proclaim that Your Name is above every name in Heaven above, on this earth and under the earth! Lord, teach us by the Holy Spirit how to pray, live, act, walk, speak and do everything in the power and authority of Your Name. Lord, You have promised that whatever we ask in Your Name You will do it. Open our understanding to be able to take hold of this unlimited promise and to act on it to pray as You would pray, do the same mighty works You did, and even greater works as You promised. Clothe us in a mantle of power and authority in Your Name, and use us to demonstrate the power of Your Name in the nations.

CHAPTER TWELVE

HOLY WRESTLING

How do you deal with unanswered prayer?

When you have prayed and fasted for something that you believe lines up with God's will and still do not receive the answer, how do you react?

Do you become discouraged and weary?

Do you begin to wonder if God really hears you or doubt whether He is concerned about meeting your need?

Does your faith in God's promises begin to waver?

In your holy pursuit of learning how to pray in the powerful dimension of prayer that Jesus taught and demonstrated, you must learn how to overcome the obstacle of unanswered prayer.

It is not God's will for you to live with one unanswered prayer! Unanswered prayer does not bring honor and glory to God!

God is raising up a people today who will build a living memorial to Him through *answered prayer!*

Jesus taught and demonstrated a level of prayer that was 100 percent on target. There was absolutely no margin for failure. Unanswered prayer was not even a concept or consideration. Jesus prayed and the Father answered every time. When He prayed before raising Lazarus from the dead, He said, *"Father, I thank thee that thou hast heard me. And I knew that thou hearest me always..."* (John 11:41-42).

Jesus lived in a dimension where the Father always heard and always answered prayer; no exceptions!

We serve a mighty God Who is unlimited, all-powerful, omnipresent and all-knowing, Who has bound Himself to His Word to answer prayer. He has promised, *"Call unto me, and I will answer thee, and show thee great and mighty things, which thou knowest not"* (Jeremiah 33:3).

There is absolutely nothing impossible with God. He has said, *"Behold, I am the LORD, the God of all flesh: is there anything too hard for me?"* (Jeremiah 32:27). Jesus said, *"...but with God all things are possible"* (Matthew 19:26).

We serve a God who has promised, *"...before they call, I will answer; and while they are yet speaking, I will hear"* (Isaiah 65:24).

Our Father has placed all of heaven's resources at our disposal and we are promised that if we ask, we will receive. Jesus said, *"And all things, whatsoever ye shall ask in prayer, believing, ye shall receive"* (Matthew 21:22). God's universal law concerning prayer is:...every one who asks receives. (see Matthew 7:8).

Knowing that God is faithful and has made full provision for you to receive answers to your prayers, what is your response when you do not receive an answer that you expected?

A SPIRITUAL DYNAMIC TO OVERCOME UNANSWERED PRAYER

There are many Christians who have resigned themselves to defeat and are living with unanswered prayer. There are various hindrances in receiving answers to prayer: lack of faith, asking with wrong motives, unconfessed sin, disobedience and unforgiveness.

However, I want to concentrate on one of the greatest reasons behind unanswered prayer: spiritual laziness!

Often when people have prayed for something for an extended period of time and they don't receive it, they give up with the excuse, "It must not have been God's will." Whenever we know that we pray in accordance with God's will we will receive. *"And this is the confidence that we have in him, that, if we ask any thing according to his will, he heareth us: And if we know that he hear us, whatsoever we ask, we know that we have the petitions that we desired of him"* (1 John 5:14,15).

This is one of the conditions of receiving answers to prayer. However, many people waver in their faith when they pray, because they are not convinced what they are asking is according to God's will. They give up, stop praying and, as a result, fail to receive what God has provided for them.

There are Christians who have failed to receive their healing, financial provision, or other things they need that are clearly revealed as being in accordance with God's will, because they have given up. There are those who have given up on their marriages, given up on their rebellious children, given up on their unsaved loved ones and have forfeited God's provision and the answers to their prayers, because they have failed to persevere in faith and stopped praying!

Are there problems or circumstances in which you have given up and have stopped praying?

Jesus taught a powerful dynamic of the Spirit we need in our lives to help us overcome every obstacle and receive the answers to our prayers.

PERSEVERANCE!

"Also [JESUS] told them a parable, to the effect that they ought always to pray and not to turn coward (faint, lose heart and give up)" (Luke 18:1 AMP).

Jesus said we are to pray and not faint!

When we pray, we are to pray with such a holy boldness that we will not give up until we receive the answer. If we do not receive the answer the first time we pray, we should go back the second time. If we do not receive the answer the third, fourth or even the hundredth time, we are to persevere in faith until we receive it.

The Father desires us to draw near to Him with a strong persistence and determination that will not give up by any seeming refusal or delay on His part.

There are some people who believe that a person should not pray for the same thing a second time. They feel it shows a lack of faith. It is true that Jesus taught that when we pray, we are to believe we have received what we have asked. He said, *"...What things soever ye desire, when ye pray, believe that ye receive them, and ye shall have them"* (Mark 11:24).

But, it is not a lack of faith to keep on asking until we receive the answer! As we look closely at Jesus' teaching we see that without question, there are also times when we must pray again and again before we get our answer.

SHAMELESS PERSEVERANCE

"The blessings that the world needs must be called down from heaven in persevering, importunate, believing prayer."
Andrew Murray

To receive from God you must be willing to persevere in faith!

Jesus said we are to pray and not faint, or give up!

After the disciples approached Jesus with their request, "Lord, teach us to pray..." Jesus taught them this parable:

> *...Which of you shall have a friend, and shall go unto him at midnight, and say unto him, Friend, lend me three loaves. For a friend of mine in his journey is come to me, and I have nothing to set before him? And he from within shall answer and say, Trouble me not: the door is now shut, and my children are with me in bed; I cannot rise and give thee. I say unto you, Though he will not rise and give him, because he is his friend, yet because of his importunity he will rise and give him as many as he needeth.*
>
> Luke 11:5-8

The word "importunity" in verse eight is very important. It basically means "shamelessness". It refers to the persistent determination in prayer that will not be put to shame by any apparent refusal or delay on God's part.

Look at verse eight in the Amplified Version, *"I tell you, although he will not get up and supply him anything because he is his friend, yet because of his shameless persistence and insistence, he will get up and give him as much as he needs"* (Luke 11:8 AMP).

Notice that Jesus taught this parable and persistence in prayer after the request of the disciples, "Lord, teach us to pray." After giving them the example of how to pray, which we refer to as The Lord's Prayer, Jesus then taught this parable.

In this parable the man went to his friend's house with great confidence and expectancy. He fully believed when he presented his need, that his friend would help him out and give him what he needed.

His plea was urgent! He could not go back home empty-handed. But his urgent request was met by flat denial! He was shocked and no doubt surprised at his friend's response. He had never expected denial from his good friend.

Instead of turning around and going back home without the three loaves of bread he needed, he continued to persevere and press his demand until the door was opened and his need was met. The man was totally shameless in his persistence.

I can imagine the man saying: "What do you mean you can't get up and help me! I'm desperate! I don't have anyone else to turn to for help. You've got to help me out. I'm not going to leave until you get up and help me. I'm going to stay here all night if that is what it takes!"

HOLY WRESTLERS

In this illustration Jesus stressed that although the man would not get up and help his friend on the basis of their friendship, because of his friend's importunity...his shameless persistence that refused to give up...he would get up and give him whatever he needed.

Jesus' teaching is very clear. When we do not immediately receive an answer to our prayers, or we face a prolonged delay, we must not allow ourselves to become weary or spiritually lazy and give up. With this same persistence we are to continue to come before God and press our petitions with increased intensity and faith until we receive the answer.

This type of persistent prayer never faints or grows weary. It is motivated and sustained by a faith that will not let go.

"Wrestling in prayer is not an impulse of energy, not a mere earnestness of soul; it is an inwrought force, a faculty implanted and aroused by the Holy Spirit. Virtually, it is the intercession of the Spirit of God in us."
E. M. Bounds

I like to think of this type of prayer as holy wrestling. It is the ability to hold on, press on and wait in faith until the answer is manifested. It is a taking hold of God Himself.

Jacob is one of God's holy wrestlers. He wrestled in prayer all night and prevailed with God. He refused to let go. At the breaking of day, when the angel of the Lord told Jacob to let him go, Jacob said, *"I will not let thee go, except thou bless me"* (Genesis 32:26). The angel blessed him then and there!

Elijah was a holy wrestler. He prayed seven times in succession before he prevailed and God opened the heavens and sent rain after three and a half years of famine and drought.

After he prophesied to King Ahab that it was going to rain, Elijah went up to the top of Mt. Carmel.

> *...and he cast himself down upon the earth, and put his face between his knees. And said to his servant, Go up now, look toward the sea. And he went up, and looked, and said, There is nothing. And he said, Go again seven times. And it came to pass at the seventh time, that he said, Behold, there ariseth a little cloud out of the sea, like a man's hand.*

1 Kings 18:42-44

Elijah did not know how long it was going to take. He continued to wrestle, to persevere in faith, knowing God would send rain in answer to his prayer.

Daniel was one of God's holy wrestlers. He prayed and fasted 21 days before the answer came. His prayer was heard the very first day. But, Daniel didn't know that. Did he stop praying? No! He persevered in faith. On the fifteenth day he didn't say, "I've been fasting and praying fifteen days now and God hasn't responded. I might as well stop praying." No! Daniel believed God was going to hear and answer his prayer. He didn't know how long it was going to take, but was determined to persevere until he received the answer.

After 21 days an angel arrived with the answer. The angel told Daniel that after the very first day his prayer was heard, but that he had been wrestling with a demonic principality for 21 days until Michael, the Archangel, came to help him.

Have you ever wondered what would have happened if Daniel had stopped praying on the twentieth day?

One thing is certain; he would have missed the answer God desired to give him.

PRAYER THAT REFUSES TO GIVE UP!

Immediately after Jesus told this parable of the man who went to his friend's house at midnight for three loaves of bread, He again stressed the importance of persistence in prayer. He said, "*Ask and keep on asking, and it shall be given you; seek and keep on seeking, and you shall find; knock and keep on knocking, and the door shall be opened to you*" (Luke 11:9 AMP).

The words "ask", "seek" and "knock" are progressive and indicate a continuing advance in prayer. We must pray with an intensity that doesn't weaken with time but increases in urgency until we receive the answer.

When we have asked and prayed fervently for an answer and have not yet received it, we are to seek...to increase our fervency and intensity in prayer. After we have cried out to God and sought Him with even greater passion, from the depths of our beings, and still do not receive the answer, we are to rise up in the Spirit to another level in prayer and knock. With even greater passion and intensity we are to keep knocking...keep pressing...keep wrestling...keep persevering in prayer until we receive.

Blind Bartimaeus is a man who persevered in prayer. One day as he sat by the road begging, he heard the sound of a multitude walking down the road. When he heard that Jesus was passing by, he shouted out with a loud voice, "...*Jesus, thou Son of David, have mercy on me*" (Mark 10:47). But, Jesus kept on walking. He did not respond. It seemed as if He had not heard Bartimaeus. The people around Bartimaeus tried to shut him up.

He had reached a point of desperation! He had no other place to turn. He didn't care about what people might say or do to him. He shouted louder, with even greater intensity, "...*Thou son of David, have mercy on me*" (Mark 10:48). This is prayer that has advanced beyond the "asking" stage. It is prayer that refuses to give up.

Bartimaeus' persistency captured Jesus' attention. When He heard Bartimaeus' cry of faith, He stopped walking and told those around Him to call Bartimaeus to come to Him.

As soon as Bartimaeus heard that Jesus was calling for him, he threw off his outer garment and came to Jesus. Jesus asked Bartimaeus what he wanted Him to do for him.

Jesus already knew what Bartimaeus needed. It was evident Bartimaeus was blind but Jesus wanted him to keep pressing through in his faith. Bartimaeus told Jesus, "*I want to receive my sight.*" Bartimaeus knew that Jesus would heal him. This is prayer that goes beyond the "seeking" stage. Jesus responded to his desperate cry of faith, *"Go thy way, thy faith hath made thee whole"* (Mark 10:52). Immediately, Bartimaeus' eyes were healed!

Bartimaeus' persistence prevailed over all the opposition he faced and as a result received his eyesight. If he had only half-heartedly cried out and had listened to the surrounding crowd, he would have died a blind beggar. But, he refused to give up and persevered in faith until he received what he needed.

This type of wrestling or persistence in prayer is not just based upon natural determination or persistence. When we wrestle in prayer we are not trying to overcome the Father's reluctance to answer our prayer. We are coming before a loving Father who takes great joy in answering our prayers and pouring good things into our lives. Jesus said, *"...how much more shall your Father which is in heaven give good things to them that ask him?"* (Matthew 7:11). He said, *"...it is your Father's good pleasure to give you the kingdom"* (Luke 12:32).

Wrestling in prayer is persevering in the Spirit, in faith knowing that what the Father has promised He will do. And this is the type of faith that God delights in.

Wrestling in persistent prayer is not fleshly energy or just an earnestness of soul, it is a spiritual energy that the Holy Spirit releases within you that enables you to persevere and continue to press through in faith until your prayer is answered.

PERSEVERING PRAYER THAT BREAKS THROUGH ALL RESISTANCE!

"It is not enough to begin to pray, nor to pray aright; nor is it enough to continue for a time to pray; but we must patiently, believing, continue in prayer until we obtain an answer."
George Mueller

In Jesus' parable of the unjust judge and the widow, He stressed again the need for a shameless persistence in prayer that refuses to give up.

Jesus used a widow to emphasize a deep level of need. A widow during that time often had no family or other resources they could depend upon. I imagine the widow in this story had, no doubt, reached rock bottom. With no one to turn to for help, she went to the unjust judge and pleaded her case saying, *"...Avenge me of mine adversary"* (Luke 18:3).

The widow's cries fell on deaf ears. The unjust judge refused to do anything to help her for a period of time, *"And he would not for a while..."* (Luke 18:4) We do not know how much time passed. But the widow did not give up! She kept persevering with a shameless persistence and determination not to stop until the unjust judge did something to help her.

The unjust judge, seeing that she was not going to give up and go away, said to himself, *"...Even though I don't fear God or care about men, yet because this widow keeps bothering me, I will see that she gets justice, so that she won't eventually wear me out with her coming"* (Luke 18:4 NIV).

The widow pressed her way through and broke through all resistance by her perseverance.

Jesus, in this parable, is not teaching us that God is like the unjust judge. He is teaching us to be like the widow – to continue to persevere in prayer until we have the answer. The widow had no other alternative. When we pray, we need to come to God with total dependence upon Him knowing He has bound Himself by His Word to answer our prayers. And, we must pray with this same persistence until the answer comes.

Jesus explained the parable by saying:

> *...Listen to what the unjust judge says. And will not God bring about justice for his chosen ones, who cry out to him day and night? Will he keep putting them off? I tell you, he will see that they get justice, and quickly.*
>
> Luke 18:6-7 NIV

If the unjust judge responded to the persistent cries of the widow, whom he didn't know, how much more will God respond to his "chosen ones," His beloved children, who persistently cry out to Him! God sees our faith that continues to persevere regardless of the obstacles, and honors it by granting our requests.

DESPERATE PRAYERS!

"Persistent prayer is not an accident, but the main thing, not a performance, but a passion, not a need, but a necessity."
E. M. Bounds

The Syrophenician woman is a tremendous example of what it means to persevere in prayer. She was desperate! Her daughter was at home, demon-possessed. When she heard Jesus was on the coasts of Tyre and Sidon, she came to the house where He was staying and cried out with a loud voice, *"...Have mercy on me, O Lord, thou Son of David: my daughter is grievously vexed with a devil"* (Matthew 15:22).

Her desperate cry was met with silence. *"But he answered her not a word..."* (Matthew 15:23). This apparent refusal would have been enough to discourage most Christians today. She could have walked away discouraged and defeated, thinking Jesus wasn't really concerned about her or her daughter's condition.

But, she could not bear the thought of her daughter being demon-possessed the rest of her life. She had, no doubt, heard that Jesus had opened blind eyes, healed the sick and cast out demons. He was her only hope of ever seeing her daughter set free from the demon tormenting her.

The woman continued to cry out with a loud voice and with such shameless persistence, the disciples came to Jesus and begged Him to send her away. She didn't care what the disciples or other people thought about her. She didn't care if they thought she was making a spectacle of herself. She continued to cry out.

The woman was a Gentile and Jesus told His disciples that He had been sent to the *"…lost sheep of the house of Israel"* (Matthew 15:24). But, this did not stop the woman. She pushed her way through the disciples, came and fell at Jesus' feet and worshipped Him. She again cried out in desperation, *"Lord, help me!"* (Matthew 15:25).

Jesus looked at her and said, *"…It is not right to take the children's bread and toss it to their dogs"* (Matthew 15:26 NIV).

Again this woman faced what seemed to be total rejection. At this point, most people would have given up all hope and walked away! But, this Syrophenician woman didn't!

She was desperate!

Instead of throwing her hands up in despair and going back home to her demon-possessed daughter, she refused to go away! She refused to give up! She was determined not to leave without receiving the answer and continued to persevere in faith.

She said to Jesus, *"Yes, Lord; but even the dogs eat the crumbs that fall from their masters' table"* (Matthew 15:27 NIV).

She would not take "no" for an answer! She knew she was not part of the House of Israel, but she believed that the power and blessings of God were so great; there was enough for her as a Gentile to receive the miracle she needed for her daughter.

Jesus looked at her strong, persistent faith – the type that will not give up but continues to persevere in spite of the circumstances and said, *"…O woman, great is your faith! Be it done for you as you wish"* (Matthew 15:28 AMP).

The woman overcame every obstacle she faced and took possession of what she needed and desired because of her persistent faith. Her daughter was delivered and set free that very hour! She went home rejoicing, believing and expecting to see her daughter totally healed and set free.

EFFECTUAL, FERVENT PRAYER

"Prayer in its highest form and grandest success
assumes the attitude of a wrestler with God.
It is the contest, trial, and victory of faith."
E. M. Bounds

This wrestling – persevering in faith will enable you to overcome every obstacle you face in getting your prayers answered. It is not ordinary prayer. It is prayer that is fervent – full of passion and the fire of the Spirit.

It is the "...*effectual fervent prayer of a righteous man availeth much*" (James 5:16). The word "effectual" means to be able to produce a desired effect.

Do you need healing for your body or a loved one?

Do you need God to answer a family problem?

Do you want to see your city and nation transformed by God's power?

To receive the answers you need you must pray effectual prayers that produce results. There must be a spiritual fervency in your prayers that will enable you to persevere in faith regardless of how long you must wait for the answer.

The word "fervent" means "very hot". It is marked by heat. It is marked by deep, sincere emotion. If you are going to pray to get a desired result, you must pray with a hot heart – with incredible emotion and a deep, sincere desire.

Fervency is located in the heart, not in the brain. Fervent prayer goes beyond head knowledge. It is not an expression of the intellect. The Holy Spirit comes as a fire to dwell within us. We are to be baptized with the Holy Ghost and with fire (see Luke 3:16).

Adoniram Judson had a revelation concerning the power of fervent prayer. He said:

A travailing spirit, the throes of a great burdened desire, belongs to prayer. A fervency strong enough to drive away sleep, which devotes and inflames the spirit, and which retires all earthly ties, all this belongs to wrestling, and prevailing prayer. The Spirit, the power, the air, and food of prayer is in such a spirit.

God has used holy wrestlers in prayer such as Martin Luther, John Knox, Charles Wesley, Jonathan Edwards, Charles Finney and praying John Hyde to help usher in a mighty move of God through their prevailing prayer. They refused to give up! They refused to stop praying! They persevered in intense, fervent, passionate prayer until the answer came.

God greatly used David Brainerd to bring a mighty revival among the North American Indians, as they had never before experienced. He worked among the Indians in the forests of Northern Pennsylvania.

Sometimes on a winter night Brainerd would go out into the forest and kneel in the cold snow when it was a foot deep. He would wrestle in prayer with such fervency that he would be wringing wet with perspiration even out in the cold winter night hours.

Father Nash and Abel Clary, who worked closely with Charles Finney, were holy wrestlers. They would slip quietly into town and find two or three people to enter into a covenant of prayer with them.

On one occasion, when they went into a city where Finney was going to have a meeting, they rented a dark cellar in a woman's house where they could shut themselves in to pray. There they wrestled and battled the forces of darkness and travailed for souls.

When Finney got into town, the lady who rented Father Nash and Abel Clary the room came to him expressing concern for the two men. She told Finnee, "Brother Finney, do you know a Father Nash? He and two other men have been at my boarding house for the last three days, but they haven't eaten a bite of food.

'I opened the door and peeped in at them, because I could hear them groaning and I saw them down on their faces. They have been this way for three days, lying prostrate on the floor and groaning. I thought something awful must have happened to them. I was afraid to go in and I didn't know what to do. Would you please come see about them?"

Finney replied, "No, it isn't necessary. They just have a spirit of travail in prayer."

Charles Finney said that the keys that unlocked the heavens and brought great revival was the prayers of Father Nash and those who agonized and travailed before God's Throne.

This type of fervency, travail and wrestling in prayer is not an energy a person works up in the flesh. It is born of the Spirit of the living God. *"Likewise the Spirit also helpeth our infirmities: for we know not what we should pray for as we ought: but the Spirit itself maketh intercession for us with groanings which cannot be uttered"* (Romans 8:26).

The fervency and earnestness God is looking for is not something we work up, it is the fervency and travail the Holy Spirit creates in us!

"Wrestling in prayer refuses to be denied.
It is a holy boldness that dares to remind God of His
divine responsibilities, dares to quote to God His
unbreakable promises, and ventures to hold God
accountable to His Holy Word."
Wesley L. Duewel

This is a level of prayer where we come into such unity with the Holy Spirit in prayer; the Spirit takes over and begins to intercede with groanings and intensity that is beyond our natural capacity.

CHRIST WON FOR US
THE ANSWER TO EVERY PRAYER

The greatest example of the fervency of agonizing, travailing prayer is Christ's prayer in the Garden of Gethsemane. This is undoubtedly the greatest prayer ever prayed.

"Wrestling in prayer enlists all the powers of your soul. You reach beyond the visible to the very throne of God. With all your strength and tenacity, you lay hold of God's grace and power." Wesley L. Duewel

The fate of mankind hung in the balance!

No man ever agonized in prayer as Christ, the Son of God, did in the Garden of Gethsemane.

Earlier during His High Priestly prayer He had lifted up His eyes to heaven and said, *"...Father, the hour is come; glorify thy Son, that thy Son also may glorify thee"* (John 17:1).

In that glorious, majestic prayer, He laid out His petitions and interceded on behalf of His disciples and for you and me.

He said, *"Neither pray I for these alone, but for them also which shall believe on me through their word"* (John 17:20). (In chapter thirteen I will take you into the depths of this prayer).

What a contrast to His agonizing prayer in the Garden of Gethsemane where He fell to the ground and cried out, *"...Abba, Father, all things are possible unto thee: take away this cup from me: nevertheless not what I will, but what thou wilt"* (Mark 14:36).

It was a cry that came from the depths of His Being. The word, "Abba" is only used three times in the Bible. And, this is the only record we have of Jesus ever using it in prayer to His Father. It is an Aramaic word denoting deep intimacy and the term used for father or "Daddy". It was a word the Jews did not use to address God because they thought it was disrespectful.

In His hour of greatest agony Jesus used this intimate term of endearment to cry out to His Father.

It was an hour of unspeakable sorrow and He had taken the inner circle of those closest to Him, Peter, James and John, to be with Him.

His agony was overwhelming. He *"... began to be sore amazed and to be very heavy"* (Mark 14:33). The Greek word for "sore amazed" does not mean that He was astonished and surprised, but it suggests that His amazement went to an extremity of horror, that makes a man's hair stand on end and his flesh to tremble. It means to be amazed to the point of almost immobility.

Jesus was overcome with sorrow. He told Peter, James and John, *"...My soul is exceeding sorrowful unto death: tarry ye here, and watch"* (Mark 14:34). It was as if He was swallowed up in an ocean of sorrow. There was no source of consolation. His Spirit cried out beneath the crushing weight of the unspeakable load He carried.

There in the Garden, while His disciples slept, Jesus agonized in prayer. He prayed fervent, emotional prayers from the depths of His Spirit. Lying on His face on the ground He wept, groaned and travailed in deep agony. *"Who in the days of his flesh, when he had offered up prayers and supplications with strong crying and tears unto him that was able to save him from death, and was heard in that He feared"* (Hebrews 5:7).

As He poured out His soul, it was as if His Father's face was hidden. Alone He must drink the bitter cup of the wrath of God. There in the Garden He took the sin of the world upon Himself and became sin for us. He bore the penalty of sin in His own body. And the Father had to turn His face from Him.

See Christ there in the Garden. Beneath Him on the ground is the crimson red of the mixture of His blood with His tears. He agonized and travailed in prayer until His sweat became drops of blood. *"And being in an agony he prayed more earnestly: and his sweat was as it were great drops of blood falling down to the ground"* (Luke 22:44).

The reason for the depth of His agony was more than the dread of excruciating pain and physical suffering. He would soon have to endure the cross. He chose Gethsemane. He willingly came to earth and took upon Himself flesh and blood knowing He would suffer and die to redeem man from sin.

Three times He cried out, if possible, the bitter cup of God's wrath be removed from Him. And, three times He prayed, "Nevertheless, not My will but Yours be done" (see Luke 22:42).

The sorrow and agony He felt was because it was necessary for Him to drink the bitter cup, not from Judas, not from the Jews, but from His own Father's hand. As God, He was perfectly holy. And as man, He was holy and undefiled, and without sin. Yet, He had to bear sin and be made a sin offering.

Isaiah prophesied, *"Yet it pleased the Lord to bruise him: he hath put him to grief: when thou shalt make his soul an offering for sin…"* (Isaiah 53:10). *"…The Lord hath laid on him the iniquity of us all"* (Isaiah 53:6). *"He shall see of the travail of his soul, and shall be satisfied: by his knowledge shall my righteous servant justify many; for he shall bear their iniquities"* (Isaiah 53:11).

Jesus was about to "taste death for every man" (see Hebrews 2:9). He was going to bear the curse and suffer the wages of sin for every man. He wasn't afraid to die. Jesus was in agony because He knew His Father could not look upon sin and would have to turn away from Him for a moment. He didn't want to break His fellowship with the Father.

As Jesus agonized in prayer, an angel was sent to strengthen and prepare Him for what He was to endure on the cross. The battle for mankind was won there in the Garden of Gethsemane as He agonized and wrestled in prayer.

Through His strong crying and tears He became obedient unto death – the death of the cross. He secured His position as our Great High Priest. He was highly exalted and given all power and dominion. He secured the right to be able to say to us *"…whatsoever ye shall ask in my name, that will I do, that the Father may be glorified in the Son"* (John 14:13).

Jesus prayed, *"Not as I will"*, so that He could say to us, *"If ye abide in me, and my words abide in you, ye shall ask what ye will, and it shall be done unto you"* (John 15:7).

His victory that day won for us the answer to every prayer as long as we abide in Him!

REFUSE TO SETTLE
FOR UNANSWERED PRAYER!

Knowing that Christ won this great victory and has secured the answer for every prayer we pray, we must never settle for unanswered prayer!

Knowing the price that Christ paid, we must rise up to a new level of prayer where the Holy Spirit takes us beyond our natural capabilities and begins to pray fervent, effectual, hot-hearted prayers that produce results!

I am persuaded that God is going to take a group of intercessors past head knowledge. He is going to take them into an experience where they will know intercession on levels unknown and unheard of that will change the circumstances of lives, nations and governments.

I am convinced beyond a shadow of a doubt that we have come to the place where something supernatural is going to be manifested when we pray.

Are you ready for God to take you beyond your spiritual capacity where He begins to pray through you?

"Here is where the real need for persevering and importunate prayer comes in. It will not rest, go away, or give up, until it knows it is heard and believes it has received."
Andrew Murray

How does the Spirit of God take over and take us beyond our own spiritual capacity? With fervency! Hot-heartedness! Deep sincere emotion! With groanings! *"…but the Spirit itself maketh intercession for us with groanings which cannot be uttered"* (Romans 8:26).

Jesus prayed in the Holy Spirit with groanings – with travail – with fervency!

If you are not moved with compassion, you cannot pray with groanings, moaning, travail and effectiveness that will bring about the desired results!

If you are not moved by the sick and afflicted; if you are not moved by the sin of the world; if you are not moved by the unsaved, you cannot pray with fervency, groanings and travail.

The Holy Spirit has been given to us to divinely energize and impart divine ability to persevere in faith, to give us a determination to not give up, to travail and pray with groanings and moanings until we overcome every obstacle and receive the answers we need.

"Wrestling prayer is the prayer in which we actually wrestle in the power of the Holy Spirit that wins out with God."
R. A. Torrey

Holy wrestling! This is the type of prayer that moves God's hand and produces results. It is the type of prayer that will enable you to overcome unanswered prayer!

Lord, teach us to pray!

Dear Lord, as we look upon You and Your travail in prayer in the Garden of Gethsemane, we cry out from the depths of our beings, teach us to pray as you prayed! Teach us to travail in the Spirit, to pray fervent, earnest, hot-hearted prayers. Release a prayer anointing upon us that will set our hearts on fire to pray with Your passion for our cities and nations. Take us beyond head knowledge into an experience where we are divinely energized and charged by Your Spirit! Teach us to persevere in prayer with a holy boldness and determination that will not give up until we see a manifestation of Your power and Spirit greater than we have ever experienced, sweep across this earth. We surrender to You and offer ourselves as vessels for Your Spirit to pray through – to travail for the lost and to bring about a harvest of souls in our cities and nations.

CHAPTER THIRTEEN

CHRIST'S SEVEN-FOLD HIGH PRIESTLY PRAYER

"The most tender and touching prayer of the Master contained in John 17 opens up to us His inmost heart. He asked for that upon which His heart was most fully set" (Charles Spurgeon).

The spiritual destiny of the world hung in the balance.

The untold agony, shame and disgrace of the cross were before Him. He had gathered His disciples together to share one final moment with them to prepare and strengthen them for what they would soon face.

He was not fearful. He was not worried. He was not trying to determine an alternate plan that would relieve Him from His suffering death on the cross. There was absolutely no doubt or confusion about what God had called and anointed Him to do. He knew He was returning to the Father and that His disciples were going to face a great onslaught of the enemy.

The prayer He prayed was divinely directed. The words He spoke contained the power for their fulfillment. I believe the moment the Father heard Him, His petition on behalf of His disciples and the Church was granted!

Christ's High Priestly prayer is sacred. It is timeless. It reveals His heartbeat, His undying love for His Church and what He plans to accomplish in our lives.

The same passion that beat in Christ's heart for His Church in His final moments on earth is what His heart yearns for now. And the Holy Spirit is now working within the Church to fulfill and to bring full completion to all that He prayed.

A PRAYER OF SPIRITUAL DESTINY

In this one prayer, the veil is pulled back from our eyes, and Christ takes us into the very Holy of Holies. We are transported into the throne room and are ushered into the sacred presence of Almighty God. There, we are given a glimpse of the intimate communion between the Father and the Son, as Christ prepares to walk the road to Calvary in fulfillment of His Father's will.

"This prayer gives us a glimpse into the wonderful relationship between the Father and the Son and teaches us that all the blessings of heaven come continually through the prayer of Him who is at God's right hand and even prays for us" (Andrew Murray).

In these final moments together, Christ warned His disciples of the persecution they would soon face and also promised to send the Comforter, the third Person of the Trinity, who would remain with them and would guide them into all truth (See John 16:7-15).

He knew the hour had come when He would face Satan and defeat him. He knew and was ready to suffer the untold agony of the cross, die, and on the third day rise from the dead. He also knew that through His death and resurrection, the Father would be glorified.

Although He faced the greatest battle of the ages, when He would suffer pain no other man had ever suffered to fulfill God's plan of redemption, His greatest desire was to glorify the Father.

It was a sacred moment as Christ lifted up His eyes toward heaven and began to talk with the Father. *"...Father, the hour is come; glorify thy Son, that thy Son also may glorify thee"* (John 17:1).

"The prayer words of Jesus are sacred words. It would seem that earth and heaven would uncover head and open ears most wide to catch the words of Christ praying."
E.M. Bounds

A hushed silence fell among the disciples as they focused on every word that came from His lips. What an awesome moment in the history of mankind! In a few moments, He would walk out of the room, where He had spent time alone in intimate fellowship with His disciples, and walk across the Kidron Valley to Gethsemane. In Gethsemane He would be betrayed, forsaken and led away by Roman soldiers to be beaten, mocked, spit upon, tried and sentenced to a cruel death on the Cross.

Christ had finished the work He had been given to do and He asked the Father to restore Him to the glory He had even before the foundation of the world. When Christ came to the earth, He had humbled Himself. Although He was the Son of God, He left His glory in heaven, stripped Himself of His heavenly attributes and took on the form of flesh and blood. Now, as He prepared to return to the Father, He first asked to be restored to His former glory. Christ prayed, *"And now, O Father, glorify thou me with thine own self with the glory which I had with thee before the world was"* (John 17:5).

At this very strategic moment, when the spiritual destiny of all mankind was in His hands, the major focus of Christ's prayer was neither for Himself nor for strength to face the great battle that lay ahead of Him. His prayer was focused on His disciples and the Church.

Although He came to die for the sins of the world and reconcile sinners to the Father, He did not pray for the world. He did not pray for the sinners or the ungodly. He prayed for all those who would believe in Him. He prayed for you and me.

Every word He spoke to the Father on behalf of His disciples and for the Church is significant and pregnant with divine purpose.

This great High Priestly prayer must not be taken lightly. It reveals Christ's heart and His undying love for His Church, for you and me. He told the Father, *"...I pray not for the world, but for them which thou hast given me; for they are thine"* (John 17:9). He said, *"Neither pray I for these alone, but for them also which believe on me through their word"* (John 17:20).

In His final hours upon the earth, Christ prayed for you! Let the full significance of His words go deep into your spirit. In that sacred moment, Christ, your great High Priest, prayed for seven specific things to be fulfilled in your life.

1. DIVINE PROTECTION

Think about Christ, our great High Priest, praying for you in this crucial moment of time. He saw through the corridors of time and knew the battles His Church would face. As your High Priest, He knows your weaknesses. He knows the trial and temptations you face. He knows your infirmities and the pain you bear.

"Christ is today the interceding Sovereign of the universe.
His intercession is not symbolic, but real,
as real as it was when He interceded on earth.
He is on the throne interceding for us and waiting
for us to join Him as intercessors."
Wesley L. Duewel

Jesus knew His disciples would soon face great turmoil and the onslaught of the enemy. He warned them they would be hated, thrown out of the synagogues and face imprisonment and death.

However, He did not ask the Father to remove them out of this dangerous environment or the coming conflict. He asked the Father to keep them through the power of His name.

He said, *"And now I am no more in the world, but these are in the world, and I come to thee. Holy Father, keep through thine own name those whom thou hast given me, that they may be one, as we are"* (John 17:11). *"I pray not that thou shouldest take them out of the world, but that thou shouldest keep them from the evil"* (John 17:15).

There are two different Greek words used in this prayer for the word "keep." The word *tereo* means to preserve and *phylasso* means to guard or protect against external attack. Jesus said, *"While I was with them in the world, I kept them in thy name: those that thou gavest me I have kept, and none of them is lost, but the son of perdition; that the scripture might be fulfilled"* (John 17:12). In essence, Jesus was saying to the Father, I preserved them. I guarded and protected them through the power of Your name. Now that I am leaving, You keep, preserve, guard and protect them by Your name.

YOU ARE PROTECTED BY THE POWER OF HIS NAME!

The name of God Almighty represents all that He is – His power, His grace, His mercy and all His divine attributes. All the power and authority of God Himself resides in His name.

Jesus told the Father, *"I have manifested thy name unto the men which thou gavest me out of the world…"* (John 17:6). *"I made Your Name known to them and revealed Your character and Your very Self, and I will continue to make [You] known…"* (John 17:26 AMP).

God is all-powerful. He is all knowing. He is the mighty Creator. He spoke the universe into existence. There is no greater power in heaven or in earth. This is the power that is behind His name!

In His prayer Christ asked the Father to keep, preserve, guard and protect us from all the powers of the evil one through the unlimited power of His name! Do you realize what this means to you?

In answer to Christ's prayer, you are being kept, preserved, guarded and protected from all evil by the power of Almighty God! Nothing can defeat or destroy you!

Christ did not pray and ask the Father to remove you from difficult circumstances, trials or temptations. He did not ask that you would never have to face the power of the enemy. He did not ask the Father to remove you from the evil, ungodly society in which we live. He placed you where you are and gave you a mission to fulfill.

Regardless of what you may face, there is absolutely nothing that can defeat or destroy you. You can face any fiery attack of Satan: persecution, disaster or personal tragedy, knowing God will keep you. Every trace of doubt or fear will disappear and you will live your life in total confidence when you know that you are being kept by the power of Almighty God.

The Apostle Paul was persecuted, stoned, beaten, shipwrecked and imprisoned. At one point in his life, his closest friends deserted him. But he never wavered in his faith. He had total confidence that God would not only deliver him out of the hand of the enemy, but also would keep, preserve and protect him. Listen to his confession of faith: *"And the Lord shall deliver me from every evil work, and will preserve me unto his heavenly kingdom..."* (2 Timothy 4:18).

Knowing that the Father heard and has answered Christ's prayer, claim this promise by faith. Face every problem, every circumstance, every weakness, every temptation and every attack of the enemy with absolute confidence, knowing He will keep you!

2. SANCTIFICATION

The second thing Christ asked the Father to do for us was to "sanctify" us.

272

Sanctify them through thy truth: thy word is truth. As thou hast sent me into the world, even so have I also sent them into the world. And for their sakes I sanctify myself, that they also might be sanctified through the truth.

John 17:17-19

Think about the eternal significance of this prayer. In the final hours before He was to lay down His life on the cross, Christ lifted His eyes toward heaven and cried out to the Father, "Sanctify them!"

The word "sanctify" means to consecrate or set apart, to dedicate for holy service to God. Jesus said, *"And for their sakes I sanctify myself"* (v. 19). He was sinless, pure and undefiled by sin or the world. *"For such an high priest became us, who is holy, harmless, undefiled, separate from sinners, and made higher than the heavens"* (Hebrews 7:26). His sanctification was that He was setting Himself apart, consecrating and dedicating Himself to fulfill the divine purpose of God by laying down His life as a holy sacrifice for man's sin.

In His intimate intercession with the Father on our behalf, Christ asked Him to sanctify us, to set us apart from the world. Jesus said concerning His disciples, *"They are not of the world, even as I am not of the world"* (John 17:16).

Those who truly belong to Christ and are part of His Church have separated themselves from the world. The Apostle John wrote, *"Love not the world, neither the things that are in the world. If any man love the world, the love of the Father is not in him"* (1 John 2:15).

The call of the Spirit is clear:

"...Come out from among them, and be ye separate, saith the Lord, and touch not the unclean thing; and I will receive you, And will be a Father unto you, and ye shall be my sons and daughters..."

2 Corinthians 6:17, 18

Do not be deceived. Christ is coming for a pure, chaste Bride that is holy and wholly set apart for Him. Christ gave Himself for the Church, *"That he might present it to himself a glorious church, not having spot, or wrinkle, or any such thing; but that it should be holy and without blemish"* (Ephesians 5:27).

IT IS TIME FOR GOD'S PEOPLE TO CRY OUT, "SANCTIFY US!"

Jesus is coming soon! As we prepare ourselves for His coming, we must focus on this important factor of Christ's intercession for us. We must lift our voices and cry out to God, "Sanctify us!" The Word declares, *"Follow...holiness, without which no man shall see the Lord"* (Hebrews 12:14). *"Sanctify yourselves therefore, and be ye holy: for I am the Lord your God"* (Leviticus 20:7).

The Holy Spirit will flow through you and pray through you only in proportion to the extent you allow God to sanctify and cleanse you. God will not release His power to flow through unclean vessels. As long as there is unconfessed sin in your life, you will not be able to pray effectively.

In His prayer, Christ reveals how we are sanctified. He prayed, *"Sanctify them through thy truth: thy word is truth"* (John 17:17). Christ knew we could not attain holiness through our own efforts. It is a supernatural work of the Holy Spirit. That is why He asked the Father to sanctify us through the truth and then said, *"Thy word is truth."*

We are sanctified, set apart from the world, cleansed and made holy through the truth, the Word of God. Christ sanctifies and cleanses us by the *"...washing of the water by the word, that he might present [us] to himself a glorious church, not having spot, or wrinkle"* (Ephesians 5:26, 27).

Knowledge of the Word is not enough. You can know the truth of the Word, but it will not change you until it is applied to your life. We are sanctified as we know the truth of the Word, submit ourselves to

274

the Holy Spirit and walk in obedience to it! This can only be accomplished through the power of the Holy Spirit working within us.

3. CHRIST'S JOY IN FULL MEASURE!

The third thing Jesus prayed was that His joy would be fulfilled in our lives. Jesus told the Father, *"I am coming to you now, but I say these things while I am still in the world, so that they may have the full measure of my joy within them"* (John 17:13 NIV).

Christ's purpose for your life is that you will have the full measure of His joy!

Christ knew that after He returned to the Father, His disciples and all who professed His name would be thrown into a sea of great turmoil. He knew they would be persecuted, beaten, imprisoned, thrown to the lions and martyred for the sake of the gospel.

As He sat and ate with them on their last evening together, He warned them that they would be hated, thrown out of synagogues and killed. He knew their hearts were filled with sorrow because He was leaving them. He had told them that they would weep and lament as a woman in travail. But He also promised them, *"...Your sorrow shall be turned into joy"* (John 16:20).

Jesus knew their hearts were already overwhelmed with sorrow. He had told them, *"And ye now therefore have sorrow: but I will see you again, and your heart shall rejoice, and your joy no man taketh from you"* (John 16:22).

In essence, Jesus was saying, "You may be overcome by sorrow now, but just wait! I will see you again. On the third day, when I come up out of the grave, something is going to happen to you! You are going to have joy greater than anything you have ever known. You will have My joy that cannot be destroyed! It is going to be full measure! It is going to be deep inside your being, and nothing, no power on earth, no evil principality; nothing will be able to take it from you!"

275

HIS JOY WILL SUSTAIN YOU IN YOUR DARKEST HOUR!

Christ, knowing what His disciples faced, prayed they would have His joy in full measure because He knew it would sustain them in their darkest hour. Christ also looked down through the corridor of time and saw what we would face in this end-time hour.

He knows the sorrows, heartaches; trials and testing you have gone through. He has seen the struggles, the pain and the hours you have cried in despair. He has seen the battles you have faced. But He has planned for you to have His joy deep inside your being that will sustain you regardless of the battles, trials or circumstances you may face.

"Jesus places us in the arms of His Father, on the care of His Father, and in the heart of His Father."
E. M. Bounds

"The joy of the Lord is your strength!" (Nehemiah 8:10). One of Satan's greatest weapons against the Church today is a spirit of discouragement. He knows that if he can cause you to get your eyes on your problems, sickness, financial problems, or problems in your family relationships, instead of focusing on God's promises and His love for you, you will become discouraged.

In the circumstances you are facing right now, do you have His joy flooding your soul? Christ wants you to have His joy in full measure so that you can rejoice even in your darkest hour of pain and sorrow. His joy is supernatural joy that comes from His Spirit living within you. It is not a joy that the world can give. It is a joy that only He can give. It is a joy that will make you sing and rejoice even when it seems as if everything around you is crumbling. His joy will enable you to walk in victory over every obstacle you will face.

276

Christ knew you would need His joy in full measure to overcome every fiery dart of the enemy and endure every trial in 100 percent victory.

4. UNITY IN THE CHURCH

The fourth thing that Christ prayed for us was that His Church would be united together as *one*. Hear the cry of His heart:

That they all may be one; as thou, Father, art in me, and I in thee, that they also may be one in us: that the world may believe that thou hast sent me. And the glory which thou gavest me I have given them; that they may be one, even as we are one.

John 17:21,22

In those final, crucial moments with His disciples, He prayed for His Church to be vitally united together as one. Christ knew what they would face: fiery trials, persecution and death for the sake of the gospel. He knew they would face the onslaught of the enemy in an attempt to crush and totally destroy the Church.

Christ also saw the inner struggles His Church would face throughout the ages that would weaken and dilute its power. Knowing the battles we would face, He prayed for the one ingredient that would make the Church a powerful, indestructible force capable of not only withstanding every attack of the enemy, but of taking the world for the kingdom of God – UNITY!

CHRIST'S PRAYER WILL BE FULFILLED!

Let His heartbeat ring in your ears: *"That they all may be one...that they also may be one in us"* (John 17:21), and *"...that they may be one, even as we are one"* (John 17:22).

277

Christ prayed for unity that would be such a dynamic, dominant force in the Church that it would be a living witness to the world that He was sent by God and was Who He claimed to be. It is not a man-made, superficial unity. This type of unity will never be produced through men's striving to attain it or through their futile attempts to bring all churches and denominations together under one structure. We will always have differences in doctrine and methods of worship and church administration. Such unity that Christ prayed for in the Church cannot be produced by natural means or methods, but by the divine flow of His Spirit living within us!

As God's Spirit is being poured out on the Church, one of the true manifestations of His Spirit will be one of love and unity drawing members of the Body, ministries and churches of all denominations together as *one in the spirit!*

Regardless of what we see outwardly, unity in the Spirit is coming to the Church. There is no doubt Christ's prayer for His Church will be fulfilled!

Christ not only prayed for His Church to be divinely united together with Him as one body, He poured out His blood, making it possible! Through His sacrifice on the cross, every true born-again believer has been *"...made to drink into one Spirit"* (1 Corinthians 12:13).

And it is that *same* Spirit within every true believer that draws us together and unites us as one body. Regardless of the unique distinctions, characteristics and differences with the Church of Jesus Christ today, there is only *one* Body, *one* Spirit, *one* Lord, *one* faith, *one* God and Father! True born-again believers have all been redeemed by the blood of Jesus, called by His Spirit and made *one* with Him.

United prayer is the seed that will produce a harvest of souls. The Body of Christ must unite through intensified prayer, weeping and travailing together, as never before, on behalf of the lost in our cities and nations. It is our united prayers that will activate God's power and enable us to reap the end-time harvest of souls.

5. FULL SPIRITUAL MATURITY

The fifth thing that Christ prayed would be manifested in His Church is that we will be brought to full maturity where we are a full manifestation of Christ to the world.

Jesus prayed, *"I in them, and thou in me, that they may be made perfect in one…"* (John 17:23). The Greek word for "perfect" means to be brought to full maturity.

By His Spirit, members of the Body of Christ are all joined together in one body. Paul told the Corinthians, *"For by one Spirit are we all baptized into one body, whether we be Jews or Gentiles, whether we be bond or free; and have been all made to drink into one Spirit"* (1 Corinthians 12:13).

Every born-again believer is joined by God's Spirit to Christ, who is the "Head" of the Church. God's purpose is that members of the Body of Christ grow together in unity until we reach full spiritual maturity, where we have been incorporated and joined together into one "perfect man."

Before Christ ascended into heaven, He placed the fivefold ministry in the Church to bring us to a position of "perfection," whereby we are doing the work of the ministry and building up the Body of Christ. Paul said the fivefold ministry was given:

> For the perfecting of the saints, for the work of the ministry, for the edifying of the body of Christ: till we all come in the unity of the faith, and of the knowledge of the Son of God, unto a perfect man, unto the measure of the stature of the fullness of Christ.
>
> Ephesians 4:12-13

Do you realize the significance of what this means to you?

Satan's objective is to keep us in a position of spiritual ignorance where we cannot see or understand God's plan and purpose. He does not want the Church to reach the full stature of Jesus Christ, because he knows he is defeated and fears what will happen when the Church takes its position as full-grown sons of God!

279

IT IS TIME FOR THE CHURCH
TO REACH FULL MATURITY!

Before the foundation of the world, according to the good pleasure of His will, God planned for the adoption of children through Jesus Christ (see Ephesians 1:3-6). He desired to have a people through whom He would manifest His Power and glory to the world.

God planned for you to be conformed and changed into the image of Christ. *"For whom he did foreknow, he also did predestinate to be conformed to the image of His Son, that he might be the firstborn among many brethren"* (Romans 8:29).

The "perfection" Paul was referring to is the position of maturity we reach when we have come to full age, where we stand, full-grown. This full maturity is nothing less than Christ's own perfection.

Through Christ's supreme sacrifice, He has already fulfilled everything necessary to make it possible for you to be perfected and to reach the full stature of Jesus Christ.

This is not something that is a remote possibility, or something that can be achieved through your own personal efforts. However, you can know that it will happen because as Christ was preparing to return to the Father, He prayed, *"I in them, and thou in me, that they may be made perfect in one…"* (John 17:23).

Christ's prayer for His Church will be answered!

The key to reaching the full stature of Jesus Christ is your union with Him. In Christ, you are filled with the fullness of the Godhead and reach full spiritual stature where you are a full manifestation of Christ to the world.

Christ intends His Church to be a full manifestation of His mind, His vision, His will, His anointing, His consecration, His power and authority, His faith, His wisdom, His righteousness, His love and all that He is!

The key to reaching this position of full maturity is your union with Christ. You must remain in Him where there is a continual flow of His life in and through you to the world.

6. A FRESH MANIFESTATION OF GOD'S LOVE

The sixth thing that Christ prayed to be manifested in the Church was God's love. How we need a fresh manifestation of God's love in the Church today! We must have it to bring us into true unity where we will be able to reach the world with the gospel before Jesus returns!

Time after time, He emphasized the importance of loving one another. Jesus told the disciples: "*A new commandment I give unto you, That ye love one another, as I have loved you, that ye also love one another. By this shall all men know that ye are my disciples, if ye have love one to another*" (John 13:34-35); "*This is my commandment, That ye love one another, as I have loved you. Greater love hath no man than this, that a man lay down his life for his friends*" (John 15:12-13);"*These things I command you, that ye love one another*" (John 15:17).

Jesus prayed:

> *O, righteous Father, the world hath not known thee: but I have known thee, and these have known that thou hast sent me. And I have declared unto them thy name, and will declare it: that the love wherewith thou hast loved me may be in them, and I in them.*
>
> John 17:25-26

The type of love Christ prayed to be manifested in the Church was not a natural love. It was a supernatural love. It is the same love that the Father had for Christ. The disciples were to love one another as Christ loved them. This supernatural love was to be the distinguishing factor, setting each of them apart from the world as one of His disciples.

Jesus did not tell them that the world would recognize them because of the power that was manifested or the miracles they performed. He told them that people would know and recognize them as His disciples by the love that was manifested by them one to another. He said, "*By this shall all men know that ye are my disciples, if ye have love one to another*" (John 13:35).

The type of love our Father manifested to us that made Him willing to send His only begotten Son to the world, to be beaten, mocked, spit upon and crucified on our behalf is the type of love Christ prayed would be in us. "*Behold, what manner of love the Father hath bestowed upon us, that we should be called the sons of God...*" (1 John 3:1).

God's love was a powerful energizing force in the lives of the disciples and believers in the Early Church. It was the major key to the power of God that was manifested through them. They had so much love they were willing to lay down their lives for one another. They were so filled with love for God, they were willing to be thrown to the lions, thrown into prison, beaten, tortured and burned at the stake. It was God's love burning within them that united them together as a mighty, united force that could not be defeated. They operated in the power and authority of God because they walked in love.

They did not merely say they loved one another. They demonstrated it! Their love for one another was a demonstration of the reality of the gospel and a witness to the world that Christ was Who He claimed to be. There was no earthly power that could quench that love.

OUR PRAYERS MUST BE FUELED BY GOD'S LOVE

When we take the mask off, we cannot say that this same dimension of God's love is being manifested in the Church. It is sad to say, but true, that as our churches have grown in size, in many instances they have also become cold and impersonal.

Within a great majority of our churches, the people do not even know one another. They have not made time to build relationships. In many churches there is jealousy, bitterness, resentment, unforgiveness and hatred among the members. There is a spirit of competition, jealousy and bitterness among ministers of the gospel.

In some cities, there is more of a demonstration of love coming from the people of the world than from the Church. If the Church does not have this type of love for one another that Christ demonstrated, how will we ever be able to reach the millions of unsaved people we have never seen?

John wrote, *"If a man say, I love God, and hateth his brother, he is a liar: for he that loveth not his brother whom he hath seen, how can he love God whom he hath not seen?"* (1 John 4:20).

If we truly have God's love in our lives, there will be a true manifestation of it through us to one another. What we need in the Church today is more than the surface, phony words coming out of our mouths. John wrote, *"My little children, let us not love in word, neither in tongue; but in deed and in truth"* (1 John 3:18).

If all we do is tell our brothers and sisters we love them and fail to show it through our actions, it isn't truly God's love. God demonstrated His great love by sending us His most valued and treasured possession – His only Son.

How can we pray effectively, *"...with all perseverance and supplication for all saints"* (Ephesians 6:18), unless we truly have God's love burning in our hearts for one another? Our prayers must be fueled by God's love; otherwise, they are just empty words and we are only going through the motions.

And when ye stand praying, forgive, if ye have aught against any: that your Father also which is in heaven may forgive you your trespasses. But if ye do not forgive, neither will your Father which is in heaven forgive your trespasses.

Mark 11:25-26

We can only pray fervently when our prayers are motivated and fueled by God's love. If there is anger, unforgiveness, bitterness or resentment in our hearts toward others, our prayers will not be heard.

When Christ prayed for the Church that we would have the same love for one another that He has for us, He knew we would need it to fulfill the Great Commission and bring in a great end-time harvest of souls. We need to pray for God to baptize and saturate us with His love so that we will manifest that love to one another and so the world will have a demonstration of God's love as a witness that Christ is alive and He is the mighty resurrected Son of God!

7. AN END-TIME MANIFESTATION OF HIS POWER AND GLORY

The seventh thing Christ prayed for His Church is that we will live in His presence and behold His glory. As He began His prayer He said, *"...Father, the hour is come; glorify thy Son, that thy Son also may glorify thee"* (John 17:1). Jesus knew the hour had come when He would return to the Father and He asked the Father to restore the glory He had with Him before the foundation of the world (see v. 5).

The word "glory" is translated from the Greek word *doxa*, which refers to all that God has and all that He is. It is referring to all His divine attributes. When Jesus came to earth, He laid aside the glory He had with the Father and took on the form of man. Although He was God in the flesh, He laid aside His divine attributes.

While He was on earth He was a reflection of God's glory. The glory of God shone forth and was manifested in both Jesus' character and the things He did. God's power and glory were revealed as He healed the sick, proclaimed the words of life, cast out devils and raised the dead. He revealed His glory through the love, mercy, forgiveness, joy, peace, authority and power He demonstrated. Paul described Jesus as *"...being the brightness of his glory, and the express image of his person...*" (Hebrews 1:3). As Christ was a visible manifestation of God to men on earth, He intends you to be a visible representation and reflection of His glory to the world.

Because of His obedience even unto death, God exalted Christ and restored to Him the glory He had before He came to earth. He is in a highly exalted position. In this glorified position He now possesses all the divine attributes He laid down before He came to earth. Christ intends His glory to be reflected through you. In His prayer for the Church, He told the Father, "*And the glory which thou gavest me I have given them; that they may be one, even as we are one*" (John 17:22).

Through His Spirit living within us, He has given us His glory. God's purpose through Jesus' death and resurrection was to bring many sons into glory (see Hebrews 2:9-10). He planned to bring you into a relationship as a true son or daughter, whereby the glory of Christ, who dwells within you, will be reflected in an outward expression to the world.

God has planned for you to be conformed into the image of Christ. "*For whom he did foreknow, he also did predestinate to be conformed into the image of his Son...*" (Romans 8:29). As you yield to the Spirit working within you, you are changed, transformed "*...into the same image from glory to glory, even as by the Spirit of the Lord*" (2 Corinthians 3:18). Your body is a vessel, a channel through which the glory of God can be manifested to the world because of Christ living in you!

Christ also prayed that we would live with Him and behold His glory. He said, "*Father, I will that they also, whom thou hast given me, be with me where I am; that they may behold my glory...*" (John 17:24).

Christ intends for His Church to be a full manifestation of His glory to the world in this end-time hour! The world will see His glory as His power and anointing are released through our lives in this powerful new dimension of prayer, in healing the sick, casting out demons and proclaiming the gospel!

"To let His disciples have the joy of knowing what His intercession for them in heaven as their High Priest will be, He gives them this precious legacy of His prayer to the Father."
Andrew Murray

We also have the promise that when He appears, we will appear with Him in glory. Paul said, *"When Christ, who is our life, shall appear, then shall ye also appear with him in glory"* (Colossians 3:4).

We will see Him as He is in all His power and glory and we will be like Him! *"...But we know that, when he shall appear, we shall be like him; for we shall see him as he is"* (1 John 3:2).

All that Jesus prayed in this great prayer for His Church will be fulfilled! Do not take this prayer lightly. Christ gave you this prayer as your spiritual legacy. Receive it and act on it. Each of the seven things He included in this prayer He intends to be manifested in your life.

1. Pray and believe God to keep, preserve, guard and protect you through the power of His name!

2. Pray and ask God to sanctify, cleanse and set you apart from the world through His Word!

3. Pray and believe God to release His joy into your life in full measure!

4. Pray for the unity in the Spirit to be manifested in the Church!

5. Pray and ask God to bring you to full maturity, by His Spirit working within you until you are a full manifestation of Christ to the world.

6. Pray for God to baptize you with His love and that it will be manifested through you to your brothers and sisters in the body of Christ!

7. Pray for Christ's power and glory to be manifested through you to the world!

Lord, teach us to pray!
Dear Lord, we have entered the Holy of Holies and have caught a glimpse of You as our Great High Priest and Your prayer for Your Church. Thank You for Your great love and that You ever live to intercede on our behalf. We receive Your seven-fold prayer for us and release our faith now to receive its fulfillment. Thank You for Your keeping power and the divine protection we have through the power of the Father's Name. We praise You for sanctifying and setting us apart in this hour. We ask You to release Your joy in all its fullness into our lives. We pray that You will release a spirit of unity and a fresh baptism of Your love within Your Church and bring us to full spiritual maturity whereby we are manifesting Your power and glory to the world.

SPIRITUAL INDEX ON PRAYER

GENESIS

Gen. 22:5	Abraham is about to sacrifice Isaac
Gen. 32:26	Jacob wrestles with an angel

EXODUS

Exo. 14:21-22	God parts the Red Sea
Exo. 20:1-17	God issues the Ten Commandments to Moses
Exo. 24:12	God summons Moses to the mountain
Exo. 24:16-18	Moses remains on the mountain 40 days and nights
Exo. 25:22	God communes with Moses above the mercy seat
Exo. 29:43	God commands Moses to meet Him at the tabernacle, sanctified by His glory
Exo. 32:1-6	Aaron leads the people into idolatry
Exo. 33:9-15	Moses' divine encounter with God

LEVITICUS

Lev. 16:13	God's instructions to Aaron on the mercy seat
Lev. 20:7	Sanctify yourselves

JOSHUA

Josh. 10:12-14	Joshua prays the sun and moon to stand still

1 KINGS

1 Kings 8:22-49	Solomon's prayer at the dedication of Temple
1 Kings 17:1	Elijah prophesies drought for three years
1 Kings 17:20-22	Elijah prays to God to raise a widow's dead son
1 Kings 18:1	God instructs Elijah to meet Ahab
1 Kings 18:36-38	Elijah's prayer that brought fire from heaven
1 Kings 18:42, 44	God sends rain to the earth

2 KINGS

2 Kings 4:32-34	Elisha's prayer for a dead child

2 Kings 19:14-19	Hezekiah's prayer for deliverance from King Sennacherib (also see Isaiah 37:14-20)
2 Kings 20:9-10	Hezekiah prays the sun's shadow to go backwards
2 Kings 20:11	God returns the sun's shadow 10 degrees back

1 CHRONICLES

| 1 Chr. 23:30-31 | Levites instructed to praise and worship God morning and evening |

2 CHRONICLES

2 Chr. 5:13-14	The shekinah glory of God fills the temple
2 Chr. 7:12	God appears to Solomon and assures him that his prayer has been heard
2 Chr. 7:14-15	God's promise to hear and answer prayer
2 Chr. 14:11	King Asa prays warfare prayer against a strong enemy
2 Chr. 14:12	God smites Asa's enemy
2 Chr. 16:9	The eyes of the Lord run to and fro
2 Chr. 20:15-22	The battle is the Lord's

NEHEMIAH

| Neh. 8:10 | The joy of the Lord is your strength |

JOB

| Job 1:20 | Job loses everything |
| Job 13:15 | Job continues to trust God |

PSALMS

Psalm 18:6-9 12-13, 17-19	David cries for help; God answers his prayers
Psalm 27:4	David's prayer to dwell in God's Presence forever
Psalm 34:1	David praises the Lord continually
Psalm 50:23	God identifies those who honor and glorify Him
Psalm 63:1-2	David's soul thirsts for God
Psalm 99:9	David recognizes the holiness of God
Psalm 100:2-4	David's instructions

| Psalm 113:3 | David praises God from the rising and setting of the sun |

ISAIAH

Isa. 45:11	"Command ye me"
Isa. 53:6-12	Isaiah prophesies the travail and intercession of Jesus
Isa. 59:15-17	Isaiah prophesies Jesus as the Chief Intercessor
Isa. 65:24	God hears and answers prayer

JEREMIAH

Jer. 29:10-13	God's promise to answer prayer
Jer. 32:27	Is there anything too hard for God?
Jer. 33:3	Jehovah wants to show you great and mighty things

EZEKIEL

| Ez. 22:30 | God seeks for those who stand in the gap |
| Ez. 36:26 | God promises a new covenant with Israel |

DANIEL

| Dan. 3:16-18 | Daniel and his companions refuse to worship |

JOEL

Joel 2:12-13	God calls His people to repentance and intercession
Joel 2:15-17	Sanctify a fast and call a solemn assembly
Joel 2:18, 23, 25-26	Rejoicing, restoration, and blessings
Joel 2:28-29	God pours out His Spirit on all flesh

ZECHARIAH

| Zech. 12:10 | The Holy Spirit is a Spirit of supplication |

MATTHEW

| Mat. 5:43-45 | Pray for your enemies |

MARK

Mark 11:25-26	Forgiveness essential to prayer
Mark 13:32-33, 37	Jesus' command to watch in prayer
Mark 16:17-18, 20	Signs and wonders shall follow those who believe

LUKE

Luke 2:36-38	Anna served God with prayer and fasting night and day
Luke 3:16	Baptized with the Holy Ghost and with fire
Luke 4:1-13	Jesus spent 40 days in fasting and prayer
Luke 4:14	Jesus returns from fasting and praying in the power of the Holy Spirit
Luke 4:32-36	Jesus teaches in Capernaum
Luke 6:12	Jesus spends all night in prayer
Luke 6:38	Jesus speaks on proper giving
Luke 7:14-15	Jesus heals a widow's son
Luke 9:28-36	Jesus transfigured while praying
Luke 10:19	Jesus gives power through prayer
Luke 11:1	Disciples cry out "Lord, Teach Us To Pray!"
Luke 11:2-4	The Lord's Prayer
Luke 11:5-9	Jesus teaches to persevere in prayer
Luke 12:32	The Father's good pleasure is to give you the Kingdom
Luke 12:42-44	Jesus in the Garden of Gethsemane
Luke 13:12-13	Jesus heals the woman with the issue of blood
Luke 18:1-8	Jesus teaches a parable concerning persevering prayer
Luke 18:42-43	Jesus heals a blind man
Luke 19:42-44	Jesus weeps over Jerusalem
Luke 21:36	Watch and pray always
Luke 22:31-32	Jesus' prayer for Peter
Luke 22:39-46	Jesus' prayer in Gethsemane
Luke 23:34	Jesus prays forgiveness for His enemies
Luke 24:49	Jesus' final instruction to His disciples

JOHN

ACTS

Acts 3:13, 16	How faith in Jesus Christ strengthened Peter
Acts 4:4	Those who heard the Word believed
Acts. 4:7	The Sanhedrin question Peter and John
Acts 4:10	Peter answers the Sanhedrin
Acts 4:29-31	Peter and John pray for holy boldness, signs and wonders
Acts 5:16	Revival comes to Jerusalem
Acts 5:42	Peter and John boldly proclaim the Gospel
Acts 6:4	Disciples make commitment to give themselves to prayer
Acts 8:6	Believers receive and heed Philip
Acts 9:40-41	Peter's prayer that raised Dorcas from the dead
Acts 10:38	Jesus went about doing good in the power of the Holy Spirit
Acts 12:5-17	Church prays without ceasing for Peter's release from prison
Acts 14:10	Paul heals a crippled man
Acts 16:25-40	Paul and Silas' midnight prayer
Acts 19:11-12	God works special miracles through Paul
Acts 19:13-15	Seven sons of Sceva attempt to cast out a demon

ROMANS

Rom. 1:9	Paul prays without ceasing for the Church
Rom. 3:24-25	Justified by the Blood of Jesus Christ
Rom. 5:17	Christ intends for the believer to reign in this life
Rom. 8:15-16, 26-34	Work of the Holy Spirit in intercession
Rom. 12:1	Paul instructs believers to offer their bodies as living sacrifices
Rom. 15:30-31	Paul's prayer asking believers to strive with him in prayer

1 CORINTHIANS

1 Cor. 2:10, 12	The Holy Spirit gives spiritual vision and discernment (also see 1 John 2:20)
1 Cor. 2:13	The Holy Spirit teaches us to pray in the Spirit

| 1 Cor. 2:14 | The natural man's lack of understanding |
| 1 Cor. 12:13 | The Body is unified in one Spirit through Christ |

2 CORINTHIANS

2 Cor. 3:18	We are changed from glory to glory
2 Cor. 4:18	Focus on the things that are eternal, not temporal
2 Cor. 5:7	We walk by faith, not by sight
2 Cor. 5:21	Jesus knew no sin and became sin for us
2 Cor. 6:17, 18	Wholly set apart for Jesus
2 Cor. 10:3-4	The weapons of our warfare are not carnal

GALATIANS

| Gal. 4:19 | Paul travails for the believers |

EPHESIANS

Eph. 1:3-6	Believers are adopted through Jesus Christ
Eph. 1:15-23	Paul's unceasing prayer for the Ephesian believers
Eph. 2:6-7	The believer becomes joint-heirs with Christ
Eph. 2:18	We have access to the Father
Eph. 3:14-20	Paul's prayer for strength in inner man
Eph. 4:8	Jesus' great triumph
Eph. 4:12-13	Come into the fullness of God
Eph. 5:18-19	Paul's instruction to praise and worship God continually
Eph. 5:25-27	Jesus comes for a holy church without spot or wrinkle
Eph. 6:11, 18	Pray always in the Spirit, on all occasions, with all types of prayer

PHILIPPIANS

Phi. 2:6-7	Jesus humbled Himself and was made in man's likeness
Phi. 2:8-11	Jesus is exalted and sits with the Father
Phi. 3:10	Paul's greatest desire

Phi. 4:6 — Do not worry – pray with thanksgiving

COLOSSIANS
Col. 1:17-18 — Jesus existed before all things and is seated at the right hand of the Father
Col. 2:15 — Jesus made a bold display of victory over the enemy
Col. 3:4 — Believers will appear with Christ in glory
Col. 4:2 — Continue in prayer with thanksgiving

1 THESSALONIANS
Ths. 3:10 — The disciples give themselves to prayer
Ths. 5:16-18 — Pray without ceasing and in everything give thanks

1 TIMOTHY
1 Tim. 2:1 — Paul's admonition that intercession be made for all men

2 TIMOTHY
2 Tim. 4:18 — Paul's confession of faith

HEBREWS
Heb. 1:3 — Paul describes Jesus
Heb. 2:9-10 — Jesus bore the curse of sin for every man
Heb 2:14, 16-18 — Jesus laid down His divine nature
Heb. 4:14-16 — Come boldly to the throne of grace for mercy
Heb. 5:7 — Jesus prayed fervently with strong crying and tears
Heb. 7:16-17 — Jesus became High Priest of the New Covenant
Heb. 7:21 — God confirmed Christ's eternal priesthood
Heb. 7:24-26 — Jesus ever lives to make intercession for us
Heb. 8:1 — Jesus is seated in position of the highest honor, supreme power and authority at the right hand of the Father
Heb. 9:11-12 — Jesus obtained eternal redemption for us
Heb. 10:12-14 — No further sacrifice is needed
Heb. 10:19-22 — God summoning us to draw near to Him through the blood of Jesus

Heb. 11:6	Without faith it is impossible to please Him (also see James 1:6-7)
Heb. 12:2	Jesus is the author and finisher of our faith
Heb. 12:14	Believers must cry out to God to be sanctified
Heb. 13:12	Sanctifiedby the blood of Jesus Christ
Heb. 13:15, 18-19	Paul's request for prayer that he would be soon restored to the churches
Heb. 11:33-35	Mighty warriors of faith

JAMES

Jas. 4:3	Praying with wrong motives
Jas. 5:14-15	Prayer of faith will save the sick
Jas. 5:16	The fervent prayer of a righteous man
Jas. 5:17-18	Elijah's prayer that opened the heavens and brought rain

1 PETER

1 Peter 1:18-19	Redeemed by the blood of Jesus
1 Peter 2:9	You are a chosen generation
1 Peter 3:18-19	Jesus died for man's sins to bring him to God

2 PETER

2 Peter 1:4	God has given us great promises
2 Peter 3:9	God is patient toward us, wanting all to repent

1 JOHN

1 John 1:7	Cleansed by the blood of Jesus
1 John 2:15	Love not the world
1 John 3:1	The Father's love enables us to be called sons of God through Jesus Christ
1 John 3:2	We shall see Him as He is
1 John 3:8	Jesus destroyed the work of the devil
1 John 3:18	Love in deed and in truth
1 John 4:20	Believers must love their brother
1 John 5:14-15	Assurance that God hears our prayers
1 John 15:14-15	We can come boldly to the Father through Jesus

JUDE
Jude 20 — Praying in the Holy Ghost

REVELATION
Rev. 1:6 — Believers become kings and priests unto God through Jesus Christ

Rev. 3:20 — Jesus' invitation to sup with us

Rev. 4:8 — Angelic praises from the Throne

Rev. 5:8 — Prayers of saints released before seals are opened

Rev. 5:9-10 — Made kings and priests unto God through the blood of Jesus Christ

Rev. 5:13 — Every knee will bow under the name of Jesus

Rev. 8:3-4 — Prayers of saints offered upon Golden Altar before the Throne

Rev. 8:5 — Prayers bring God's power upon the earth

Rev. 12:11 — Victory over Satan through the blood of the Lamb

...and God gave me a vision!

There is a greater anointing upon me now than ever before to pray for your needs.

Never before, in my more than 56 years of frontline ministry have I carried a deeper burden for the Body of Christ than I do now. I have prayed, fasted, interceded, agonized, and fought spiritual warfare against satanic powers...

...and God gave me a vision!

A vision of Jesus Christ, our Great High Priest, praying for all your needs.

God said, *"Place the needs of my people upon the altar before My Presence. Jesus is praying for all their needs to be met."*

Every need, every disease, every family problem, every circumstance... God wants me to lift your need for Jesus to pray for you. Do not delay. Write all your needs on the following page and mail it to me today!

For prayer call:
1-858-HELPLINE
1-858-435-7546

Brother Cerullo,

Please place these requests on the Miracle Prayer Altar in the World Prayer Center and pray for these needs:

_____

_____

_____

_____

_____

❑ Enclosed is my gift of $/£_____ to help yoiu win souls and to support this worldwide ministry.

Name _____

Address_____

City_____ State/Province_____Postal Code_____

E-mail _____

Fax_____Phone Number (___) _____

Mail today to:

MORRIS CERULLO WORLD EVANGELISM

San Diego: PO. Box 85277 • San Diego, CA 92186
Canada: PO. Box 3600 • Concord, Ontario L4K 1B6
U.K.: PO. Box 277 • Hemel Hempstead, Herts HP2 7DH

Web site: www.mcwe.com • **E-mail:** morriscerullo@mcwe.com

For prayer call: **1-858-HELPLINE**
435-7546

HELPLINE FAX: 1-858-427-0555

HELPLINE EMAIL: helpline@mcwe.com

Tear off and and mail this in today!